The Wild Palisades of the Hudson

The Wild Palisades of the Hudson

By
John Serrao

LIND PUBLICATIONS
Westwood, New Jersey 1986

Lind Publications
192 Third Avenue
Westwood, New Jersey 07675

Library of Congress Cataloging-in-Publication Data

Serrao, John, 1949-
  The Wild Palisades of the Hudson.

  Bibliography: p.
  Includes index.
  1. Palisades (N.J. and N.Y.) 2. Natural history—
Palisades (N.J. and N.Y.) 3. Hiking—Palisades
(N.J. and N.Y.) I. Title.
F127.H8S47   1986   917.49′21   86-7350
ISBN 0-910389-01-2

Printed in the United States of America
10 9 8 7 6 5 4 3 2 1

*To my wife, Felicia, for her strong support and encouragement
throughout this project, and for her love throughout our life together.*

*And to my parents, for instilling in me the desire to pursue
the career of my lifelong interest.*

CONTENTS

ACKNOWLEDGMENTS

I am grateful to the following people for sharing their knowledge and advice with me while I was gathering background information in the preparation of this book. First of all, for their invaluable service in reviewing sections of the manuscript in their areas of expertise: Jerome Wyckoff (geologist-author and editor); John Spring (President of the Bergen County Historical Society); and Charles "Buzz" Quadri (Superintendent of the Palisades Interstate Park, N.J. section).

For confirming some wildlife occurrences and suggesting additional possibilities: Harry Darrow (butterflies); Stiles Thomas (migrating hawks); Phil Meisner of the Rockland Lake Nature Center (reptiles and amphibians in the vicinity of the Lake); Richard Zweiffel (Curator of Herpetology at the American Museum of Natural History); Sidney Anderson (Curator of Mammals at the AMNH); and Ken Chambers (Education Dept. of the AMNH).

For revealing some of the more out-of-the-way trails and small natural areas on the Palisades: Richard Olsen (Assistant Supt., P.I.P., N.J. section); Fred Corring (Head of Maintenance, P.I.P., N.J. section); George Zobelein (former Chairman of N.Y.-N.J. Trail Conference); and especially Jeanne Ross (Director of Services, P.I.P.,

N.J. section) for answering many of my questions regarding the Park's facilities, schedules, etc.

Four long-time friends and "old-time hikers" also shared their knowledge of the Palisades with me starting 10 years ago, and opened my eyes to what a treasure this region really is: Ted Nelson, Bill Zuegel, Col. "Tarv" Tarvin, and Julia Lamb.

Eric Sundberg of the Rockland County Park Commission was especially helpful with regard to the backgrounds and exact boundaries of the sections of the Palisades ridge belonging to the Rockland County Park system.

A special thanks also goes to Susan Goodman, reporter for the *Bergen Record,* whose feature article about me brought this book to the attention of its eventual publisher—Bob Tebbenhoff of Lind Publications. I am also grateful to Dan McDonough for his fine work in developing all the black and white photos from my color slides.

Finally, I owe a debt of gratitude to my wife, Felicia, and three children, Vanessa, Holly, and Roy, for sacrificing many evenings and days off without me during the past year while I toiled away in completing this book.

INTRODUCTION

In the midst of the nation's most densely populated region, the Palisades of the Hudson River has miraculously retained an atmosphere of primitive wildness and seclusion, and an amazing variety of wildlife. From the tops of these world-famous cliffs, a hiker can look across the river and view New York City's skyscrapers, bridges, traffic jams, and crowded apartment houses. Hundreds of feet below, the Hudson River nears the end of its 300-mile journey from its headwaters in New York's Adirondack Mountains to Manhattan's harbor, one of the world's busiest seaports.

Yet, on foggy days when views of the concrete, brick, and steel are obscured, the hiker can easily imagine being in some faraway wilderness. Dense forests of 200-year-old oaks extend back from the sunny cliff edge into deep, shaded coves and ravines. Here the sturdy oaks are replaced by dark groves of swaying hemlock trees, or immense tulip-trees which tower 125 feet above the colorful woodland wildflowers. Brooks slowly meander through maple-gum swamps, or rush down steep hemlock gorges and cascade over the cliffs into the river hundreds of feet below. In early spring, small woodland ponds fill with rain and melting snow and become breeding sites for noisy wood frogs and secretive spotted salamanders. Flying squirrels and screech owls hide in deep cavities gouged out of trees by pileated woodpeckers. Red-tailed hawks soar above the Palisades in winter searching for rabbits and squirrels, and the skies above the cliffs are filled each autumn with hundreds, and sometimes thousands, of migrating hawks of a dozen kinds. At dusk, powerful great horned owls emerge from hidden evergreen roosts to scan the woods for nocturnal prey ranging in size from mice to skunks. On fern-covered rock slopes, black snakes and copperheads warm themselves each spring in the morning sun, while red foxes raise their pups here in the many natural caves and crevices.

Herds of deer still thrive in more rugged northern sections of the Palisades, and even an occasional bald eagle spends the winter roosting on the cliffs and fishing in the Hudson. Though certainly not virgin (most sections were cut at least once since the first Europeans settled here in the 17th century), the protected forests of the Palisades today represent outstanding examples of mature northeastern hardwood forests. And not only do they support a great diversity of plants and animals, but their proximity to millions of people makes them a natural oasis for outdoor recreation and spiritual refreshment. In June 1983, the Palisades was officially designated a National Natural Landmark by the United States Department of the Interior.

Chapter I

Geology and Landforms

ORIGIN OF THE HUDSON'S WESTERN WALL

In his widely used 1952 Scenic Folder of the New York region, *The Palisades*, Columbia University geologist A. K. Lobeck claimed that few places in the world offer views of so much geological and topographical diversity as the top of the Palisades. This viewpoint is echoed by geologist George Harlow in his introduction to the 1984 edition of the *New York Walk Book*. To the east of the Palisades, directly across the Hudson Valley, are the ancient gneiss, schist, and marble rocks upon which Westchester, the Bronx, and Manhattan were built. Beyond them can be seen the sandy, glacier-deposited hills of Long Island. From a few vistas on western slopes of the Palisades and from the tops of the highest summits near the ridge's northern end, there are also views of the Hackensack Valley, New Jersey's volcanic Watchung Mountains, and the billion-year-old granite and gneiss rocks of the Ramapos and Hudson Highlands. And, extending north and south for about 50 miles, is the magnificent monolith known as the Palisades, the most famous and distinctive nat-

View of Hook Mountain from Lamont Sanctuary (Lamont-Doherty Geological Observatory in foreground; Piermont Marsh and Pier on Hudson)

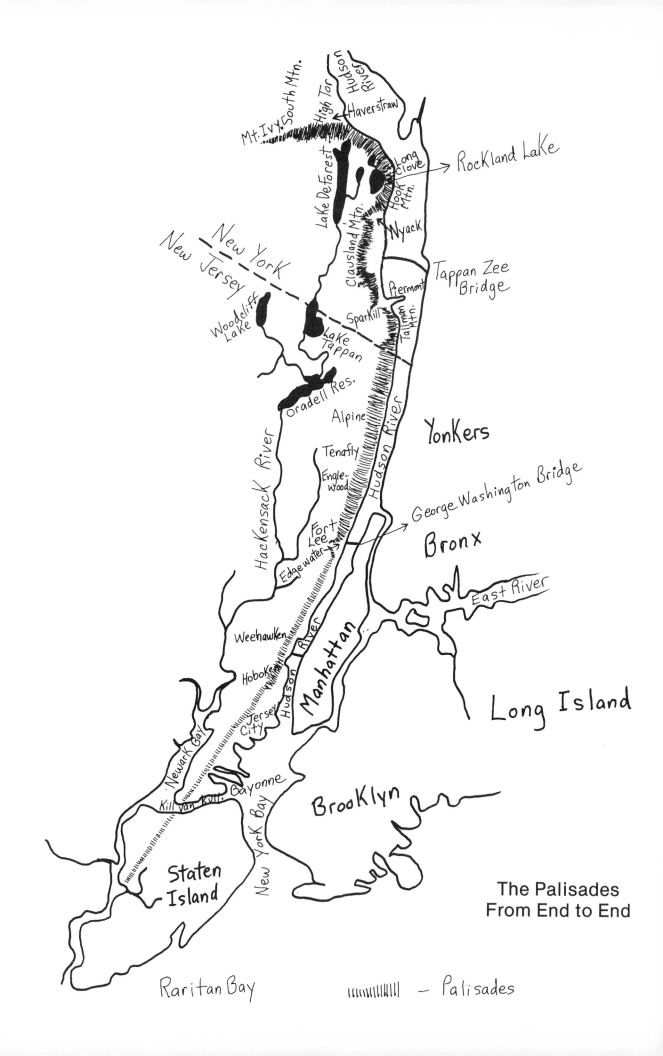

Mt. Ivy

South Mtn.

High Tor

Hudson River

Haverstraw

Lake DeForest

Long Clove

→ Rockland Lake

New York

New Jersey

Clausland Mtn.

Hook Mtn.

Nyack

Woodcliff Lake

Piermont

Tappan Zee Bridge

Sparkill

Tallman Mtn.

Lake Tappan

Oradell Res.

Alpine

Hudson River

Yonkers

Tenafly

Englewood

George Washington Bridge

Hackensack River

Fort Lee

Bronx

Edgewater

East River

Weehawken

Hudson River

Manhattan

Hoboken

Long Island

Jersey City

Newark Bay

Bayonne

Kill van Kull

New York Bay

Brooklyn

Staten Island

Raritan Bay

||||||||||| — Palisades

The Palisades
From End to End

2

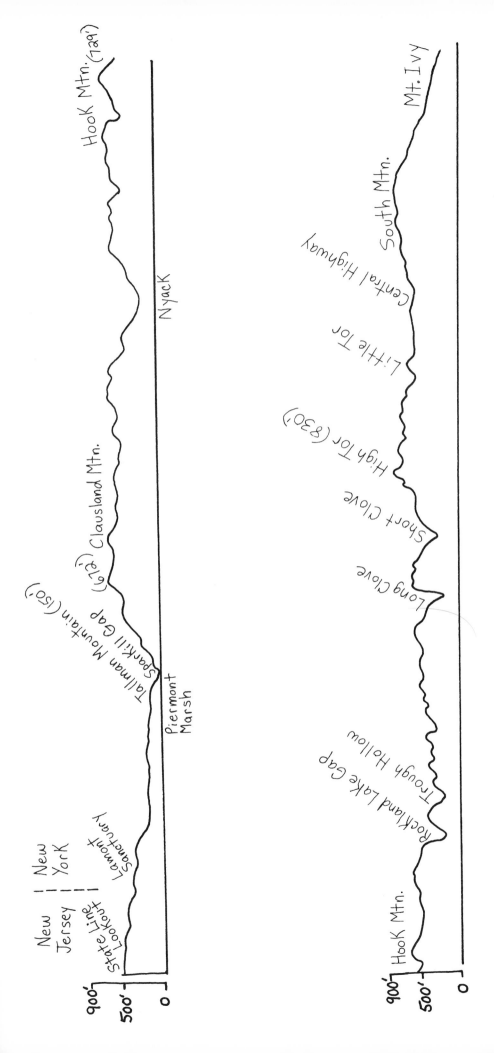

Longitudinal Profile of the Palisades, from State Line Lookout, N.J., north to its end in Mount Ivy, N.Y.

(Adapted from H. Thompson, 1959, "The Palisades ridge in Rockland County, N.Y.". *Annals of N.Y. Academy of Science*, vol. 80: page 1110.)

3

Occurrence of Dikes and Sills in Palisades

(from *Rock Scenery of the Hudson
Highlands and Palisades*, by
Jerome Wyckoff)

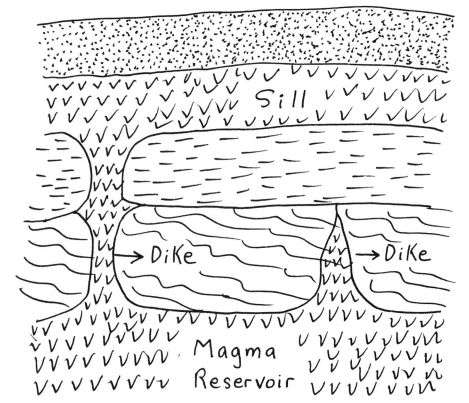

The modern geological theory of plate tectonics and continental drift suggests that during this Triassic period, North and South America, Africa, Europe, and much of Asia were joined together into one super-continent, "Pangaea." About 195 million years ago this great land mass started to break into separate chunks of land which very slowly drifted apart to form the individual continents and today's Atlantic Basin. Strong volcanic activity accompanied these crustal movements in the region, which was later to include the Palisades. Hundreds of cubic miles of hot, molten rock, or "magma," was suddenly released from great confining pressures and escaped upward from the depths of the earth through giant fractures or cracks which were forming.

Some magma erupted out onto the earth's surface as extensive sheets of lava, which would eventually become New Jersey's Watchung Mountains. On the other hand, on several occasions much magma failed to reach the surface. Instead it was squeezed horizontally, or "intruded," as a 1000-foot-thick, sandwich-like "sill" between layers of the sandstones and shales. Wedged between these sedimentary rocks, the molten liquid slowly cooled and hardened underground into the igneous Palisades rock known as diabase. Meanwhile, the entire region was tilted downward about 17 degrees to the west by the earth's crustal movements along the Ramapo fault.

Since then, the powerful forces of erosion have produced the landscapes we see today throughout our region. Softer rocks and sediments have been weathered and washed away, leaving the harder rock masses beneath them to emerge and stand out as prominent ridges, such as New Jersey's Watchungs and Snake Hill along the New Jersey Turnpike. Thus, water, ice, and wind gradually removed the thick upper covering of weaker sandstones and shales and exposed the top of the more resistant diabase sill of the Palisades. Meanwhile, the Hudson River (or a more ancient precursor flowing along the same boundary between the different types of rock formations found along its present east and west shores) cut more and more deeply through this westward-dipping rock sandwich. The

ural landmark in the metropolitan New York region.

A person peering over the edge of this vertical precipice, with some sheer drops exceeding 300 feet near the New York-New Jersey state border, may find it hard to believe that the Palisades was once thousands of feet below the ground. Over 200 million years ago during the earth's Late Triassic (the "Age of Dinosaurs") and early Jurassic periods, northeastern New Jersey was a basin, part of a vast chain of lowlands extending from Rockland County, New York, southward through eastern Pennsylvania into Virginia. Into this "Newark Basin" poured layer upon layer of sands and dark muds washed down from highlands to the east and from the nearby Appalachian Mountains, which were then perhaps 10 to 15 thousand feet high. Over millions of years of continuous deposition, the lowland accumulated thousands of feet of these sediments, the bottom layers of which became compressed and compacted beneath the tremendous weight and were consolidated into hard sandstones and shales.

river removed all the sandstones and shales bordering the eastern side of the underground sill and finally exposed that entire edge – the steep cliffs of the Palisades. The spectacular height of these cliffs is a result of the river's eroding out the relatively soft sedimentary rock from around the edge of the hard diabase.

It is thought by some that the Palisades sill once extended farther eastward over New York City and even Westchester; if so, erosion has removed all of this rock. Today the Palisades escarpment forms the more or less continuous west wall of the Hudson River for about 50 miles. It emerges as a very low ridge from beneath the ground near Travis, Staten Island and crosses the Kill van Kull to Bayonne, New Jersey. Then for the next 18 miles the cliffs gradually increase in altitude northward and move closer to the Hudson River past Jersey City (50 feet high), Hoboken, Weehawken (150 feet), and North Bergen. Just south of the George Washington Bridge an ancient natural fault, or break, in the Palisades causes the cliffs to suddenly drop down and dip inland away from the river again. Erosion along this fault permitted the development of the river-shore community of Edgewater. North of this fault, at Fort Lee (where the early silent "cliff-hanger" movie serials and Mack Sennett comedies were filmed) the Palisades finally becomes the famous rampart of rock that rises 300 feet perpendicularly from the Hudson.

The cliffs continue uninterrupted for more than 12 miles past Englewood, Tenafly, and Alpine before reaching their steepest height of 530 feet near the New Jersey-New York state line. After this the ridge dips sharply down to Sneden's Landing on the river, climbs again as the 150-foot Tallman Mountain, and is then abruptly interrupted by the deep Sparkill Gap near Piermont. Here the Palisades moves a little inland and temporarily loses its wall-like character, becoming a series of hills and ridges known as Clausland Mountain, which includes Mount Nebo and the Blauvelt section of Palisades Interstate Park. The Palisades returns as the Hudson's western wall in Nyack. This is where the stark precipice of rock once called "Verdrietege Hoogte" (Grievous Point, in Dutch), now

simply Hook Mountain, rises cliff-like 729 feet from the north end of the Tappan Zee. The town of Nyack is beautifully situated in a natural "amphitheatre" facing the Hudson River, with the cliffs of Hook Mountain enclosing its rear.

At this point the Palisades ridge finally begins to curve westward and inland in a hook-like shape away from the Hudson River along its broad Haverstraw Bay. Moreover, here is where erosion has removed not only the upper sandstone layers, but also the horizontal component of the diabase. The Palisades is exposed down to the vertical channels or shafts which were the ancient roots of the laterally spreading sills of molten magma. Thus, instead of a horizontal sill, here the diabase is seen as a vertical, wall-like "dike" in which the

Palisades sinking beneath ground in Mount Ivy, N.Y.

molten magma was injected upward *through*, rather than between, the sandstone layers. Unlike the generally flat, table-top topography which erosion has created by exposing the top of the horizontal sill in the southern Palisades, the ridge here is much narrower, with 360-degree vistas at the sharply exposed summits. Both the ridge-top in the Hook Mountain area and its adjacent swamps and lakes (Rockland, Congers, and Swartout) produce the headwaters of the Hackensack River.

Continuing inland above the eastern shores of Rockland Lake, the Palisades is interrupted by several small gaps and then a deep valley (caused by erosion along an ancient fault zone) called Long Clove, from which it climbs to its highest altitude on High Tor (830 feet) behind Haverstraw, N.Y. Then come Little Tor, South Mountain, and at last the end of the Palisades ridge at Mount Ivy, where the cliffs plunge beneath the ground near the Mahwah River at the Ramapo Mountain front.

ROCKS THAT LOOK LIKE ROWS OF TREES

The native Lenni Lenape Indians called the cliffs "we-awk-en," the middle syllable of which means "rocks that look like rows of trees." The exposed face of the Palisades is indeed actually composed of a series of long, vertical columns which, with a little imagination, appear like a continuous row of upright stakes or posts, especially if viewed from across the river. This resemblance to a walled-in colonial fortification or Indian stockade, or "palisade," has given

the cliffs their famous name. These rock patterns are matched by cliffs in Morocco and by Fingal's Cave in Scotland. Not only are these widely separated rock masses strikingly similar in appearance and composition, but they all originated about 195 million years ago, when their land masses were joined into a single continent!

The columnar appearance of the Palisades was caused by the manner in which the magma froze into solid rock deep be-

Palisades cliffs north of Alpine Boat Basin – note vertical rock columns

neath the ground. Since it was unexposed to the air, the cooling process took many thousands of years. As the liquid magma cooled and solidified, it contracted and shrank and experienced great tensional stresses. These stresses were relieved by long vertical fractures extending hundreds of feet and essentially breaking up the rock mass into a series of roughly polygonal, prism-shaped columns several feet wide.

Much later, when the Palisades diabase was exposed to the air by erosion, these vertical contraction "joints" became natural lines of weakness in the rock mass. Water seeps into these cracks and corrodes and weakens the rock. Also, as water freezes into ice during the colder months, it expands with a force of 2000 pounds per square inch! Masses of rock are thus pried apart and tumble into huge piles or "talus" at the base of the steep cliffs. As surrounding blocks of diabase fall away over the years, a few vertical columns become isolated as picturesque pillars at the cliff edge. One such pillar, called "Bombay Hook," north of Alpine, stands 70 feet high. There are also less conspicuous, horizontal fissures which intersect the vertical fractures of the diabase, often causing the columns to break off into natural steps or stairways during weathering. This phenomenon was responsible for the Palisades diabase being termed "trap rock," from the Swedish word "trapp" for stairs. Much of this weathering by rain and frost takes place during the spring thaw, when rock slides sometimes carry down hundreds of tons of diabase to the bottom of the cliffs. This annual removal of sections of the vertical columns is causing the Palisades to gradually retreat

Isolated diabase pillar near Lamont Sanctuary, N.Y.

westward. At the same time, erosion and weathering continue to undermine the cliffs wherever the underlying sediments — the softer shales and sandstones, or the bottom part of the diabase "sandwich" are exposed.

ROCKS OF THE PALISADES

Out of the layers of Triassic sedimentary rocks between which the Palisades sill was intruded have come some remarkable discoveries. In 1910, along the river bank at Fort Lee, N.J. (near Old Dupont Dock), three Columbia University students found the 200-million-year-old fossils of a crocodile-like phytosaur, *Rutiodon*, washed out of the lower cliff by heavy rains. This is now on exhibit at the American Museum of Natural History in New York City. Ancient lake deposits in an abandoned quarry

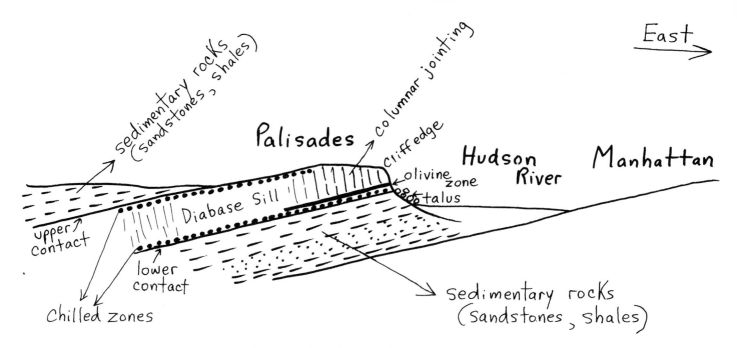

Cross Section of Palisades

(from "The Geology of the Palisades" by Henry Sharp, *New Jersey Nature News*, June 1962, p. 51)

at North Bergen, N.J. have yielded coelacanth fish fossils and, in 1960, the fossil skeleton of the earliest known winged vertebrate, a gliding reptile named *Icarosaurus.*

These sedimentary rocks are mostly of two types: arkosic sandstones (derived from granite and gneiss), composed mainly of the minerals feldspar, mica, and quartz; and shales, darker and representing finer deposits of mud at the bottoms of ancient lakes. The iron oxide, hematite, often gives the sandstones a reddish color, and is characteristic of rocks formed in a semi-arid environment. It was this "Newark sandstone" which was the principal building material of many of New Jersey's historic Dutch farmhouses and, around the turn of the 20th century, of New York City's well-known "brownstone" apartments and houses.

The igneous rock of the Palisades sill itself is called diabase. Its two dominant minerals, dark pyroxene (or augite) and lighter plagioclase feldspar, are present in equal proportions and thus impart a mottled, "salt-and-pepper" texture to the rock. In mineral composition it is actually identical to the volcanic basalt of the Watchung Mountains, but since the latter cooled more quickly as above-ground lava, its crystalline texture is much finer than that of diabase.

Diabase cooled off rather slowly below the ground, so that its individual minerals are large enough to be seen with the naked eye. Very durable and resistant to weathering, diabase was the valuable "Belgian bluestone" used during the late 19th century for buildings, ships' ballast, and cobblestone roads. Today it is used mostly as large blocks in the construction of seawalls and as crushed gravel for concrete and pavement. The value of its rock brought almost complete destruction to the Palisades, as quarries blasted away column after column of the ancient diabase. Thanks to the formation of the Palisades Interstate Park Commission in 1900, only one quarry now remains on the Palisades, in Haverstraw, N.Y. Barges from this quarry bearing the name New York Trap Rock Company can often be seen along the Hudson River. Most trap rock today comes from large quarries around the Watchung Mountains.

When the molten magma was first squeezed between the Triassic rock layers, its intense heat "metamorphosed," or chemically altered sedimentary rocks for dozens of feet above and below the two actual contacts with the enclosed sill. Shales were baked into a very hard, flinty, gray rock called hornfels, composed of such minerals as feldspar, biotite, quartz, and hornblende. Sandstones, less affected by the heat, were changed to hard quartzite. At the same time, since the magma lost its heat more quickly wherever it contacted these sediments, it cooled and solidified into diabase first at the top and bottom of the thick sandwich, and later in the interior. Thus, its texture at these two "chilled zones" is denser and finer-grained—almost like the basalt of the Watchung Mountains. Away from the two contact zones the cooling process was slow enough to permit the various mineral crystals to grow and settle out of the hot liquid in a definite order by gravity. For example, olivine was one of the first minerals to crystallize. Fairly heavy, it settled mostly to the bottom of the mass, composing as much as 25% of the diabase above the lower contact.

Exposed to close examination along various roads and trails, the Palisades is an international geological landmark. The cliff face north of the George Washington Bridge is one of the world's classic areas to study these two interesting geological processes by which molten magma changes the rocks with which it comes into contact and crystallizes into various minerals as it cools. In designating the Palisades a National Natural Landmark in 1983, the U.S. Department of Interior called the cliffs "the best example of a thick diabase sill in the United States."

At several points along the Hudson, especially the two Shore Paths which follow the river at the base of the cliffs from Fort Lee, N.J. to the New York State border and from Nyack to Haverstraw, the unaltered reddish and buffy sandstones and dark shales of the Triassic Lowland can be viewed. The lower contact zone is largely obscured by talus and rock slides. Below the cliff along the Henry Hudson Drive between Fort Lee and Alpine, however, and in a creek bed off Undercliff Avenue (along an abandoned trolley route) in Edgewater, N.J., road cuts and erosion have revealed some good examples of where the molten magma contacted the sediments. Here, the vertical columns of diabase rest right on top of the baked shales and sandstones, which show the distinctive horizontal layers in which they were deposited during the Triassic period. The contrast of vertical columns atop horizontal layers is distinctive and unique.

In these same exposures, about 40 feet above the lower contact zones, the olivine layer often stands out as a crumbly, sandy, brownish, 15-foot-thick layer within the diabase. Because olivine quickly deteriorates when exposed to air or water, this "rotted zone" tends to undermine the rest of the Palisades and cause rock slides. As for the upper contact zone, millions of years of erosion have removed not only the thousands of feet of sedimentary rocks which once covered the Palisades, but as much as half of the diabase sill's original 1000-foot thickness as well. There is one place in New Jersey, however, where the upper contact zone is still visible: at the deep road cut where Interstate 95 passes beneath Jones Road at the Englewood-Leonia border. Here, some of the horizontal layers of met-

Olivine layer, or "rotted zone" in cliffs, Edgewater, N.J.—note upper rocks being undermined

Vertical diabase columns atop horizontal sedimentary layers, along Henry Hudson Drive, N.J.

amorphosed shales and sandstones can still be seen covering the vertical diabase columns. The entire rock formation here gradually dips westerly out of sight beneath the ground at the 17-degree angle to which it was tilted 195 million years ago. In New York state, the upper contact zone can be seen about 2 miles southeast of Haverstraw, at the south portal of the West Shore branch of the New York Central Railroad's tunnel through the Palisades.

THE GREAT GLACIER

In more recent geological times, after our present major landscape had been formed, the earth's climate turned cooler and huge glaciers gradually covered much of the northern hemisphere with thousands of feet of ice. The last (or latest) of these ice sheets started to melt away from northern New Jersey only about 12 to 15 thousand years ago, so its effects on the Palisades can still be seen today. Soils and rocks were scoured and plucked away, plant and animal life was destroyed, the exposed bedrock was smoothed, rounded, and polished, and most of the talus which sloped gradually from the cliff down to the river was bulldozed away. Thus, the Palisades was left bare, lifeless, and extremely steep, and any flora, fauna, and talus here today has accumulated during the last 12 to 15 millennia.

As the glacier slowly melted back northward, any materials carried in the ice were deposited. Some Palisades diabase rock can be found today on Long Island, where it was transported by the ice sheet. "Glacial drift"—rock debris in the form of boulders, gravel, sand, and silt carried by the glacier—was deposited on the Palisades and still contributes to the area's soil structure and quality. Large boulders—some carried by the ice from as far away as the Shawangunks and Ramapos, others from nearby–also were scattered on the Palisades. Called "erratics," these transported chunks of sandstone, conglomerate, gneiss, and granite can easily be recognized as they rest atop the contrasting diabase bedrock. "Haring's Rock," a huge sandstone erratic which is 10 feet tall, 10 feet around, and weighs 15 tons, is visible on a marked trail off East Clinton Avenue in Tenafly's Lost Brook Preserve. Whereas the bedrock was smoothed by the sands carried in the glacier ice, grooves and striations were gouged into the diabase by pebbles embedded in the bottom of the moving ice sheet. Both fine scratches and large grooves, some of which are over 6 inches deep and several feet wide, are especially evident on the 830-foot summit of High Tor, the Palisades highest peak.

When northern New Jersey and southern New York started to emerge from the deep freeze as the glacier retreated, fresh rock slides started new talus slopes below the Palisades. Icy streams of meltwater from the glacier washed away much of the glacial drift. Some drift formed temporary dams in places, creating glacial ponds. The large "Kelders Swamp" (now an artificial pond in Greenbrook Sanctuary in Tenafly,

N.J.) is thought to have originally been a glacial lake. As temperatures warmed and the ice melted northward, plants gradually recolonized the barren cliffs–first crusty lichens and primitive mosses, then dwarf shrubs, and finally larger shrubs and trees in the accumulating soil layer.

By studying ancient pollen sediments deposited at various boggy sites in the eastern United States, scientists (palynologists) have suggested the following sequence of plant succession following the retreat of the glaciers. First there was a sub-arctic landscape of low, tundra-type shrubs and herbs, with some spruce in milder lowlands. Then, starting about 12,000 years ago, came a boreal forest of spruce, fir, and pine, with a ground cover of grasses, sedges, birch, alder, willow, and various herbs and mosses. About 9,000 years ago, pines dominated as the climate grew warmer and drier. Then, 2,000 years later, hemlock dominated the forest, with many hardwoods like beech, maple, and oak gradually "migrating" northward from their southern glacial refugia. In the succeeding few thousand years to the present as the climate continued to warm up, the forests were gradually dominated by various oaks and chestnut, associated with maples, birches,

Glacial scratches and grooves atop High Tor, Haverstraw, N.Y.

beech, ashes, hickories, and other species commonly encountered today (chestnut has now been eliminated by a fungus blight introduced in the 1900s).

Today only the scratches and grooves on the polished diabase and the erratic boulders offer evidence that the dense forests and abundant wildlife of the Palisades are only recent additions to these ancient rocks.

THE HUDSON RIVER

Many geologists believe that the Hudson River's present southward course past the Palisades and Manhattan and into the Atlantic Ocean is comparatively recent and only one of several former courses taken by the river since its ancient past. Before the Ice Ages, the river flowed south through the Hudson Highlands (as it does today) but then veered west after emerging from these mountains near Piermont, cutting its course across the Newark Basin behind the Palisades and then turning east again to enter Raritan Bay south of Staten Island. According to one theory, however, a different stream, eroding its way northward east of the Palisades, intercepted or "captured" the Hudson south of the Highlands and diverted the river into its present course.

Another theory blames the glaciers for changing the Hudson's course by blocking the river's westward turn at Piermont with rocks and debris and causing it to dam up and form a freshwater lake. When the ice melted, the river broke through at the Narrows much farther south and relinquished its westward jog in favor of today's more straightforward route. The notch which the Hudson supposedly cut into the Palisades where it once veered westward is today a broad, magnificent gorge over 500 feet deep. Called the Sparkill Gap (the Sparkill Creek now flows through it), this former "Hudson Water Gap" is spanned by Route 9W about 4 miles south of Nyack, N.Y. It is the only sea-level gap in the Palisades.

Forest View area of Palisades, from Hudson River, near Alpine, N.J.

During the Ice Age the glaciers cut into and deepened the Hudson River valley hundreds of feet below sea level. Then, when the ice started to melt, the lower valley became filled with Atlantic Ocean water, converting the former freshwater river into a brackish basin or estuary from Manhattan all the way up to Newburgh, N.Y. Atlantic Ocean tides actually reach 150 miles up to Troy, N.Y., but saltwater intrudes only half this distance because of the Hudson's substantial freshwater flow north of the Highlands. There is relatively little downstream current in the lower fourth of the Hudson except after heavy rains and spring runoff. The mean vertical tide range in the Palisades region of the Hudson averages 3 to 4 feet. From 30 parts per thousand in the sea off New York Harbor, the salinity of the water decreases to about 23 parts per thousand at Manhattan's Battery, to 15 parts per thousand at Yonkers about 25 miles north, and then to only one or two parts per thousand at West Point. Of course, the northward extent of this salt front depends on the degree of freshwater flow in the river: in spring, the Hudson is fresh all the way down to Haverstraw, but by autumn seawater sometimes extends as far north as Hyde Park.

Thus, after originating in the Adirondack Mountains as a wilderness stream, the Hudson flows southward as a freshwater river for three-quarters of its 300-mile length. Then, as its lower fourth gradually merges with the sea, it becomes a calm estuary, subject to the pulls and pushes of the tides—a "stream that flows both ways," as the Indians called it. Because of this, the Hudson's role in eroding the steep cliffs of the Palisades has effectively ceased since the last Ice Age. The Hudson is now said to flow in a "drowned valley" and some geologists consider this valley as true a fiord as those in Scandinavia. A fiord is a river valley deepened below sea level by glacial erosion and then filled by the sea as the ice melted. The only other one on the east coast of the United States is Somes Sound in Maine's Acadia National Park. Because of its depth, the lower Hudson River is navigable by large ships all the way up to Albany, and during its heyday, few river valleys approached it in its volume of traffic.

A wide assortment of sediments is washed into the river along its 300-mile journey. From these sediments, various minerals and organic nutrients are released into the water and churned up by the ocean tides to yield an extremely productive habitat for plants and animals. Its mixture of both saltwater and freshwater allows an extraordinary variety of fish to inhabit the river. Over 130 species have been collected by Texas Instruments (see Table I). Shiners, sunfish, carp, perch, catfish, bay anchovy, bluefish, flounder, American eel, needlefish, short-nosed sturgeon, and many others all call the Hudson "home". Even sea anemones and blue-claw crabs can live in the lower Hudson's brackish waters. Ospreys, herons, kingfishers, and several species of gulls fish the river, and thousands of canvasback ducks congregate in the waters each winter.

Black-crowned Night Heron on old piling

13

For some species of marine fish, such as striped bass, alewife, blueback herring, Atlantic sturgeon, tomcod, and shad, the Hudson estuary represents a major spawning and nursery habitat, supplying fish for oceanic and coastal waters. Some of the Hudson's most productive and interesting wildlife habitats are right below the Palisades. The shallow, 3-mile-wide Haverstraw Bay-Tappan Zee region is one of the most important nursery areas in the river. According to naturalist-fisherman Robert Boyle (author of *The Hudson River*), the 2-mile-long Piermont Marsh con-

TABLE I
136 FISH SPECIES IN THE HUDSON

Here is a list of fish species, 136 in all, collected by Texas Instruments in the Hudson. It does not include tarpon and ladyfish species reported by others last summer (1980). (From Newsletter of Hudson River Fishermen's Association, Spring 1981)

Alewife	Red Hake	Atlantic Croaker
Bay Anchovy	Central Mudminnow	Longhorn Sculpin
American Shad	White Bass	Round Herring
Bluefish	Rough Silverside	Hickory Shad
Bluegill	Summer Flounder	Atlantic Herring
Brown Bullhead	Crevalle Jack	Reef Silverside
Pumpkinseed	Silvery Minnow	Striped Anchovy
Black Crappie	Fallfish	Conger Eel
Carp	Weakfish	Striped Killifish
American Eel	Comely Shiner	Warmouth
Goldfish	Common Shiner	Bluntnose Minnow
Golden Shiner	Mimic Shiner	Walleye
Hogchoker	Lookdown	White Mullet
Tessellated Darter	Grass Pickerel	Yellow Bullhead
Banded Killifish	Sea Horse	Gray Snapper
Emerald Shiner	Logperch	Channel Catfish
Largemouth Bass	Trout Perch	Pollack
Mummichog	Northern Hogsucker	Seaboard Goby
Atlantic Menhaden	Fathead Minnow	Naked Goby
Northern Pike	Redfin Pickerel	Yellowtail Flounder
Chain Pickerel	Tautog	Windowpane
Blueback Herring	Four Bearded Rockling	Spotted Hake
White Sucker	Striped Cuskeel	*Prionotus,* sp.
Atlantic Silverside	Green Sunfish	Northern Stargazer
Rainbow Smelt	Northern Kingfish	Northern Sandlance
Smallmouth Bass	Spot	Fat Sleeper
Shortnose Sturgeon	Moonfish	Fourspot Flounder
Spottail Shiner	Brook Stickleback	Atlantic Mackerel
Atlantic Sturgeon	Northern Porgy	Black Sea Bass
Striped Bass	Winter Flounder	Smallmouth Flounder
Fourspine Stickleback	Tidewater Silverside	Rock Gunnel
Atlantic Tomcod	Sea Lamprey	Inshore Lizardfish
White Catfish	Gizzard Shad	*Umbra* sp.
White Perch	Silver Hake	Silver Lamprey
Yellow Perch	Striped Mullet	Rainbow Trout
Satinfin Shiner	Threespine Stickleback	Rosyface Shiner
Rock Bass	Brown Trout	*Fundulus* sp.
Northern Pipefish	Butterfish	*Myoxocephalus* sp.
Redbreast Sunfish	White Crappie	*Menidia* sp.
Atlantic Needlefish	Brook Trout	Syngnathid Unid.
Silver Perch	Longnose Dace	Mackerel Scad
Northern Puffer	Creek Chub	*Ammodytes* sp.
Blacknose Dace	Black Bullhead	Cunner
Bridle Shiner	Striped Searobin	Flying Gurnard
Cutlips Minnow	Northern Searobin	Shield Darter
Spotfin Shiner		

tains—in addition to fiddler crabs, waterfowl, and a variety of marsh, shore and song birds—the most northerly concentration of saline plants in New York state, including marsh elder, cylindrical bulrush, and four species of *Spartina* (salt marsh or cord grass).

Unfortunately, just when the Hudson seemed to have recovered from the pollution it suffered after World War II, the dangerous industrial chemical PCB (polychlorinated biphenyl) was discovered in the mid-1970s. Its sources were two General Electric capacitor plants near Fort Edward on the upper Hudson. They have since stopped discharging this poison into the waters and started a massive, multimillion dollar project of dredging it from "hotspots" in the river. Since 1976, however, most commercial fishing (except shad and sturgeon) has been banned by the New York State Department of Environmental Conservation until the river is cleaned up and restored to health once again. (Some bans were lifted in 1982 after a significant decline in PCB levels was found.)

A second, perhaps more insidious, danger to the river's biology has been the construction of massive power plants along the banks. As millions of gallons of riverwater are sucked into these plants for cooling purposes, many thousands of fish are killed by being suffocated or crushed against the intake screens. After 18 years of hearings, court cases, and arguments between the Hudson's electric utilities and environmental-fishermen groups, a landmark "Hudson River Peace Treaty" was signed in December, 1980. Besides agreeing to install special intake screens to reduce fish kills, and to cut down or even shut down operations during key fish-spawning weeks, the utilities will also support an independent foundation for Hudson fishery research and an experimental striped bass hatchery. Furthermore, Con Edison finally dropped its plans to construct a pumped storage plant on the Hudson's Storm King Mountain in Cornwall, New York. This controversial project had been fought by environmentalists since 1964 on the grounds of both fishery and scenic damage. In return for these terms, the environmental groups agreed to stop pushing for the construction of costly cooling towers at the Hudson's power plants on Roseton, Bowline, and Indian Points. Thus, the battle which many spokesmen claim was the foundation of the modern environmental movement at long last ended in a compromise.

Piermont Marsh, from top of Tallman Mountain

THE PALISADES TODAY

Whether hiking atop 830-foot High Tor in the north or studying a small diabase outcrop on Staten Island, a visitor to the Palisades today is experiencing the result of almost 200 million years of geological changes. And the forces of nature are still very much at work in shaping these cliffs. Freezing and thawing continue to topple the diabase columns, cause rock slides, and add to the talus pile beneath the cliff's steep eastern face. Thus, the cliff face continues to retreat westward as more and more of its rock is lost each year. Iron-bearing minerals in the diabase oxidize and turn brownish or reddish-yellow when exposed to the air, thus marking the place where rockfalls have occurred (long-exposed surfaces are dirty gray).

Erosion by water, ice, and wind removes soil and rock, while the decay of wood, leaves, and animals adds new organic matter to the ground. Streams carry many stones and boulders from the cliffs into the lower valleys. Although most drainage from the Palisades is off its long, westward-tilting slope into the Hackensack Valley, several narrow streams flow opposite this dip in the terrain and fall over the cliffs into the Hudson. Since these don't drain as extensive an area as those on the western slope, they tend to dry up in midsummer. Some of them meander slowly through low swamps in depressions or flat areas atop the cliffs. Others, flowing along natural lines of weakness, such as faults or fractures, have carved deep, steep-sided gullies and ravines, or "cloves," (from the Dutch "kloof" for cleft, gap, or ravine) on their way down to the river. One such stream, Green Brook, which emerges from Greenbrook Sanctuary in Tenafly, N.J., forms a spectacular series of cascades as it tumbles 250 feet over the Palisades. Impressive and beautiful to behold, these Falls also serve as a reminder that the powers of erosion continue to change the face of the Palisades.

North Brook Falls, Alpine, N.J.

Chapter II

History

THE NATIVES AND FIRST EUROPEANS

The lower Hudson Valley has certainly experienced some of the most important and singular events in American history. From some of the earliest colonial settlements to truly decisive Revolutionary War occurrences, to the growth of industries which helped build our young nation, and finally to the formation of one of the world's first and finest urban parks, the Palisades possesses a history matched by few other places in this country.

Humans first entered the lower Hudson Valley with the retreat of glaciers. These so-called "Palaeo-Indians" were hunters and may well have contributed to the extinction of the mammoth and mastodon, remains of which have been unearthed in Bergen County. The clovis projectile points of their weapons have been found in oyster and clamshell heaps dating back to 5,000 B.C. along the Hudson near Haverstraw Bay and Twombley's Landing north of Alpine. By 1500 B.C. these hunters were replaced by woodland Indians who integrated agriculture into their way of life and replaced the spear with the bow and arrow. These were the people who inhabited the region when Europeans first viewed the Hudson River and its Palisades.

The white men found the region's natives to be a peaceful people and described them as "handsome," "well-favored," and "loving." Strong and well-proportioned with reddish skin and jet black hair, they wore animal skins and often decorated themselves with feathers, tattoos, and necklaces of animal teeth and claws. These were the Tappan clan of the Munsee division of the Lenni Lenape, or Delawares, the largest eastern tribe of the Algonquin Nation. The Indian population of the entire lower Hudson region was estimated to be about 6,000. Although they occasionally set fire to the forests on the top of the Palisades to improve hunting conditions, their settlements were in the fertile Hackensack Valley and along the bays, tributaries, and shores of the Hudson. Here, beneath the steep cliffs which sheltered them from northwest winds, they fished and gathered shellfish in the bountiful waters and tended farms planted with maize and squash. Their villages consisted of groups of bark wigwams sometimes surrounded by a log palisade. Some of the trails which they used in travelling between the Hackensack and Hudson Valleys later became the first colonial roads on the Palisades. The names of some modern cities and towns of the Palisades, like Hoboken, Weehawken, and Nyack, have their origins in the language of the Delawares.

It is debated whether or not Verrazano preceded the Portuguese explorer Gomez as the first European to view the Palisades from the Hudson River in 1524. At any rate, the first good description of the region comes from the log of Robert Juet, aboard Henry Hudson's "Half Moon" in 1609. He detailed the journey of the famous ship south from Nova Scotia and New England, into New York harbor and up the Hudson past the "pleasant land with grass and flowers and goodly trees." Henry Hudson sailed the river all the way up to Albany, exploring the region and trading with the natives. It wasn't too long before the first Dutch settlements were established along the Palisades. In 1630 Michiel Pauw started an agricultural colony named Pavonia along the shore of the Hudson in present-day Jersey City and Hoboken. Thirty years later a stockaded settlement called Bergen was founded on a hill (Jersey City Heights) overlooking Pavonia and became New Jersey's first town.

In the present Bergen County region of the Palisades, the first organized hamlet was Vriessendael (today's Edgewater) founded in 1640 by Captain David DeVries as a plantation extending from the Hudson River westward across the ridge to Overpeck Creek. DeVries also possessed a second tract (today's Tappan) 15 miles north of his plantation on meadowland he bought from Indians in the Sparkill Creek valley opening from the Hudson River through the Palisades. Lands below the Palisades in present-day Nyack and Haverstraw were settled in the late 1600s. From these colonies the Dutch spread westward into the Hackensack Valley and north and

Hudson River Shore Path, looking north to Forest View

south along the Hudson's shores. Like the Indians before them, these Europeans found the Hudson convenient for trade and transport and rich in natural resources. Very few people settled the so-called "mountain top." The thin, rocky soils, rugged topography, and primeval forests of the Palisades summit represented physical—and possibly emotional—barriers to these early Europeans, and thus saved the woods from destruction.

The Lenni Lenape taught the Dutch much about the native medicinal herbs, game animals, and methods of agriculture. The Indians traded furs of beaver, otter, mink, and muskrat for axes, knives, hoes, iron pots, glass bottles, flint, and steel—all items which radically changed their lives. Treaties and agreements were symbolized with belts of wampum—small beads of shell made from periwinkles, clams and whelks—which was also used as money and necklaces. Unfortunately, as the Dutch farms and orchards spread along the Hudson "under the mountain," treaties were often ignored or breached by the white man. The Indians, to whom the idea of private property was completely alien, were gradually displaced, cheated, and plagued by European diseases and liquor.

Skirmishes were fought and outright massacres ordered by the Dutch authorities. The Indians retaliated by destroying both Pavonia and Vriessendael by 1645.

Inevitably, the Europeans expanded their new realm and forced the Lenni Lenape with all their unique traditions to disappear from their Palisades homelands forever. By 1710 most of the land along the Hudson from Sandy Hook to Bear Mountain was taken from the Indians. Many of the Munsee people migrated west to Pennsylvania and Ohio, and then were forced to move on still farther to Wisconsin and Canada or Kansas and Oklahoma. A few remained in isolated communities in the Ramapo Mountains of New Jersey. Though their descendants intermarried with many different nationalities over the years, they still retain a pride in their Indian heritage and strong feelings of independence and self-reliance.

With an abundance of trees for timber and fuel, fish, shellfish, game, and produce for food, and Palisades rocks for homes and seawalls, these early settlers became quite prosperous in this land of plenty. As travel and trade in these items increased along the river, stone docks were extended into the Hudson to serve as landings. Many of these docks were built where faults or gaps in the Palisades ridge permitted easy access to the river from more populated western valley settlements. Waldberg or Snedeker's Landing was established near the Long Clove south of Haverstraw. Slaughter's or Rockland Landing was built near Trough Hollow, a gap connecting the river to Rockland Lake.

Tappan Landing or the Sloat was at the eastern end of a valley (Sparkill Gap) leading through the ridge to the village of Tappan and represented a main shipping point for farm produce originating in the interior of Rockland and northern Bergen Counties. Near another gap in the ridge, Sneden's Landing was established in 1719 as the western landing of a ferry from New York (Dobb's Ferry). Burdett's Ferry was operated in the 18th century from Edgewater, N.J., where a picturesque fault or ravine cuts through the Palisades and provides easy access to Fort Lee and the country beyond the cliffs. During the Revolutionary War this landing was used by

American Troops as a connecting link between Fort Lee on the overlooking cliffs and Fort Washington across the river.

On the other hand, some of the docks such as Lower Closter or Huyler's and Upper Closter or Alpine were built right below the cliffs and were connected to the western valleys via steep trails which ascended the Palisades. All of these river landings became important means of communication and trade between New York City and the wild back country.

A few thriving farms and villages below the cliffs lasted until the early 1900's when the Palisades Interstate Park bought them. For example, the fishing village of Undercliff, extending northward from below Englewood Cliffs, N.J., had remained in the

Van Wagener headstone, Undercliff Cemetery (former fishing village)

19

same family (Van Wagener) since before the Revolutionary War. The old family cemetery is still there beside a picnic area, with headstones dating back to the early 1800's. Throughout the Palisades, from Jersey City to Englewood to Haverstraw, one can still follow these historic trails, stop at the old river landings, and visit examples of beautiful old Dutch and colonial architecture.

THE REVOLUTIONARY WAR

When Thomas Paine wrote, "These are the times that try men's souls" in late November of 1776, he and the remaining 3,000 men in General George Washington's army were retreating from the British after an extremely close encounter on the Palisades. It was indeed one of the lowest points of the Revolutionary War. On November 16, from Fort Lee Bluff (Point Bluff) on the Palisades, 250 feet above the Hudson, the General had watched helplessly as the Americans under General Magaw were forced to haul down the flag in surrender to the British at Fort Washington directly across the river. The Fort Constitution redoubt and encampment site (later named Fort Lee after General Charles Lee) was built there the previous summer where the Palisades extend farthest out into the river. It was meant to complement Fort Washington (built on the highest elevation along Manhattan's shore) and to assist that fort in preventing the British from controlling the lower Hudson Valley, which was considered the key to the whole rebellion. Sunken sloops, two large gun ships, chained logs, and other impediments were strung across the river to block the British fleet from sailing up the Hudson. But on November 5, six weeks after capturing the American fort at Paulus Hook on the river below present-day Jersey City, British ships managed to break through the blockade while being bombarded by artillery from Fort Lee Bluff and Burdett's Landing.

Meanwhile, after capturing Fort Washington, British and Hessian troops advanced toward Yonkers where, on November 19, under the cover of darkness and heavy fog, Lord Cornwallis crossed the Hudson over to the Palisades with over 5,000 men. The ancient small stone house where legend has it that Cornwallis rested that night is still preserved at the Alpine Boat Basin (old Closter Dock) as a Palisades Interstate Park museum. Before dawn on a rainy November 20th, Cornwallis and his troops scaled a precipitous path up the Palisades, hauling arms and a heavy cannon. Whether they ascended via Upper Closter Dock Road or Lower Closter Road (Huyler Road) 1½ miles farther south is still the subject of local historical debate. The Bergen County Historical Society claims that Lower Closter Dock and Road were the sites of the British landing and ascent. They have published several accounts based on contemporary maps, documents, and diaries, and have erected historical markers on old Huyler Road to demonstrate this claim. Other well-known local historians, however, maintain that Upper Closter Dock and Road were used, and still others suggest that perhaps both roads were used by the British in scaling the cliffs.

At any rate, American patriots (possibly from Sneden's Landing farther north) fortunately discovered the surprise landing and warned Major General Nathaniel Greene at Fort Lee. Greene sent word to General Washington who was then at his headquarters in Hackensack about 6 miles away. Washington ordered that Fort Lee be evacuated, and then immediately left Hackensack to meet the American soldiers on their bitter and hasty retreat westward from the last American-held post on the lower Hudson. Moments later, Cornwallis completed the march over the top of the Palisades down toward present-day County Road, then to Fort Lee, only to find the fort and its supplies just abandoned. Thus, although the

British now had control of the lower Hudson Valley and New York City, the possible end of the American fight for independence was narrowly averted.

Farther north in New York State, groups of patriots who called themselves the Minute Men and the Shore Guard were effectively guarding the shore below the Palisades and preventing the British from landing in the hamlets of Nyack and Haverstraw to replenish their provisions. Beacon lights at lookouts atop Hook Mountain and High Tor warned the Americans of the approaching British fleets. Haverstraw Bay was the scene of the Hudson's only naval battle during the War – an indecisive but costly encounter between the British fleet and five American ships.

Tappan was the headquarters for the American Army at various times during the War and contains several historic buildings on Oak Tree Road. There is the '76 House Restaurant (Mabie's Tavern), where the Orangetown Resolutions were adopted in 1774 to protest acts of the British government and where Benedict Arnold's co-conspirator, the British spy, Major John André, was imprisoned in 1780. The nearby DeWindt House (built in 1700) was occupied by George Washington several times during the Revolution, including André's trial and execution. At Sneden's Landing in Palisades, N.Y., a ferry across the Hudson to New York was operated by the Tory, Molly Sneden. At the end of the War this same landing became the site where the American flag was first saluted

Cornwallis House, Alpine Boat Basin

by direct order of the British Parliament in 1783. The graves of Revolutionary War soldiers are preserved in Rockland County's oldest cemetery, on Old Mountain Road in Upper Nyack.

POST-REVOLUTIONARY DEVELOPMENTS

After the War for Independence was won, the Palisades region experienced increased development and activity as its natural resources became more valuable to the growing cities. Near the top of the cliffs the forests were still mostly unbroken, with only two developed settlements, Fort Lee and Liberty Pole (Englewood), both situated in back of the cliff edge. But along the Hudson River, fishing hamlets thrived as the market for striped bass and shad in New York City grew. By the mid-1800s the fishing village of Undercliff contained over 800 people and extended along the river for 11 miles from Fort Lee to Sneden's Landing – an almost unbroken line of stone and frame dwellings, shingled cottages, boatyards, wharves, and fishing shacks. Powder

High Gutter Point, a former "pitching point" north of state line

Huyler. This landing became a very busy riverfront community, with a dry dock for ship building, a tavern, a general store, winter skating parties, and three or four families as permanent residents. Each day during the fruit season, as many as 40 to 50 oxen-drawn wagons full of farm produce were taken down Huyler Road to be unloaded onto sailing vessels or steamboats. People bound for New York rode large farm wagons, which carried up to 24 passengers, to the cliff edge. Here they boarded smaller rigs which descended this old road to Huyler Landing. Today this road is maintained as a historical trail, but the 130-year-old building at the Landing was lost to fire in 1973.

Upper Closter, or Alpine Dock, was also a regular landing place for Hudson River sloops and schooners, and the Kearny House there ("Cornwallis Headquarters") became a popular inn. In the 1860s another steep road was built down to the river along a narrow fault or gulch in the cliffs. Known as Lambier's Road, it connected William Lambier's farm and residence (still located on present-day Hudson Avenue in Tenafly, N.J.) to the Buckingham Long Dock. By this time as many as 150 sloops could be seen on the Hudson at one time, carrying timber, stone, and produce from the interior.

Throughout the 19th century, the Industrial Era gradually transformed the character of many quiet Palisades hamlets and villages. Starting in 1815 a brickmaking industry succeeded in making Haverstraw the most prosperous community on the west banks of the Hudson. By 1900, 40 brick yards produced 360 million bricks annually and employed over 2,400 workers. This prosperity ended, however, when concrete and steel replaced brick after the turn of the century. Today none of the brickworks remain. In the 1830s Rockland Lake became the site of an important ice industry which harvested cakes of pure, crystal-clear ice from the spring-fed lake. The ice was transported to Hudson River boats first via a chute and later, in the 1850s, via a cog or gravity-incline railway which ran through Trough Hollow, the gap in the Palisades connecting the lake to Rockland (Slaughter's) Landing 300 feet below. At one time, the lake's Knickerbocker Ice Company em-

houses along the shore became sites for religious meetings and dances. Today the landings and cemeteries still bear the Dutch names: Van Wagener, Bloomer, Huyler.

Farmers in the western valley behind the Palisades brought their produce down to the Hudson for shipment to the city, and the roads descending the valleys, or cloves, and steep cliffs to reach the landings became heavily travelled. Captain John Huyler purchased a confiscated Tory's farm in 1784 on present-day County Road in Cresskill, that included Lower Closter Landing. These properties were passed on to his son Peter in 1818 and grandson George in 1872. The old Indian trail connecting Cresskill, the cliffs, and the river was improved, and the name of both the Landing and Road was changed from Lower Closter to ployed over 2,000 people, but this industry also disappeared in the 1920s with the development of mechanical refrigeration. Remains of the old ice docks and transporting machinery can still be seen along the Nyack Shore Path.

The village of Piermont (formerly Tappan Landing or simply the Sloat) was built in 1841 as the eastern terminus of the Erie Railroad which would run down from Dunkirk, N.Y., on the shore of Lake Erie. A mile-long pier was built over the Hudson's extensive shallows here and into its deeper, navigable channel, where passengers and freight were transferred from trains to boats bound for New York City. Coal from Pennsylvania mines was transported here by the Erie Railroad and loaded on barges for New York. The pier was also the site of a thriving ferry landing for steamboats crossing the river or heading north. In 1859 the Northern Railroad of New Jersey was completed to its junction with the Erie Railroad at Piermont, resulting in an end to the isolation of many Bergen and Rockland County towns, an era of skyrocketing land values, and the decay of many Hudson River landings (Closter, Huyler's, Sneden's). In 1862, ten years after a change in the railroad's charter allowed it to make a direct connection to Jersey City, this city became the eastern terminus of the Erie. That year, half the populaton of Piermont moved away.

The 19th century will also be remembered as the era of the Hudson River steamboats, which landed to pick up freight and passengers all along the Palisades (e.g., Haverstraw, Nyack, Piermont, Closter). Throughout the 1820s, '30s and '40s, steamboats flourished on the Hudson, making it one of the busiest thoroughfares in America. Some of the first steamboats were built at landings right in Nyack and Haverstraw. Ferries also operated from Westchester to Rockland Counties and from New York City to Fort Lee and Jersey City, exchanging both people and resources between the rapidly expanding communities on both sides of the Hudson. The steamboat era ended with the coming of the Hudson River railroads in the 1850s.

Increased demands for wood as railroad ties, as timber in ship building, and especially as fuel for Hudson River steamboats, industries, and New York City fireplaces put added stress on the Palisades forests. In 1825 an estimated 100,000 cords of wood were cut for steamboat fuel in the lower Hudson Valley. In 1846 almost 11,000

Ruins of 19th century estate atop Palisades in Greenbrook Sanctuary, N.J. – note forsythia blooming in background and day lily leaves

Former quarry below Hook Mountain, N.Y.

Throughout the late 19th century, spurred on by the emergence of a new, wealthy leisure class and promoted by the railroad, spacious summer resorts and large landscaped estates were built in communities like Nyack along the river and Englewood Cliffs atop the Palisades. Such residences boasted views of the imposing cliffs and the beautiful Hudson and were within commuting distance via railroad from the developing cities on the other side. Greycliff, the first of the cliff-top estates, was built by New York publisher William Dana at Englewood Cliffs in the late 1850s. In the 1860s a big, 300-room hotel, the Palisades Mountain House, was constructed near Greycliff, close to the present site of St. Peter's College. Accessible both by railroad and a zigzag road down to the steamboat landing on the Hudson, the Mountain House served as a retreat for prominent New Yorkers and a scenic, spacious site for political gatherings. In 1884 it burned down and became the site of the William Allison mansion, now a park. In the 20th century, another large resort hotel, the Riviera, was built on top of the cliffs in this region, but it was removed when the Palisades Interstate Parkway was built in 1954.

At the opposite extreme was a rural community of free blacks who lived in the Skunk Hollow section near the state line throughout the 19th century. Located about a quarter-mile from the cliff edge, this community began about 1806 with a small group of mostly former slaves. Though the land was very marginal, they were able to farm it and establish a very stable, close-knit community with homes and a church built from the native timber and diabase rock. The population peaked at about 75 inhabitants in the latter half of the 19th century and was abandoned in the early 1900s. Now most of the land with its stone walls, foundations, and cellar holes is owned by the Palisades Interstate Park.

By and large, however, these cliff-top communities and estates were few and far between, and for the most part the summit of the Palisades north of New York City remained heavily wooded and unsettled by the turn of the century. In fact, an 1894 report by New Jersey's state forester classified the Palisades as 11,000 acres of unbroken forest and among the best in the entire state.

cords from Hook Mountain and the Tors were consumed by the Haverstraw brickyards, which were also responsible for the destruction of much terrain by excavating great holes to get clay. Cordwood was either carried to the boat docks down the steep roads, conveyed to the river by wood slides, or actually tossed from the top of the cliffs down narrow ravines to the river. These so-called "pitching points" were located where the cliffs were steepest and the river deep along the shore, such as High Tom in Englewood Cliffs, DePeyster's and Ruckman Points in Alpine, and High Gutter Point at the New Jersey-New York state line. Wealthy New Yorkers acquired tracts of forest on top of the Palisades, each with its own pitching place to supply wood for their fireplaces in the city.

Meanwhile, another activity was spreading along the cliffs which did threaten to destroy its scenery and wildlife. The sandstone underlying the cliffs had long been used for buildings and forts. Beginning in the early 1800s, quarries next began to remove much of the loose diabase talus sloping down from the cliffs for ships' ballast, buildings, Belgian-block pavements, and Manhattan piers and seawalls (such as the one around Governor's Island). As quarrying flourished, boarding houses were built along the river to house the quarry men, and the Dutch residents at Undercliff supplied them with quarry sloops to transport the rock to New York. The construction of forts in New York harbor during the War of 1812 created a new demand for diabase.

When the construction of roads and skyscrapers in New York City demanded more of this hard, valuable "trap rock" as rock fill for highways, riprap for railroad beds (like that of the New York Central), and broken stone for concrete, the devastation rapidly increased. In the Hook Mountain area alone, there were 31 quarries along the river from Grandview to Upper Nyack in the 1830s. Quarrying reached a peak in the 1890s concurrent with the development of dynamite and improved steam-crushing and earth-moving equipment, making it possible for the cliffs themselves to be blasted away. From Weehawken, north to Hook Mountain and High Tor, scores of quarries exploded the cliffs and toppled one after another of the picturesque rock columns and pillars. Citizens of both New York and New Jersey saw their unique geological and scenic monument being rapidly destroyed. It was left to New Jersey's Women's Clubs to save the day.

THE PALISADES INTERSTATE PARK

In his book, *American Sublime,* Prof. Raymond O'Brien explores the events leading up to the formation of the Palisades Interstate Park from the perspective of our nation's evolving sense of landscape aesthetics. O'Brien maintains that the birth of the modern conservation and preservation movements in our country in the late 19th century – movements of which the creation of the Interstate Park was perhaps the most stunning example – must be viewed in the context of which natural features were considered beautiful and worth saving for posterity.

Contrary to views espoused by many historians, O'Brien believes that the early Dutch settlers did not necessarily fear the Palisades but actually praised and appreciated its natural beauty. On the other hand, the English and Puritan settlers, who spread down into the Hudson Valley from New England and largely replaced the Dutch in the late 17th and 18th centuries, feared the forests and scorned anything as useless as aesthetics. By the 1820s, however, the Ro-

mantic Era took hold in America and influenced the spread of new attitudes toward natural beauty. The concept of "sublime" beauty – wild, untamed, raw, and awe-inspiring scenery as opposed to the tamer and more sentimentalized notion of "picturesque" beauty – was sought by travellers and landscape artists. Rising majestically out of the Hudson River, the Highlands and the sheer cliffs of the Palisades with their associated waterfalls and rock pillars came to be idolized as the epitome of sublime beauty. Soon the lower Hudson Valley acquired a universal reputation as a prime source of aesthetic inspiration and national pride, and as an area containing some of the finest scenery in the world. It was here that these new attitudes and tastes were nurtured and tested throughout the 19th century.

The Hudson River school of landscape artists, including Durand, Church, Willis, Cole, and Downing, was an influential force in spreading the sublime images of the Palisades and Hudson Highlands. By the

Women's Federation Monument atop Palisades, south of state line

was established in 1885. And, reacting against the quarrying which was destroying one of the country's most famous examples of grand scenery, preservation-minded groups successfully brought about the creation of what O'Brien regards as the culmination of the Romantic ideal of the sublimely aesthetic landform–the Palisades Interstate Park.

After an 1894 proposal to make the Palisades a military reservation failed to pass the House of Representatives, the New Jersey Federation of Women's Clubs fought for legislation to protect the Palisades. In 1900 their efforts resulted in the formation of an Interstate Park Commission by Governors Roosevelt (New York) and Voorhees (New Jersey). Five commissioners per state were appointed with the powers to acquire whatever territory was deemed necessary to preserve the shorefront and cliffs. South of Fort Lee, the Palisades shorefront was already mostly ruined by factories, warehouses, ship terminals, quarries, and pollution, and the cliffs themselves largely obscured by apartments and crowded settlements. The Commission's goal was to establish a continuous and permanent Interstate Park between Fort Lee, N.J. and Piermont, N.Y. Almost immediately, the Commission's first president, George Perkins, Sr., convinced his business partner, J. P. Morgan to contribute over $120,000 for the purchase of the Carpenter Brothers Quarry at Fort Lee where 12,000 cubic yards of rock were being blasted away daily. This was one of the most destructive and visibly active of the quarries, even staging elaborate public ceremonies during the blasting away of such dramatic cliff landmarks as the Washington and Indian Head columns north of Fort Lee. Carpenter Brothers was bought out on Christmas Eve, 1900, for $132,500. In 1901 the New York and New Jersey state legislatures appropriated $400,000 and $50,000, respectively, for additional purchases. Thus began an era of active land acquisition aided in no small way by such philanthropic families as the Allisons, Perkinses, Harrimans, Twombleys, and especially the Rockefellers.

In the early years of the Park, land was bought for 200 to 500 dollars per acre, and only a million dollars was needed to pur-

mid-19th century, the Hudson Valley's fame increased by leaps and bounds as appreciation of its beauty and wildness was augmented by pride in its historic significance and an interest in its unique geology. Finally, beginning with the creation of the first national parks (Yosemite in 1864 and Yellowstone in 1872), a national preservation and conservation movement originated in this country, with roots in the Romantic concept of sublime beauty. As more and more of the country's wildlife, resources, and scenery were being squandered, misused, or thoughtlessly destroyed, a growing number of people became concerned that the most stunning, sublime scenery be preserved forever. Thus, the Adirondack Preserve with its magnificent high peaks and numerous lakes and rivers chase the first 13½ miles of cliffs, talus slope, and shorefront. By 1905, 75% of the land from Fort Lee to the New York State line had been given to, or purchased by, the Park, including Lydia Lawrence's gift of her "Cliffside" estate near Sneden's Landing. By 1909 most of the remaining fishermen's houses were bought out by the Park. The Park Commission then took steps to stop the quarrying which was destroying the cliffs in the New York sections of the Palisades. Further gifts and acquisitions in these sections resulted in state parks at Hook Mountain and Blauvelt by 1915, Tallman Mountain by 1930, and at both High Tor and Little Tor in 1943. The 1950s saw Fort Lee Bluff and Rockland Lake saved by the Park from development. In recognition of its monumental achievements in preserving one of America's most scenic wonders, the Palisades Interstate Park was designated New Jersey's first National Historic Landmark in Conservation.

Today there are over 6,200 acres of public recreational lands in the Palisades region of the Interstate Park system, preserving a long, almost continuous section of the ridge from Fort Lee, N.J., north to Haverstraw, N.Y. (North of the Palisades, the Interstate Park comprises another 75,000 acres of land in the Hudson Highlands and Shawangunk Mountains, including Bear Mountain, Harriman, Storm King Mountain, and Minnewaska State Parks.) Women's Federation Monument, north of Alpine, N.J., is a small stone castle at the cliff edge commemorating those Women's Clubs which were the impetus behind the creation of this great park. In more recent years (since the mid-1960s), the Rockland County Park Commission has followed the lead of the Interstate Park by preserving 2,000 acres of woodland in Rockland County. Half of this lies along the Palisades ridge and serves to fill in most of the gaps between the lands in the Interstate park system. (See final chapter for more specific details about each of these Parks—past background, current facilities, and natural highlights—as well as other county- and town-owned natural areas preserved along the Palisades)

PUBLIC RECREATION – THE EARLY YEARS

It didn't take long for the Palisades to be developed into a major recreational park. By the 1920s, three steamships were carrying over a million people a year on excursions from New York City to landings below Hook Mountain and Bear Mountain. The Park operated these tours until 1931 when the ships were sold to private operators. Along the shore from Fort Lee to Alpine, old docks were refurbished, new ones were built, and the seawall was strengthened by the Park. Bathing beaches and bathhouses were established shortly after 1900 at Hazzard's Beach, Ross Dock (Carpenter's Beach), Englewood-Bloomers, Undercliff, and Alpine. These recreational centers were equipped with refreshment stands, parking lots, playgrounds, rest rooms, picnic areas, grills, and even gas stations at Alpine and Englewood. Photographs taken at these sites during their heyday are reminiscent of today's crowded beaches on Long Island. After Hook Mountain was acquired, similar facilities were created in Upper Nyack and Haverstraw along the river.

Boat basins were constructed at the Englewood and Alpine Landings and later (1931) at Forest View just north of Alpine. This latter area was situated on the shore beneath the Park's most magnificent cliff scenery and rugged talus forests. It contained a large ballfield, fireplaces, pavilion, rest rooms, picnic tables, and camp grounds. Tent camping was also permitted along the river at Powder Dock, Canoe Beach, Twombley's Landing, Excelsior Point, Englewood Cliffs, and, starting in 1931, at Ross Dock's "Camp Colony" below Fort Lee, where organized groups could reserve campsites for a week or entire season. In 1927 a popular trailer park for motor tourists was opened atop the Palisades in Englewood. All of these sites were provided with picnic areas, and pavilions were added to Alpine, Undercliff, and Excelsior Grove. During the Depression years of the 1930s, much of the construction and maintenance work in the Park was performed by federal work crews like the Civilian Conservation Corps (C.C.C.) and Works Progress Administration (W.P.A.). Much of their fine stone work has lasted to this day.

The recreational sites were most accessible from the river by steamboat, motorboat, or canoe. Ferries carried passengers from New York City to Edgewater/Fort Lee, Hazzard's Beach, and Englewood, and from Yonkers to Alpine and Forest View. Besides boat, access to these sites was made possible by a charming 13-mile trail skirting the river's edge from Fort Lee to the New York state line. Named the Shore Trail, this path also led the hiker to some of the Park's most spectacular and primeval cliff, forest, and talus scenery north of Alpine. In 1916 the scenic Henry Hudson Drive was built above the Shore Trail from Fort Lee to Alpine, where it connects to a road leading up

to the top of the cliffs (where the Park's New Jersey Headquarters building is now located). This Drive joined the two ferries at Englewood and Alpine and made it possible for people to visit some of the Park's facilities by automobile. From both the Shore Trail and the Drive, hikers could reach the top of the Palisades via several old trails and roads which wound up the cliffs to afford spectacular vistas of the Hudson River and New York skyline.

During the Park's first two decades most of its attention was focused on lands below the cliff edge, including the cliff face, talus slopes, and river shore. Not only were these areas being rapidly destroyed by quarrying and thus in most immediate need of protection, but the recreational opportunities along the river were more varied. Two of the first areas acquired by the Park on top of the Palisades in New Jersey were Women's Federation Park in Alpine (1909), to commemorate the role of the Women's Clubs in saving the cliffs, and the Greenbrook area. The latter comprised 165 acres in Tenafly and Alpine, and was noted for its outstanding scenery, rugged terrain, dense forests, and 250-foot "Greenbrook Falls." The Park acquired this area in 1917 as one of its first cliff-top purchases and planned to

Rock steps on trail descending Palisades from Women's Federation Monument to Hudson River shore

develop it into a major recreational center, including an artificial 15-acre lake. These plans were dropped, however, and the southern end of the area was used in 1933 as a base by the Civilian Conservation Corps (who worked below the cliffs to stop erosion on the talus slopes) and as a bomb demolition center by the Army following World War II. In 1946 the Park permitted the private, non-profit Palisades Nature Association to develop the entire 165 acres into Greenbrook Sanctuary, one of the state's finest centers for environmental education, nature preservation, and outdoor field studies.

By the 1930s more of the Park's attention gradually shifted to the top of the Palisades as the real estate boom following the completion of the George Washington Bridge into New York City brought the threat of residential and commercial exploitation to these prime lands. In 1935 John D. Rockefeller donated to the Park a long, 700-acre strip of land atop the Palisades which he had purchased to prevent its development. Although his gift had no strings attached, Rockefeller expressly desired that someday a parkway be built along the top of the Palisades to permit the public to safely and conveniently enjoy the area's scenery and to form one continuous park by linking all of its sections. During the next few years this idea became more and more attractive. Garden clubs and nature societies were persuaded to support the "Parkway Plan" as the only way to legally buy out both the planned and existing developments (such as the Riviera Resort Hotel in Englewood Cliffs) which separated the Park's various sections. Park Commissioner and spokesman, Col. George Perkins stressed that the Parkway would enable more people to enjoy the Palisades and, through condemnation procedures, would guard the area against quarrying, tree-cutting, residential developments, and commercial resorts or nightclubs. Following Rockefeller's 1935 gift, 90% of the lands on top of the Palisades were in park hands and the remaining 10% could only be added by condemnation for parkway purposes. In this way, said Perkins, the entire Palisades would become one linear park rather than 15 separate parcels.

The Parkway would be a scenic drive

Palisades cliffs in spring, looking south from state line

with overlooks, woodland paths, landscape screening, reforestation plantings, picnic nooks, and no billboards or commercial traffic. It would consist of two one-way drives, separated by a wooded island 30 to 300 feet wide. After running for 12 scenic miles atop the Palisades from Fort Lee to the New York state line, the Parkway would then swing away from the Hudson and traverse the Ramapos and Hudson Highlands for its remaining 26 miles to the Park's New York Headquarters at Bear Mountain. Finally, in responding to those who asked why the existing Route 9W couldn't simply be modified to serve the same purposes, Perkins explained that a widened 9W route would not only be more dangerous with all its private entrances and driveways and lack of a center island, but

29

Hikers along Nyack-Haverstraw Shore Path

despite these efforts, the necessary funding was granted by the state legislatures in 1946. Construction started in 1947 in New York and the following year in New Jersey. By 1958 the Parkway was opened as a limited-access, scenic route, with New Jersey exits to the Englewood and Alpine Boat Basin Recreation Areas, the Henry Hudson Drive, and scenic overlooks in Englewood (Rockefeller Lookout), Alpine, and the State Line. Today, although the Parkway has become a major commuter artery between New Jersey and New York City, it has attained a reputation as one of the most scenic, pleasant parkways in the east.

Concurrent with the completion of the Parkway, the blue-blazed Palisades Long Path was cut from Fort Lee northward along the entire length of the ridge. This path extends beyond the northern end of the Palisades in Mount Ivy and into the Hudson Highlands. It passes some spectacular vistas, ancient forests, and remains of old estates which were razed as the top of the Palisades passed from private to public ownership.

The geological significance, historical importance, and natural beauty of the cliffs, forests, and river made the Palisades extremely attractive to millions of visitors. In 1908, 4,000 campers used the Palisades on weekends and holidays, and by 1921 well over a million people a year visited the Palisades. This number included 254,000 bathers, 20,000 canoeists, and 4,700 motorboaters. In 1928 over a million cars reached the Palisades by ferries from New York City (130 St. and Dyckman St.) to Fort Lee and Englewood, and from Yonkers to Alpine. The Henry Hudson Drive below the cliffs became a very busy tourist road. The group campsites at Ross Dock were used by more than 3,000 people in 1932.

It was about this time, however, that several factors brought a decline in the use of the Palisades. The opening of the George Washington Bridge across the Hudson in 1931 was followed by an immediate reduction in the number of vehicles using the New York City ferries. Hazzard's Beach was closed in 1938 shortly after the 158 Street-Fort Lee ferry was stopped. In 1941 the Dyckman Street-Englewood ferry closed down because of gasoline and tire rationing during the War. A pedestrian ferry

twice as costly due to the need for extensive straightening of sharp curves and leveling of dips. Furthermore, this alternative would not solve the old problem of eliminating the private developments atop the cliffs and consolidating the Palisades Interstate Park.

In 1945 and 1946 a very determined party of opposition, at the core of which were nature lovers, hikers, and property owners on the Palisades, was created against the construction of the Parkway. First the Committee for the Preservation of the Palisades and then the New Jersey Association for Parks and Parkways were formed to condemn the Parkway on the grounds that it was unneeded, financially wasteful, and environmentally destructive. Politicians, they said, were sacrificing the Palisades to provide easy access to the new Bear Mountain parks for the cities masses, resumed operation in 1949 but closed down two years later for lack of passengers, as people now used buses and cars to cross the river over the George Washington Bridge for more distant weekend excursions. The Alpine ferry suffered the same fate in 1956, a year after the opening of the Tappan Zee Bridge.

During World War II, with its gas rationing and other restrictive measures, the Park naturally experienced a reduction in its number of visitors, and both the Ross Dock Camp Colony and the Englewood-Bloomer bathing area were closed. After the war, pollution of the Hudson River forced the closing of all the beaches, and the campgrounds and recreational areas along the river from Fort Lee northward were gradually abandoned. Water pollution also caused the number of commercial shad fishermen along this same stretch of the river to drop from 20 in 1947 to 5 in 1957. When the Palisades Parkway opened in 1957, offering convenient access to sports fields and swimming pools in the larger, more intensively developed New York sections of the Park, the New Jersey sections suffered further reductions in visitors.

In recent years the Park has experienced somewhat of a revival in both visitor use and the upgrading of recreational facilities. Increases in the price of fuel have caused millions of outdoor enthusiasts from the cities to take a renewed interest in the natural wonders just minutes away. Government funding and private grants have made it possible for the Park to operate summer youth programs to improve the hiking trails, playgrounds, and picnic areas, and simultaneously offer fresh air and outdoor education to urban teenagers. Cross-country ski trails have been added at Blauvelt and Rockland Lake State Parks and State Line Lookout, and bike paths to the state parks at Hook Mountain, Tallman Mountain, and Rockland Lake. The two remaining boat basins at Englewood and Alpine have been expanded to a combined capacity of 252 boats, and facilities at both these sites are being refurbished. Rockland Lake State Park has become one of the most popular and heavily used parks, with facilities for swimming, golf, jogging, biking, fishing, ice-skating, and nature study. In 1984, over 60,000 people used the two golf courses, and 24,000 visited the Nature Center.

Each year from May to late September the excursion ship, *Dayliner*, carries about 50,000 people from New York City to Bear

Mute swan on nest in Rockland Lake, N.Y. (Hook Mountain in back)

Mountain. In 1976 a major visitor center opened at Fort Lee Historic Site with exhibits, a 200-seat auditorium, information desk, and programs. Almost 54,000 people visited the site in 1979, including over 2,000 students enrolled in American history programs. That same year the attendance in the New Jersey section of the Palisades alone was over 2.2 million people. Membership in the Palisades Nature Association which operates Greenbrook Sanctuary approached 3,000 families in 1985.

Today, as in 1900, there is an abrupt transition in scenery and land use at Fort Lee. Southward, the scene is blighted by factories, high-rise apartments, warehouses, and crowded settlements. Northward, the Palisades is preserved as park land, perhaps even more densely forested now than in 1900. The beauty and wildness of much of the Palisades remain unaltered and people are now rediscovering this area's potential for outdoor recreation, education, and renewal of the spirit. (See final chapter, "A Palisades Tour Guide" for more specific details about these places)

Chapter III

Habitats of the Palisades

THE PALISADES FORESTS – AN OVERVIEW

When the Europeans first explored and settled the Hudson Valley, the Palisades was covered with fine old forests, possibly interrupted here and there by openings resulting from hurricanes, lightning, or fires set by Indians. Many of the oaks, sugar maples, chestnuts, and hemlocks were undoubtedly over 300 years old and 12 feet in circumference. Today, over eight decades after the creation of the Palisades Interstate Park, the forests have matured and covered up most of the openings left by former human habitations and activities. This writer has taken measurements and increment borings of trees in several sections of the Palisades and has discovered many specimens exceeding 200 years in age, with a few even reaching the three-century mark. Oaks, ashes, and hemlocks commonly tower over 100 feet and approach 10 feet in circumference. The most enormous trees are the tulip trees, many of which exceed 115 feet in height. A most impressive specimen – 130 feet tall and 18 feet in circumference – grows on the east side of 9W at its junction with Route 340 in Sparkill (just north of Tallman State Park). Coincidentally, just around the corner on Route 340 in front of the former Chownes Homestead (now a restaurant) stands a white ash which is 22 feet in girth and has a 97-foot crown spread! It is reputed to be 300 years old and the largest ash in the United States.

There are about 60 kinds of trees growing naturally on the Palisades. The forests of the Palisades, however, are not uniform. Differences in topography, drainage, and soils result in surprising variations in the species of trees (and, as a result, in the

Giant tulip tree (18 feet in girth, 130 feet tall) & child

shrubs, smaller plants, and animals) predominating in a given woodland. Cliff edges and rocky summits, sunny ridges and dry hillsides, fertile coves and shaded valleys, steep talus slopes and dark ravines, swampy lowlands and streamsides, rock slides and abandoned clearings are all present on the Palisades. Each habitat has its own forest covering and it is this variety that makes a Palisades hike so interesting and stimulating. (In the following sections on habitats of the Palisades, the common names of the trees appear in *A Field Guide to Trees and Shrubs* by George Petrides in the Peterson Field Guide Series.)

MIXED OAK FOREST

In the early years of this century the woodlands of the northeastern United States experienced a disaster which changed their appearance forever. A fungus, accidentally brought into this country on chestnut logs imported from overseas, infected the bark of our native American chestnut trees and spread throughout their range. In less than two decades this deadly "chestnut blight" virtually eliminated the tree that had been the dominant species in most of the upland forests throughout this part of the country. The chestnut trees on top of the Palisades were stricken about 1910, and in 1918, 6,000 feet of dead or dying chestnut logs were salvaged by the Park and used for lumber. Today some surviving root systems still send up sprouts which themselves succumb to the disease in a few years. There are a few 50-foot-tall chestnut trees, however, which this writer has found on the Palisades. Increment borings reveal them to be at least 50 years old and a very few even bear chestnuts each fall, offering at least a glimmer of hope for the return of this species to our forests some day.

Today the upland forests of the Palisades are dominated by several species of oaks, the trees best adapted to this region's comparatively hot summers, cold winters, and shallow, acid soils. In fact, all of extreme southern New York and most of northern and central New Jersey are part of that section of the United States labelled the "mixed oak" (formerly the "oak-chestnut") forest. (Farther north on this continent, the progressively cooler and moister conditions cause the oaks to gradually give way first to maples, birches, and hemlocks, and then to spruces and firs.) On exposed, well-drained hillsides and dry, sunny ridges, five species of oaks more or less dominate the Palisades woodlands. They provide shelter, acorns, grubs, and a great variety of leaf-eating insects for woodpeckers, songbirds, squirrels, and chipmunks.

Red oak, the state tree of New Jersey, is the most common and fastest growing spe-

Mixed oak forest (from left to right) white oak, red oak, black oak

cies. It is recognized by the bark's shiny ridges and dark crevices, which resemble black and white stripes or "ski runs" running up the trunk. Next in abundance is white oak with its massive trunk and limbs, and loose, flaky, light gray bark. The third, identified by its thicker leaves and rough, almost black bark, is black oak. Thriving along the cliff edge and rocky outcrops is chestnut oak, characterized by its unique, deeply furrowed bark and chestnut-like leaves. Finally, on the driest, poorest sites is the least common upland oak, scarlet oak, named for the autumn color of its deeply lobed leaves.

Smaller and of lesser importance than the oaks are two species of upland hickories— pignut (or red) and mockernut—and trees like black birch, white ash, and sugar and red maples which become more common in other habitats of the Palisades. As we shall see later, however, a few of these trees may actually be replacing the oaks in some sections as the forests continue to mature and undergo changes in their tree compositions. Beneath the large trees, the so-called "understory" of the forest is dominated by 30- to 40-foot flowering dogwoods, with bark resembling alligator skin and showy white blossoms in early May.* The lower shrub layer in an oak woodland is dominated by maple-leaf viburnum, with members of the heath family like laurel, azalea, and blueberry in more acidic soils. Characteristically lush and well-developed, the

Note-Beginning in the 1980's, dogwood trees along the Palisades began to succumb to an anthracnose fungus disease, which continues to kill them and greatly reduce their importance in the forest. Their survival is questionable.

shrub layer offers prime nesting sites for many birds (see later sections).

The Long Path, which follows the top of the Palisades ridge, continually passes through some fine examples of the mixed oak forest, especially in Tallman Mountain and Blauvelt State Parks and sections of Hook Mountain State Park north of Rockland Lake. (See last chapter for more details about these places.)

Black birch growing on bare rock—note bark lenticels

TREES OF THE CLIFF EDGE AND SUMMITS

Each morning when the sun rises over the bridges and buildings of New York on the opposite side of the river, it bathes the rocks along the cliff face and edge of the Palisades with warmth and light. In summer the colorful lizard known as the five-lined skink emerges from crevices where it has spent the night and flattens its body on the warming rocks. Red-tailed hawks leave their tree-top roosts and soar effortlessly on the thermal air masses rising from the diabase. Wild "rock gardens" of columbine and wild pink, and even an occasional patch of prickly pear cactus thrive in the spring and

Red cedar at cliff edge, near Women's Federation Monument

goldenrods which grow beneath them, most of these trees require lots of sunlight and wouldn't survive in the shade of the oak forest. Red cedar, a small, compact evergreen, grows right from cracks in the exposed diabase, both along the cliff edge (especially along the old Gurnee Quarry at the end of South Mountain in Mount Ivy, N.Y.) and from the steep face of the Palisades. Valued as fence posts before the turn of the century, many of these red cedars were cut, but their fragrant, decay-resistant stumps remain rooted in the cliff like pieces of driftwood. Below the cliff edge, gray and weathered dead cedars jut out from crevices in the face of the Palisades. Another evergreen, the scraggly pitch pine (with needles in bundles of three) is found only on the highest summits and grassy, lichen-covered "balds" of Hook Mountain and the Tors, habitats quite unlike New Jersey's "Pine Barrens" where it dominates. The light-gray, warty trunks of stunted American hackberry trees also reach out horizontally from the cliff edge for sunlight. Shadbush, or Juneberry, which bears its white cherry-like blossoms in mid-April when the shad swim up the Hudson, is characterized by a cluster of small, smooth, gray trunks with dark vertical lines.

Other trees more often associated with old fields, such as sassafras, black cherry, fire cherry, hawthorn, gray birch, and staghorn sumac, are also found along the edge of the Palisades where their need for strong sunlight is fulfilled. Occasional apple and pear trees grow from the seeds of discarded fruit cores and the fast-growing weed tree from Asia known as ailanthus or tree-of-heaven ("the tree that grows in Brooklyn") thrives in these sunny exposures. The cliff edge offers fine views of not only the Hudson River and points north, east, and south, but also songbirds feeding in the tree-tops below, ducks and gulls on the river, and hawks, geese, and monarch butterflies migrating overhead. Greenbrook Sanctuary, State Line Lookout, Women's Federation Monument, Hook Mountain, the Tors, and South Mountain all offer good opportunities to study this habitat. (See last chapter for more details about these areas)

early summer sunlight, and dewberries, lowbush blueberries, and pasture rose-hips ripen later in summer. This is the cliff edge community, probably the most unique of the Palisades environments.

With strong winds, bright sunlight, and a shallow, dry, almost nonexistent soil layer, the Palisades cliff edge and high summits represent harsh environments for plants. Nevertheless, several species of trees have specialized in conquering these adversities and thrive along the cliff without competition from members of the nearby oak community (except for occasional chestnut oaks and pignut hickories). In fact, like the grasses, rock cresses, and

THE TALUS SLOPE

One mild spring day in 1981, this writer spent several fascinating hours exploring one of the most rugged and least visited sections of the Palisades—the so-called "giant stairs" region just south of the New York state line. For over one-half mile along the Hudson, the shore and lower slopes of the Palisades were covered with huge, room-sized, angular blocks of diabase rock which had tumbled down from the cliffs above. The gently lapping waters of the Hudson washed over the algae-covered rocks and gulls cried overhead, suggesting a scene from New England's coast rather than inland New Jersey. The huge rocks had to be negotiated by hand and foot in order to make any progress and avoid a crushing fall or sprained ankle. Five-lined skinks scurried in and out of crevices among the warm rocks, and millipedes as thick as a child's finger crawled along decaying logs between the boulders. Many widely scattered trees grew at the bases of the rocks. Some of these were actually in the process of "engulfing" portions of the diabase as their trunks gradually widened over the years around the angular corners of the blocks. Along a branch of one of these trees, fully 12 feet off the ground, dangled a 6-foot-long skin of a black rat snake which had climbed up to molt.

But the most exciting discovery of all were the many deep piles of black droppings left by some kind of animal on ledges outside the caves and smaller chambers which led deep within the rock heaps. The size of the droppings, the manner of deposition, and the unique habitat itself led me to conclude that I had discovered a colony of eastern woodrats, one of the rarest mammals in the northeastern United States. Sure enough, the following week I revisited the site near dusk and saw one of these beautiful rodents in the top of a Paulownia tree reaching for seeds. Later, biologists from the New Jersey Department of Environmental Protection accompanied me there to live-trap several woodrats and thus confirm the first of only two known colonies in the entire state.

These steep talus slopes below the cliffs and rocky knolls of the Palisades are perhaps even more demanding environments than the cliff edge itself. Rocks are constantly shifting by gravity or frost action, and soil and water are very scarce commodities. Since most of the talus was bulldozed away by glaciers, today's accumulations date back to the retreat of the last ice sheets 12 to 15 thousand years ago. Some recent rock falls are completely devoid of vegetation, but older talus accumulations are covered with forests of widely spaced trees growing in the cracks and crevices. Few shrubs and herbs can survive in these harsh

Five-lined skink

The rare eastern woodrat on talus south of State Line

Giant blocks of fallen diabase near Forest View, Alpine, N.J.

environments, although some evergreen ferns and choice wildflowers like Dutchman's breeches and early saxifrage appear among the rocks in early spring. Dominating the talus slopes is the beautiful black or sweet birch, whose twigs are characterized by the sweet odor and taste of "oil of wintergreen." Easily recognized by its lustrous, dark brown bark marked with horizontal, white lenticels (breathing pores), this birch apparently grows best on rocky slopes where its roots gradually expand into and along the cracks. Black birch is normally a medium-sized tree, but on some of the more rugged, isolated talus forests such as in the Clausland Mountain area, individual trees exceed 8 feet in circumference and 100 feet in height.

Also abundant on the talus are white ash and American basswood (linden), followed by flowering dogwood, hop hornbeam (*Ostrya*), slippery elm, ailanthus, a few butternuts and towering white pines and chestnut oak on the upper slopes. On abandoned quarry slopes and some of the more recently disturbed rock slides, black locust often competes with white ash as the dominant tree. At the northern end of the Palisades ridge, near the southern limit of its range (except along the higher Appalachian Mountains), the small, green trunks of the beautiful striped maple become a common sight on the talus from Rockland Lake to Mount Ivy.

Another interesting member of the talus community is the royal Paulownia or princess tree, named after a former princess of Russia, Anna Paulovna (1795–1865). Native to China where its extremely light wood is carved for religious objects and bridal chests, it was planted in 19th century Palisades estates for the beauty of its huge, elephant ear-like leaves and lavender, trumpet-shaped flowers. Since then Paulownia has spread throughout the Palisades on rocky exposures where it grows up to 20 feet in height each year as saplings or sprouts. It is most commonly seen along the Henry Hudson Drive and it completely dominates the immense fallen rock masses above the shore between Forest View and the New York state line.

An even bigger surprise of the Palisades talus slopes is an extensive stand of American white or paper birches growing above the Shore Trail in the Forest View section of the Park, 2 miles north of the Alpine Boat Basin. The only other place in New Jersey where this northern tree grows are the mountains of Sussex and Warren Counties. Apparently, the cooler conditions in this rugged, shaded accumulation of boulders approximate those of its northern homeland in Canada, New England, and upstate New York.

The many natural caves and cavities of talus slopes serve as den sites for families of foxes, raccoons, and other animals. Beneath the rocks hide slimy salamanders, and some of the more southerly exposed talus slopes provide hibernation dens and "sunbathing" sites for black snakes, copperheads, and skinks. Many good examples of

Big sugar maple in cove forest beneath Palisades cliffs

talus slope communities can be viewed along the Palisades Shore Trail, the Haverstraw-Nyack Shore Path, and the Henry Hudson Drive. (See last chapter for more details about these areas)

FORESTS OF THE COVES, SLOPES, AND VALLEYS

When one descends from the sunny, dry ridges and exposed hillsides of the Palisades into the fertile, moist, and shaded slopes, valleys, and coves, a very different kind of forest is encountered. It is easy to imagine being in the forests of New England or northern New York rather than New Jersey when entering these cool, sheltered habitats. Although a few large white and red oaks, white ashes, and black birches are

present, the forest is dominated by Appalachian tulip trees, Canadian hemlocks (especially on the cooler, north-facing slopes), and the so-called northern hardwoods: sugar maple, American beech, and rarely striped maple and yellow birch, north of Hook Mountain. In autumn, the colors emanating from some of these coves rival those of any New England forest. Even in winter, the smooth, silver-gray trunks of

39

Giant tulip trees and hemlocks in Greenbrook Sanctuary, N.J. – note man beside tree at right

growth. The straight, deeply furrowed trunks of tulip trees exceed 10 feet in circumference and bear their large, orange-yellow, tulip-like flowers as high as 130 feet in late May. Unlike the oak woodlands, where the smaller trees are often different species than the sun-loving oaks above them, most of the trees in the understory of a mature cove forest are the same as those in the canopy. Young sugar maples, beeches, birches, and hemlocks are tolerant of shade and survive quite successfully beneath their "parents."

Whether it's spring, when wildflowers proliferate and shy songbirds return to their secret nesting places; summer, when the cooler temperatures here are more conducive to the activities of toads and salamanders than in the uplands; autumn, when mushrooms thrive in the deep leaf litter and maples, beeches, and tulip trees are ablaze in color; or winter, when the hemlocks are laden with snow or ice and streams frozen solid, these secluded coves and valleys of the Palisades are special places to be treasured for their wildness and beauty. There are some splendid cove forests in Greenbrook and Lamont Sanctuaries, Blauvelt State Park, Clausland Mountain County Park, Alpine Scout Camp, and the shaded hillsides sloping down to the Hudson above the Palisades Shore Trail and Haverstraw-Nyack Shore Path. One of the most primeval of these forests is in the Forest View area, where tall maples, hemlocks, black birches, tulip trees, and even a few white pines and white birches combine to portray a very different picture from that of the oak-hickory woodlands on the cliffs above. (See last chapter for more details about these areas)

beech offer a vivid contrast to the shaggy maple trunks and the dark, evergreen hemlocks.

With organic matter, rock debris, and water washing down into these coves from the upland forests and talus, the conditions here are much more suitable for rapid tree

RAVINES AND GORGES

Some of the streams which drain the Palisades forests cascade more than 200 feet over the cliffs into the Hudson River. During the summers they frequently dry up completely, but after heavy rains or winter

freezes these waterfalls are truly spectacular. Many of them flow through dark, steep-sided ravines where the dominant tree is that graceful evergreen of Canada and the northern United States, eastern

Interior of hemlock grove, Greenbrook ravine

hemlock. Adapted to these cool, moist, rugged sites, hemlock forms dense groves where little else can survive. The dark shade produced by these evergreens and the monopolization of the surface water by their shallow, extensive root systems make it practically impossible for any other kind of tree to invade a well-established hemlock grove. In addition, the ability of smaller hemlocks to survive indefinitely under the dark canopy of the larger trees and the longevity of the species (it has been known to reach 600 years of age) further decrease its chances of being replaced in these gorges.*

For some animals, such as white-tailed deer and ruffed grouse, the hemlock grove represents a shelter from winter storms. For others, like the great horned owl and American crow, the dense trees provide perfect places in which to raise their young. And for the hikers, there is quiet, solitude, and a soft bed of fragrant fallen needles to rest upon. When entering such forests all of the senses are stimulated and it is easy to shed the cares of everyday life and experience a renewed appreciation for the wonders of nature. Some picturesque, well-developed hemlock ravines are found in Greenbrook and Lamont Sanctuaries, Kennedy-Dells County Park, and the shaded valleys below the ridge from Rockland Lake to Long Clove. On the steep, north-facing slopes of the Blauvelt-Clausland Mountain area are some of the wildest, most rugged hemlock forests on the Palisades, with huge old trees towering above many decaying, moss-covered logs. Buttermilk Falls, a County Park south of Central Nyack, N.Y., boasts a magnificent waterfall which roars through a steep-sided ravine with big, fragrant hemlocks and northern hardwoods. After a rainfall, perhaps no other forest in the region is more reminiscent of the Adirondack Mountains of New York or the White Mountains of New Hampshire. (See last chapter for more details of these areas)

---

*Note-Starting about 1983, the hemlock trees along the Palisades and in other nearby forests of New Jersey and New York began to exhibit severe symptoms of the *Fiorinia externa* scale, a tiny white insect (accidentally introduced into this country from Japan) that plasters itself to the bottom of the hemlock needles and sucks the juices. As millions of these scales coated the trees, the hemlock forests gradually changed from their normal dark green color to grayish-white, and by 1985 individual trees began dying from the bottom branches upward. It remains doubtful that the hemlocks will be able to recover from this serious infestation, and they may very well join the American chestnut in vanishing from the Palisades forests.

WETLAND FORESTS

Almost as if by magic, there comes a day each March when the woodland pools and roadside ditches, which heretofore had been silent and ice covered, suddenly become sources of loud choruses of whistling voices. Hidden among the tussocks and clumps of moss, these unseen singers are the tiny, one-inch-long tree frogs known as spring peepers. At this same time, beneath the surface of the icy waters float the large, jelly-like egg masses of wood frogs and spotted salamanders. These are two other early-emerging amphibians which actually preceded the peepers to the pools but whose secretive, nocturnal behavior saved them from detection. These animals emerged from their underground hibernation dens in the forests following the first mild rains in March. A week or two after they enter the waters to mate and lay eggs, they return to the woods. They are the true harbingers of spring.

Spotted salamander migrating to vernal pond in March

Scattered across the ridges, valleys, and western slopes of the Palisades, the shallow depressions which nurture these amphibians tend to fill up with water from melting snow and ice and early spring rains and again after summer rains. Originally these wetlands may have been larger lakes and ponds which formed when the glaciers either dammed up valleys or carved basins on the Palisades. Now after many years of drying and filling-in with dead leaves and debris from the surrounding forests, some have dwindled to temporary "vernal ponds," devoid of plants except along their perimeters. Others are woodland swamps covered with widely spaced trees. The species of tree which does best in these low, soggy habitats is red or swamp maple, distinguished by its smooth, gray upper trunk, red flowers and twigs, and brilliant crimson foliage in autumn. Also common in the southern half of the Palisades, where it

reaches the northern most limit of its range in this country, is the sweetgum, recognized by its star-shaped leaves and spiny, woody fruits ("gum balls"). The diversity of trees in some of these swamps is perhaps greater than in any other habitat on the Palisades. There is sour gum or black tupelo with simple, oval leaves which are the first to turn a vivid red in autumn; sycamore, with loose patches of cream-colored bark; pin oak, with many long, dead lower branches hanging to the ground; American elm, with a swollen, buttressed trunk; ironwood or musclewood (*Carpinus*), named for its smooth, twisted, "sinewy" trunk; shagbark hickory, with loose, vertically peeling strips of bark; and bitternut hickory, with bright, mustard-yellow buds. There are also red mulberry, white and red ashes, and – in northern sections and in Englewood's Flat Rock Brook area – yellow birch. Beneath these trees the shrub and herb layers of wooded swamps is typically very lush, diversified, and sometimes almost impenetrable (see page 51). Many of these same trees grow along the banks of the slower-moving brooks draining the Palisades.

The wetlands represent important breeding sites for most of the salamanders, frogs, toads, tree frogs, and aquatic insects of the Palisades. Many of these amphibians breed in the spring so that their aquatic tadpoles have sufficient time to mature and metamorphose into terrestrial, air-breathing adults before the swamps and vernal ponds dry up in the heat of the summer. Other salamanders and insects breed in the gravel and stones of the brooks. Fishing spiders, turtles, water snakes, herons, and raccoons inhabit or visit these wetlands to feed on the insects and amphibians, and wood ducks breed in hollow trees here in spring. Good examples of vernal ponds and swamps are found in Mount Ivy County Park, Tenafly's Lost Brook Preserve west of 9W and the picturesque "dark pond" in the forest near the cliff edge above Rockland Lake Village. In Rockland Lake State Park a boardwalk trail encircles a very interesting maple/ash swamp with some poison sumac and possibly the only native Atlantic white cedar in the Palisades region. The most ex-

tensive swamp forests on the Palisades are the sweetgum/red maple/spicebush wetlands stretching from Route 9W almost to the cliff edge south of the Tallman State Park entrance. (See last chapter for more details on these areas)

Spring on the Palisades first arrives in the wetlands with the emergence of the first skunk cabbage flowers through the frozen ground at the beginning of March, followed by the opening of the flower buds on elm, red maple, smooth alder, hazelnut, and pussy willow, and the arrival of the first amphibians. A visit to any of the more accessible roadside ditches and swamps on a warm evening in early spring when the spring peepers produce an almost deafening chorus is an unforgettable experience.

Pin oak in swamp forest – note hanging branches

PONDS AND SHORELINES

Cattails and reeds sway in the breeze. Red-winged blackbirds sing from shoreline perches and display their bright-red shoulder "epaulets." An osprey circles overhead, peering down into the water for a fish. The calmness of the surface waters is often broken by ripples from breezes or splashes from a large-mouth bass snatching insects. A pair of mallards dips beneath the water for aquatic vegetation, the head of the male reflecting a brilliant iridescent green in the sunlight. The images portrayed by a large pond are certainly different fom those associated with woodland swamps: open, sunny, and airy versus impenetrable, dark, and still.

Only a few large, permanent bodies of water exist on the shallow, droughty soils of the Palisades and most of these were artificially created. For example, the 5-acre pond in Greenbrook Sanctuary was formed in 1956 by building a dam where three separate brooks joined after flowing through a wooded swamp. Smaller ponds on the Pali-

Osprey with pickerel in talons, Greenbrook pond

sades on the nearby Englewood (Flat Rock Brook) and Tenafly Nature Centers are likewise formed by dams. The so-called "tank farm ponds" near the southern border of Tallman Mountain State Park were originally dug in the 1920s to retain oil seepage when this area atop the cliffs was slated for development into an oil tank facility. All of these ponds are now prime habitats for the larger aquatic animals which can't survive in the shallow woodland swamps: bullfrogs, snapping turtles, Canada geese, and several kinds of freshwater fish. During the spring and fall migratory seasons the large natural lake in Rockland Lake State Park attracts a great variety of aquatic birds, including gulls, swans, coots, grebes, geese, and flocks of dabbling and diving ducks (see "Birdwatching Hotspots").

Many of the trees which grow in the shallow wetland forests are found along the wet edges of these ponds and lakes as well. Since these shores are usually more open and exposed to sunlight, some shade-

intolerant species also grow here among cattails, sedges, rushes, and tall plumes of *Phragmites* reeds. Huge cottonwoods, and several species of willow – black, white, crack, weeping, and pussy – grace the shorelines. Along the sunny banks of the Hudson River, these trees also grow among red maples, sycamores, hackberries, black locusts, box elders (or "ash-leaved maple" – a green-twigged species with three-parted leaves), and even a few catawba, apple, and osage-orange trees either intentionally planted or escaped from nearby estates. Many large, ragged-looking white mulberries join the cottonwoods and willows lining the shores of the mile-long pier into the Hudson at Piermont. The Palisades Shore Trail offers the best opportunity to experience these shoreline trees amidst algae-covered rocks and the tidal currents of the Hudson River. (See last chapter for more details about these areas)

Bullfrog, Tenafly Nature Center pond

DISTURBED FORESTS

In many sections of the Palisades, forests are still in the process of reclaiming areas formerly disturbed by either natural catastrophes or human activities. Destructive hurricanes (1938, 1950, 1976) periodically ravage the exposed Palisades and topple hundreds of shallow-rooted trees. The forest openings thus created are quickly invaded by sun-loving weeds, vines (summer and fox grape, Japanese honeysuckle, bitter nightshade, poison ivy, Canada moonseed, Virginia creeper, Asiatic bittersweet), and thorny brambles (blackberry, prickly dewberry, wine raspberry, black raspberry, multiflora rose, and common and glaucous greenbriers) which spread over the fallen trunks and up the remaining trees. Most of these vines and brambles also thrive along the sunny, open shores of the Hudson. Around the foundations of the former estates which were razed when the Park acquired the land atop the cliffs, exotic ornamental shrubs, vines, and trees like Chinese wisteria, Japanese barberry, deutzia,

45

winged euonymus, lilac, privet, forsythia, garden mock orange, European sweet cherry, highbush cranberry-viburnum, and Japanese and Norway maples are likewise expanding throughout the rubble from the old garden sites.

Abandoned fields, old clearings, quarries, and woods recently burned by lightning or human carelessness gradually revert back to forest in a series of stages called "plant succession." First to cover these sunny openings are the tough, hardy "weeds," like dandelion and thistle, and the grasses: sweet vernal grass, redtop, orchard grass, purple love grass, poverty oats, switch grass, beardgrass, perennial rye, and various species of fescues, bromes, foxtails, panics, and blue grasses. These low plants increase the organic content and stability of the soil and prepare the way for the more demanding plants: the vines and brambles, and shrubs like red-panicled (or gray) dogwood and smooth, winged, and staghorn sumacs. Next come the first or "pioneer" trees: quaking and bigtooth aspens, gray ("little white") birch, sassafras, black and fire cherries, hawthorn, red cedar, Hercules club, and European buckthorn. These are mostly small, sun-tolerant trees which do well for a few years, but since their seedlings can't survive in the shade beneath them, they soon fail to reproduce. Thus, their success

eliminates the very factor—open sunlight—which made it possible for them to become established in the old field in the first place. Unable to replace themselves, the pioneer trees gradually die off and leave the redeveloping forest to the more shade-tolerant oaks, birches, or maples which will someday form the mature Palisades forest.

Disturbed forests are excellent habitats for wildlife, from butterflies and bees to woodchucks and deer. The heavy growth of weeds, vines, and shrubs not only provides plenty of food in the form of leaves, flowers, seeds, and berries, but dense shelter and nesting sites as well. Both the Palisades Shore and Long Paths traverse several burned or cut-over areas and the overgrown ruins of estates, bathhouses and boat docks. There is about a one-mile stretch of the Long Path from High Tor to Little Tor that passes through dense thickets of brambles and early successional growth, including lots of striped maple. The Haverstraw-Nyack Shore Path passes several abandoned quarries below Hook Mountain where jumbles of fallen rock are being revegetated with black locust, white ash and other pioneer trees. One of the more interesting disturbed areas is the old cliff-top Burnett estate near Women's Federation Monument, where many ornamental pines, spruces, cedars, yews, rhododen-

Woodchuck eating grass in clearing atop Palisades

Tiger swallowtail on orange milkweed

drons, magnolias, and flowering shrubs grow among the weedy foundations. In the "Bluefields" area of Blauvelt State Park, several former fields are now overgrown with gray birches, aspens, red cedars, and apple trees. Other clearings here, which were planted with evergreen seedlings 50 or more years ago, are now beautiful groves of Norway spruce, and red, white, and Scotch pines. Near the eastern end of Ruckman Road in Camp Alpine, a former "borrow pit" is now a vast, lush meadow being invaded by pioneer trees, shrubs, and brambles, and frequented by courting woodcock in early spring. (See last chapter for more details about these areas)

CHANGES IN THE FORESTS

Besides major disturbances and natural catastrophes (such as the blight which eliminated American chestnut from the forests 70 years ago), there are more subtle changes occurring in the Palisades forests which are difficult to detect except after years of study and comparison. In 1980 and 1983 this writer participated in two separate studies designed to compare the present composition of the forests of Greenbrook Sanctuary with those of 1949 and 1955, when two major analyses of its forest communities were completed by Drs. E. P. Moore and Stephen Collins. Although red oak still appears to be the dominant tree in the sanctuary (and throughout the upland habitats of the Palisades), there has been a very substantial decrease in its dominance over the past three decades. In some sites the importance of red oak has decreased by as much as 80%, while the importance of black birch, hemlock, and sugar maple has simultaneously increased (by as much as 200% for sugar maple in some sites).

Indeed, a casual walk along some of the oak-covered hillsides of the Palisades re-

American chestnut tree, sprouts from old stump

veals that the understory has very few young oaks and is composed almost entirely of sugar maple saplings and seedlings, indicating that this shade-tolerant species may possibly someday replace the oaks in the forest. To a somewhat lesser extent, beech, black birch, white ash, and eastern hemlock are also spreading out of the ravines, coves, and slopes and invading more open sites in the upland oak woodlands. Hemlock has been increasing in abundance all over southeastern New York according to some studies, possibly because of the better fire control and increasing annual precipitation and soil moisture during the 20th century (hemlock, like sugar maple, is much more susceptible to drought and fire damage than oaks). Formerly relegated to cool, deep ravines and steep, north-facing slopes, this evergreen's seedlings and saplings are becoming increasingly common on rotting logs and clumps of moss in more upland sites.*

Ecologists suggest that these changes throughout much of New York and New Jersey are simply manifestations of the continuing natural process of plant succession. Before the 20th century—the era of

protection for the Palisades forests—the woodlands were often subjected to cutting and fire damage. More than any other trees, the thick-barked oaks recovered quickly from such disturbances. Indeed, they have been termed the "sprout hardwoods" because of their ability to sprout vigorously from fire-charred or cut stumps. These sprouts grew quickly into large trees and thus became dominant in the recovering forests. As the canopies close and shut out the sunlight, however, the oak seedlings and saplings fail to prosper and are gradually replaced by the more shade-tolerant maples, birches, beeches, and hemlocks. Meanwhile, the big oaks succumb over the years to fungus disease, gypsy-moth damage, drought, hurricanes, or other natural mortality factors. For example, red oak has become less dominant in many of the

*Note-See section on "Ravines and Gorges" for a major infestation of scale insects which may bring about not only a setback in the spread of hemlocks but even its total demise in the forests of the Palisades.

Also see section on "Mixed Oak Forest" for a fungus disease which threatens to eliminate flowering dogwood from the understory of the Palisades woodlands.

48

upland forests along the Palisades because of two severe droughts in the 1960s and early 1980s, during which periods gypsy-moth outbreaks also peaked. Red oaks were affected much more than other species (possibly a third factor was involved which was specific to red oaks in weakened condition) and many large specimens died.

Scarlet oak has likewise greatly decreased on the Palisades in the past 30 years. This species often hangs on to its dead branches for years, lacking the "self-pruning" ability of other trees. As the dead branches decay, rot spreads into the trunk and weakens the tree. Many of the large scarlet oaks along the cliffs have rotting trunks and broken crowns and easily succumb to disease or windfall. Since its seedlings need open sunlight, scarlet oak is not replacing itself in the upland forests. If forest fires and other human disturbances are eliminated, as they have been throughout much of the Palisades since 1900, the northern hardwoods (especially sugar maple) may someday replace the oaks in the canopies of many forests.

Thus, perhaps we are witnessing a natural culmination of the long process of forest succession on the Palisades, with red oak having merely dominated one transitional stage. As the process reaches a climax in the years to come, many woodlands will experience extensive changes in their tree compositions. Although the most exposed ridges, summits, and cliff edges may retain

Saw-whet owl in hemlock tree

their status as mixed oak forests, many of the more shaded slopes that are covered with red, black, and white oaks today may be sugar maple forests in the future.

The Colorful Palisades

Trail through black birches, Greenbrook Sanctuary, October.

Palisades in late October from Alpine Boat Basin.

Young racoon and polypody ferns, June.

Five-lined, or blue-tailed skink, State Line Lookout, May.

Newborn assassin bug with empty egg shells, July.

Eastern screech owl in hemlock, November.

Box turtle, male, August.

Hemlock-hardwood forest, Greenbrook ravine, late October.

Vernal pond at sunset, Tallman Mountain, early May.

American toad, male singing, Tenafly Nature Center pond, April.

Wild pinks on cliff face, Englewood, early May.

Cardinal, male, February.

Buckeye on orange milkweed, Tenafly, July 1979.

Sulphur polypore, or chicken mushroom, August.

Palisades, looking north from Picture Point, Alpine, late October.

Red sandstone and waterfall, Alpine Boat Basin, April.

Copperhead snake, Alpine, May.

Baltimore butterfly, underside, Greenbrook Sanctuary, late June 1983.

Orb-weaving spider (Neoscona), August.

17-year cicada with empty nymph shell, May 1979.

Greenbrook Pond, late October.

Northern red salamander on fern moss, June.

Pipevine swallowtail on thistle, Greenbrook Sanctuary, September 1984.

Milk snake, May.

Pink lady slippers, mid-May.

White oak leaves, late October.

Spicebush swallowtail caterpillar on sassafras, July.

Chapter IV

Other Flora of the Palisades

SHRUBS

Trees, of course, are only one component of the forest community. Below them are the much smaller, multi-trunked woody plants known as shrubs. Quite diverse and well developed beneath the canopy of a mixed oak or swamp forest, but virtually absent in the dense shade of a hemlock grove, the shrub layer is commonly dominated by one of three species on the Palisades. In both the dry uplands and moist coves it is maple-leaf viburnum, identified by its paired, maple-shaped leaves, purplish-black berries, and numerous thin, upright trunks or "shafts." Along the cliff edge and more exposed ridges are dense thickets of tall blackhaws with rough, black trunks, short, stiff side twigs, cherry-like leaves, and clusters of dark blue fruits which produce a foul, rotting odor in autumn. The most common shrub in the wet lowlands and streamsides is the fragrant, "warty"-barked spicebush, whose small yellow flowers are a welcome contrast to the gray bareness of the early April woods.

The sandier, rockier, more acidic upland soils are characterized by various members of the heath family of shrubs: black huckleberry, tall deerberry, late and early low blueberries, and the beautiful pink azalea ("pinxter flower") and evergreen mountain laurel, whose showy flowers bloom in late April and late May, respectively. Along the dry cliff edge, on rock outcrops and some sunny trail borders, are red-panicled or gray dogwood, pasture rose, American bitter-sweet, Japanese and northern bush honeysuckles, and an occasional fragrant New Jersey tea, sweet fern, or northern bayberry bush. On the highest summits and exposed ridges from Hook Mountain northward, choke cherry, scrub oak, and even a rare prickly ash and currant survive in the thin soils and crevices. The talus slope is the habitat of red elderberry, purple-flowering raspberry, Virginia creeper, poison ivy, occasional round-leaf and alternate-leaf dogwoods, the beautiful climbing fumitory, or Allegeny vine (along the Nyack Shore Path), the rare hoptree or wafer ash, and the unusual bladdernut, with hollow, papery, inflated seed capsules resembling Japanese lanterns. Clumps of tall, contorted witch hazels, waiting until October and November to bear their spidery, yellow flowers, are found on the talus and moist hillsides.

Growing around the shores and shallows of ponds and in soggy meadows are button-bush, broad-leaf spiraea (meadowsweet), bristly dewberry, swamp rose, steeplebush, silky dogwood, red and black chokeberries, rigid, silky, and pussy willows, and smooth alder, whose caterpillar-like catkins of early March are among the first blossoms of spring. Along the banks of the Hudson are northern bayberry, poison ivy, various sumacs, honeysuckles, brambles, and – escaped from cultivation – Dutchman's pipe (pipe-vine), and indigo bush. It is in the woodland swamps and stream borders that the shrub layer reaches its greatest diversity. Besides

Baby catbirds in nest in blackberry thicket

spicebush there are thickets of buttonbush, maleberry, arrowwood, American hazelnut, and occasionally beaked hazelnut and nannyberry; fragrant July flowers of swamp azalea and sweet coast pepperbush; juicy black elderberries and highbush blueberries; vivid red fruits of chokeberry and common winterberry—a deciduous holly;

and reddish, late-autumn leaves of swamp leucothoe or sweetbells.* (See also "Disturbed Forests")

---

*The common names of these shrubs appear in *A Field to Trees and Shrubs* by George Petrides in the Peterson Field Guide Series.

FUNGI

When most nature enthusiasts are watching migrating hawks or admiring the changing colors of autumn from the vistas and woodland trails of the Palisades, a smaller but growing number of people is walking in the woods with eyes searching the ground for mushrooms. Some are armed with cameras, content to bring home only photographs of these interesting and colorful spore-producing organisms. Others, especially those of Italian ancestry, carry bushel baskets to transport some of these fungi back to their kitchens where they will be transformed into delicious

meals via old family recipes. Several types of mushrooms found on the Palisades are poisonous and a few are quite deadly (some *Amanitas*). No general rule of thumb separates the edible from inedible. Mushrooms shouldn't be tasted unless their specific identification is absolutely confirmed by an expert.

Although some species of mushrooms, including the extremely tasty morels which appear in May, can be found in spring and summer on the Palisades, it is in the fall that they proliferate. Rainy autumn days are almost always followed by a great profusion of fungi popping up overnight through the rich humus and fallen leaves. Since they lack the green pigment, chlorophyll, by which plants produce their own food, many fungi are saprophytes, subsisting on dead leaves, wood, and other organic matter. A few are parasitic on the roots or wood of living trees. It is now thought that a great many species may also establish intimate and mutually beneficial relationships with the root systems of certain species of trees. They provide nutrients to the tree rootlets and receive water and protection in return.

On the ground there are clusters of delicious honey mushrooms (*Armillaria*), white puffballs, and red chanterelles; vividly colored *Hygrophorus* and poisonous *Amanita* mushrooms; stout, pore-covered boletes and dainty *Mycenas*; smooth *Russulas* and scaly "pine cone" (*Strobilomyces*) mushrooms. Erect clusters of slender coral fungi and foul-smelling stinkhorns are also present, along with stalkless scarlet cup fungi, amorphous masses of jelly fungi, and unique earth stars and tiny bird's nest fungi. One of the most familiar groups of fungi are the polypores, commonly called "shelf fungi" or "conks." These are the large, generally woody growths which extend out horizontally from tree trunks or logs. Some, like the colorful cinnabar fungus and the white-bottomed artist's conk, are perennial and add on new zones of woody growth year after year. Others are like the fleshy sulphur polypore, also called the

"chicken mushroom" for its delicious taste, which produces a new cluster of bright orange and yellow shelves from the same tree or log each year.

Amanita muscaria, a poisonous mushroom

NONFLOWERING PLANTS – THE SURVIVING PIONEERS

After the glaciers melted away from the Palisades, the first living things to recolonize the barren rocks and glacial drift were probably the lichens. These primitive, dual plants (each species is actually a combination of a fungus and an alga) can survive in the harshest environments. Over the millennia as the climate gradually warmed and a thin layer of organic matter accumulated, cold-hardy mosses and ferns, rock-

sprawling shrubs, and finally larger shrubs and trees were able to colonize the new habitats. Today the Palisades is dominated by flowering trees, shrubs, and herbs, but their ancient nonflowering ancestors can still be found from sunny cliff edge to shaded swamp. Although their identification is usually the realm of the specialist and professional rather than the amateur botanist and photographer, a knowledge of some of the more common and widespread species can make any woodland walk a more informative, enjoyable experience.

Unfortunately, many lichens have disappeared from southern sections of the Palisades, since they are very susceptible to air pollution spreading from the crowded highways, cities, and chemical plants. One of the few species which is still common is the pearl button or "whitewash lichen" (*Lecidea*), resembling a flat patch of dirty gray paint on moist rocks. In more northern sections of the Palisades, the greenish boulder lichen (*Parmelia*) spreads out like a tangled mat on exposed rocks, especially on the higher summits. Among the most beautiful lichens are those species which grow on decaying wood and assume an erect, branched form like miniature trees. Common in some of the most exposed, barren habitats, they are often named after objects which they resemble: pyxie cup or goblet lichens, powder horns, and–most striking of all–the scarlet British soldiers.

There are about a dozen easily recognized mosses on the Palisades. Largest, or longest, of all is the water moss (*Fontinalis*), whose submerged stems often reach a length of 3 feet in clear brooks. Sphagnum (peat moss) forms deep, soggy clumps in swamps. Extensive patches of the common haircap moss (*Polytrichum*),

with erect stems up to 6 inches high, thrive in sunny clearings. In more acid soils as in hemlock groves, there are spongy, deep clumps of the white pin-cushion moss (*Leucobryum*). Velvety carpets of the bright green nodding moss (*Pohlia*) and purplish-green burned-ground moss (*Ceratodon*), and tufts of the tiny, whitish shoots of the silvertip moss (*Bryum*) grow on the driest ground, bare rocks, and even old foundations. Shaded stream banks, moist soil, and rotting logs support several beautiful species: dense, "wind-blown" mats of the brush or broom mosses (*Dicranum* and *Dicranella*); clumps of the spineleaf or Catharinea mosses (*Atrichum*); juicy rosettes of the star mosses (*Mnium*); and flat, spreading mats of the dead log moss (*Hypnum*) and delicately branched fern moss (*Thuidium*).

Related to the mosses but possessing vascular tissues (for conducting water and food) like all the higher, flowering plants, are the ferns. Most of the approximately 25 species found on the Palisades are easily identified. Around ponds and swamps grow delicate, twisted stalks of the marsh fern; tall, bushy, locust-like clusters of the royal fern; big, strikingly beautiful fronds of the cinnamon fern; and low, coarse, triangular leaves of the sensitive fern. Unlike the majority of our ferns, which bear dense clusters or "dots" (*sori*) of reproductive

Boulder lichens atop Hook Mountain

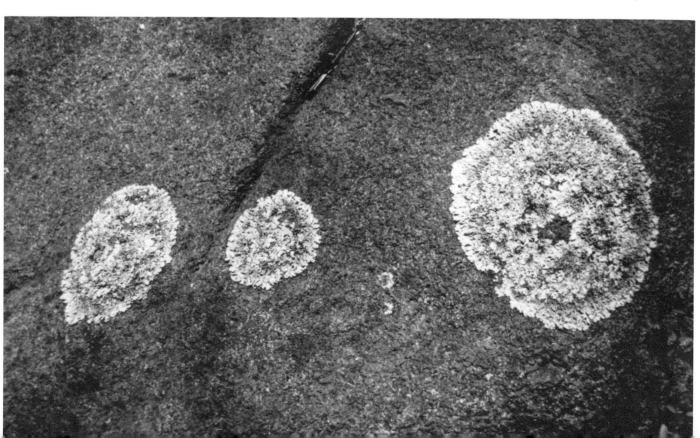

Marginal wood fern

spores beneath their leaves, both the cinnamon and sensitive ferns produce separate fertile stalks: tall, wooly, and cinnamon-brown for the former, and short with hard, bead-like clusters for the latter.

Delicate silvery spleenworts, named for their shiny elongated spore dots, grow beside Palisades streams. Shaded woodlands support clumps of lacy lady ferns, with smooth reddish stems and kidney-shaped spore dots; wide, triangular fronds of the broad beech fern; single, triangular leaves of the intricately branched rattlesnake fern; and tall clusters of the interrupted fern, whose fronds are "interrupted" with brown, spore-bearing leaflets, which leave vacant spots after they wither. Among the rocks on shaded talus slopes are three evergreen ferns: shiny, dark Christmas fern; mats of the small, leathery common polypody fern; and dark, blue-green bouquets of the very common marginal woodfern. A close relative of this last species, spinulose woodfern, also grows on the Palisades, but it is much more prevalent in northern forests. It has lacier, more sub-divided foliage than marginal woodfern and is often used by florist shops. Sunny openings in the upland oak woods are habitats for the light green New York fern, whose narrow fronds taper to tiny leaflets at both ends, and the very lacy hay-scented fern, which often covers large areas with its fragrant, yellowish-green foliage. The driest and sandiest soils are sometimes covered with the large, coarse, triangularly branched fronds of the bracken fern.

One of the earliest ferns to uncurl its fresh spring leaves from the moist crevices of steep mossy rocks is the fragile fern. This small, light green species occasionally shares its sheltered cliff habitat with dainty evergreen rosettes of the small, rare rock fern known as maidenhair spleenwort. Searching the woods, cliffs, and hidden glens of the Palisades may reveal a few of the other rare ferns: tiny cut-leaf grape ferns; evergreen ebony spleenworts; delicate, fan-shaped maidenhair ferns; and even two or three species of club mosses, those distant relatives of ferns which resemble miniature evergreen trees (they are more commonly found in moister lowland woods on the western backslope of the Palisades, e.g., the Closter and Demarest Nature Centers).*

*The common names of the ferns appear in *A Field Guide to the Ferns* by Boughton Cobb in the Peterson Field Guide Series.

WILDFLOWERS

In August of 1981 this writer discovered a very odd-looking plant growing on the border of the entrance road into Greenbrook Sanctuary. Its leaves were long, pointed, and very much like those of a yucca plant. The flowers were small, white, and borne in dense masses on several large, round heads rather like those of a button-bush. A field guide revealed its identification as rattlesnake master (*Eryngium yuccifolium*)–a plant last seen in New Jersey in 1912 and long considered extirpated from the state! Its origin is a mystery (it wasn't planted by a human), but it has flourished and flowered every year since

then, thus adding one more unusual species to the list of Palisades wildflowers.

From the emergence of the first skunk cabbage flower cluster from the icy swamps at the end of February until the withering of the last aster on the cliffs in November, over 400 species of wildflowers display their beauty throughout the Palisades. Most of the woodland flowers bloom in early spring before the trees sprout their leaves and reduce the sunlight. After spring the best areas to see wildflowers are clearings, sunny borders of roads and trails, and around ponds. In Greenbrook Sanctuary efforts have continued since 1946 to preserve as many of the native species as possible and to reestablish those species which are now rare or extinct on the Palisades due to human destruction or natural plant succession. In 1984 the Palisades Interstate Park also initiated a wildflower planting project along the wide, grassy borders of the Palisades Interstate Parkway in New Jersey. Funded by a grant from *Reader's Digest* founder, Lila Acheson Wallace, the project was expanded in 1985 to include 30 species of wildflowers planted on 12 acres of Parkway.

In the following chronological groupings (based on 10 years of records maintained by this writer) are some of those wildflowers which are most likely to be encountered by people hiking the Palisades–the common species as well as the larger, more striking ones. Included are "naturalized" flowers like coltsfoot and dandelion which are alien but well established. Excluded are garden species like snowdrops, periwinkle, daffodil, scilla, and day lily, which continue to bloom around old estates, as well as the sedges, rushes, and grasses. Keen eyes and a little luck may result in the discovery of some of the rarer Palisades woodland gems: wood lily, round-lobed hepatica, and wood betony in dry oak woods; trailing arbutus and downy rattlesnake plantain near hemlock slopes; great lobelia, Canada lily, and lizard's tail in woodland swamps; yellow corydalis, harebell, and prickly pear cactus

Skunk cabbage melting its way through snow in March

atop the highest summits; and large coral-root and smaller yellow lady's slipper in some shaded forest retreats.*

Habitat Abbreviations:
  U = Upland dry woods
  C = Cliff edge, cliff face, summits
  H = Hemlock woods
  T = Talus
  L = moist Lowlands (valley, cove, shaded slope)
  S = Swamp, stream
  P = Pond, lake, Hudson shores
  D = Disturbed areas, trails

(Species in each grouping are listed in roughly chronological order of first-flowering dates. Flowering dates of the early spring species may be as much as two weeks sooner along the shores of the Hudson than in the woodlands behind the cliff edge, because of the increased warmth and light from the morning sun rising in the east.)

Late February:
  skunk cabbage (S)

March:
  coltsfoot (D,T)
  lyre-leaved rock cress (C)

April 1–15:
  Whitlow grass (D)
  common dandelion (D)
  trout lily (L)
  spring beauty (L)
  Dutchman's breeches (T,C,U)
  early saxifrage (C,T)
  bloodroot (L)
  smaller pussytoes (C)
  common blue violet (U,L)
  early meadow rue (T,L)
  wild columbine (C,T)
  marsh marigold (S)
  wild strawberry (D)
  common chickweed (D)
  red trillium (L)

April 16–30:
  marsh blue violet (S)
  rue anemone (U,L)

Wild columbine along cliff edge

  wood anemone (L)
  Jack-in-the-pulpit (S,L,T)
  northern white violet (L,S)
  dwarf ginseng (L)
  small-flowered crowfoot (S)
  northern downy violet (D,U)
  wild pink (C)
  wild ginger (L)
  hispid buttercup (S)
  smooth rock cress (C,T)
  common winter cress (D)
  dwarf cinquefoil (D)
  smooth Solomon's seal (U,T,L)
  wild geranium (L)
  garlic mustard (D,U)
  celandine (D)
  sessile bellwort (U,L)
  yellow stargrass (U)
  yellow wood sorrel (D)

---

*The common names of the wildflowers appear in *Newcomb's Wildflower Guide* published by Little, Brown, & Co.

57

May 1–15:

- swamp buttercup (S)
- white baneberry (L)
- Canada mayflower (L,U)
- wild sarsaparilla (U)
- mayapple (L)
- false Solomon's seal (U,T,L)
- false hellebore (S)
- pink lady's slipper (U,H)
- bulbous buttercup (D)
- small forget-me-not (P,S)
- sweet cicely (T,L)
- squawroot (U)
- watercress (S)
- common fleabane (D)
- dwarf dandelion (D,C)

May 16–31:

- herb Robert (T)
- field and pale hawkweeds (D,C)
- larger blueflag (P)
- common speedwell (D)
- yarrow (D)
- rattlesnake hawkweed (U)
- white clover (D)
- yellow pond lily (P)
- blue-eyed grass (P,D)
- whorled loosestrife (U)
- oxeye daisy (D)
- tall buttercup (D,S)

- rough-fruited cinquefoil (D)
- Venus's looking glass (D)
- Indian cucumber root (L)

June 1–15:

- clammy hedge hyssop (S)
- long-bristled smartweed (D)
- partridge berry (H,U)
- Asiatic dayflower (D)
- horse nettle (D)
- Deptford pink (D)
- spreading & intermediate dogbanes (D)
- viper's bugloss (D)
- moth mullein (D)
- common milkweed (D)
- common St. Johnswort (D,C)
- tall meadow rue (S)

June 16–30:

- butterfly weed (D)
- field garlic (D)
- daisy fleabane (D)
- spotted touch-me-not (jewelweed) (L,S)
- poke milkweed (U)
- black-eyed Susan (D)
- enchanter's nightshade (L)
- common mullein (D)
- fringed loosestrife (S)
- heal-all (D)
- Indian pipes (U,L)

Wild pinks growing from crevice in cliff face

Baltimore butterfly on butterfly weed in Greenbrook Sanctuary

common cattail (P)
pokeweed (D)
swamp milkweed (P)
bouncing bet (D)

July 1–15:
spotted wintergreen (U)
butter & eggs (D,C)
purple loosestrife (P,D)
false nettle (S)
spotted knapweed (D)
Indian tobacco (D)
Queen Anne's lace (D)
seedbox (P,S)
water plantain (S)
early goldenrod (D,C)
spotted St. Johnswort (D)
wintergreen (H,U)
Turk's cap lily (S,P)
toothed white-top aster (U)
woodland sunflower (C,D)

July 16–31:
broad-leaved dock (D)
bull thistle (D)
chicory (D)
large-leaf aster (U)
sweet Joe-Pye weed (P,D)
blue vervain (P,D)
New York ironweed (P)
boneset (P,S)
evening primrose (D)

cardinal flower (S)
Virginia bugleweed (S)
marsh St. Johnswort (P)
lance-leaf goldenrod (D)
common burdock (D)
mad-dog skullcap (P)
Virginia knotweed (P,L)
thin-leaf sunflower (D,C,U)
field thistle (D)

August 1–15:
common dodder (P,S)
white snakeroot (U)
white wood aster (U)
Japanese knotweed (D)
common smartweed (water pepper) (P)
wood nettle (S)
smooth false foxglove (U,C)
tansy (D)
wild lettuce (U,C,D)
pilewort (U,D)
northern bugleweed (P,S)
silverrod (U,D)
panicled hawkweed (U)
hairy bush clover (D,C)
common arrowhead (P,S)

August 16–31:
late goldenrod (D)
panicled tick trefoil (D)
horse balm (L)

59

white lettuce (U)
hoary tick trefoil (D)
rough-stem goldenrod (D,U)
common mugwort (D)
turtlehead (S,P)
tall goldenrod (D)

September:
gray goldenrod (D,C)
small white aster (D)

blue-stem goldenrod (U,D)
beechdrops (L)
calico aster (D,P)
heath aster (D)
New England aster (D)
seaside goldenrod (on Hudson shore)
heart-leaf aster (D,U)
zigzag goldenrod (S,T)
panicled aster (D,U)
wavy-leaf aster (D)

Chapter V

Fauna of the Palisades

SPIDERS – THE DOMINANT PREDATORS

On crisp autumn mornings, when summer's green begins to yield to golden yellows, reds, and browns, and the woods once again become alive with the movements of migrating birds, there is another spectacle which stimulates the senses of those who explore the outdoors. A surprising variety of spiders reaches maturity at this time of year and on these cool mornings their webs are strikingly visible with their coverings of dew. Each strand of silk is transformed into a bead of sparkling dewdrops and the entire outline of the web glistens in the early morning light. There are webs shaped like domes, hammocks, sheets, and funnels, but the most beautiful of all are the orb webs, with their silken concentric circles and spokes radiating outward from the central hub. Each type of web is created by a certain species of spider and, indeed, the orb web is actually constructed by many different species, each with its own modifications on the basic design.

There are probably a few hundred species of spiders on the Palisades. Although even

*Pardosa wolf spider along
Palisades Shore Trail*

experts have difficulty (and disagreement) in the identification of these eight-legged relatives of insects, it is fairly easy to break them down into their family groups on the basis of appearance and behavior. Spiders are present in virtually all habitats except under water and their value in controlling insect populations is just beginning to be appreciated.

Although all spiders are predators on insects, many do not build webs to capture their prey. Hiding beneath stones, logs, and leaf litter, the wolf spiders emerge at night to lie in wait for passing insects or chase down prey like wolves. The typical wolf spider is fairly large, robust, brown, with strong muscular legs and good vision. Females are sometimes seen with their white egg sacs attached to their hind ends or with newly emerged baby spiders riding on their backs. One extremely active kind of long-legged wolf spider, the gray *Pardosa,* is commonly seen sunning itself on rocks along the shore of the Hudson. Also hiding beneath objects is another group of nocturnal hunters, the gnaphosids, or running ground spiders. Very quick and "nervous," these flattened spiders are usually velvety-black with white markings. They leave their white or pinkish, envelope-like egg sacs attached to the underside of rocks.

Crab spiders wait motionless on flowers, with legs outstretched in crab-like fashion, ready to close on any unsuspecting insects.

Able to run sideways and backwards, some crab spiders can even change color from white to yellow to blend with their backgrounds. Small stocky jumping spiders, with short legs and large, alert eyes, actively hunt insects on rocks and vegetation. Like cats, they creep closer and closer to their prey and then accurately pounce upon it when it is a few inches away. The largest hunting spiders on the Palisades are the nursery web spiders, one species (*Doloedes*) having an inch-long body and a leg-spread of as much as 4 inches. Occasionally seen stretched out on tree trunks or buildings, some species—the fishing spiders—are often found near ponds and streams where they hunt insects and, rarely, small fish and tadpoles. The female holds her egg sac in her jaws until the babies are ready to emerge, at which time she builds a "nursery web" at the top of a shrub or milkweed plant. The baby spiders remain inside this webbed enclosure for a short time while the mother aggressively stands guard outside.

Stretched between the branches of shrubs and tall weeds in summer and fall are beautifully designed orb webs. Their owners usually lie in wait in a nearby leaf until vibrations transmitted along a "trap line" indicate that an insect has been caught. Among the common orb weavers of the Palisades are unusual spiny-bellied spiders (*Micrathena*) in woods, twig-like long-jawed spiders (*Tetragnatha*) near ponds

Fishing spider (Dolomedes) with egg sac in jaws

Orb web covered with morning dew

and streams, and colorful garden spiders (*Araneus, Neoscona*) in open woods and clearings. On rare occasions the large black and yellow *Argiope* is also found resting in the center of its huge orb web. Other web spinners include funnel-web spiders (*Agelenopsis*) in grasses and weeds, dome and sheet-web spiders (Linyphiids) in shrubs, and cob-web spiders (Theridiids) beneath logs, loose bark, and on buildings. One species of cob-web spider, the dangerous black widow, is found in the Hackensack meadowlands but not in the Palisades woodlands. In fact, no spider on the Palisades is dangerous to humans.

INSECTS – THE MOST ABUNDANT ANIMALS

There comes a time each summer, during the uncomfortably hot and humid "dog days" of late July and August, when many of the animals of the woods and fields seem to disappear. Birds have finished raising their broods and are no longer singing to defend territories or making frequent trips to the nest to feed hungry babies. Salamanders sink down into the mud to escape the heat in a state of dormancy called estivation. Many snakes become nocturnal for the same reason, and all the frogs have completed their breeding seasons also. There is one group of animals, however, which becomes more evident during this time of year than at any other – the insects. Cicadas buzz in the tree tops and crickets chirp in the grass. Dragonflies patrol the ponds, and the wildflowers in clearings and roadsides are covered with bees, flies, wasps, beetles, and butterflies gathering pollen and nectar. Indeed, the "dog days" may well be called the "insect days" of summer.

There are more insects in the world than all other animals put together. In forest communities like the Palisades, insects are extremely important, first as primary herbivores, converting plant tissue into animal

63

*Span worm (large inch worm)
mimicking twig*

tissue, and secondly as food for the next link in the food chain, the predators: bats, shrews, skunks, birds, toads, salamanders, turtles, fish, spiders, and even carnivorous insects. It is impossible to give a survey of the many types of insects found on the Palisades, but a few of the most commonly encountered and easily recognized representatives of each habitat will be mentioned.

Some insects begin their lives as gill-breathing nymphs in ponds and streams, emerging in spring as air-breathing, winged adults. Examples are pesty black flies, delicate mayflies, and stoneflies, some of which emerge as early as March. Later in summer, damselflies and powerful dragonflies emerge from ponds to patrol the air for mosquitoes and other small flying insects. Many insects such as diving beetles, backswimmers, water bugs, water scorpions, and water striders or "skaters" also spend their adult lives in aquatic environments. At the other extreme are those insects which live inside decaying wood or deep beneath the soil, like the 17-year cicada, which last emerged in teeming, deafening hordes on the Palisades in 1979. Rolling over a rotting log along a trail will often uncover a colony of termites or carpenter ants, the white grubs of scarabs like the May, June, and dung beetles, swift wood

roaches, purplish- or greenish-black ground beetles, long-legged camel crickets, or even a hibernating queen yellow jacket or hornet in winter. The loose bark of dead trees often hides darkling and click beetles, large underwing moths, and the hieroglyphic-like tunnels of bark and engraver beetles.

Feeding on the foliage is a fantastic variety of herbivorous insects: grasshoppers, leaf beetles, aphids, treehoppers and leafhoppers in the lower vegetation; Japanese beetles on wild grape and tent caterpillars on cherry; walking sticks, katydids, and countless caterpillars (including inchworms, webworms, and cankerworms) in the tree tops. Some of the caterpillars transform into beautiful butterflies or colorful giant moths like the luna, cecropia, promethea, and tulip tree silk moths. Others, like the hairy larvae of the gypsy moth, are not so pleasant or well liked. This destructive insect from Europe and Asia periodically builds up to great numbers on the Palisades (early 1960s, '70s, and '80s) and defoliates thousands of oaks, birches, sweetgums, and even hemlocks. The forests may look pitifully bare, but soon starvation and a virus disease spreads through the population and the menace is reduced for another eight to ten years. Some trees are weakened and die, especially if defoliated three years in a row, but others grow in their places. Rather than participate in massive, aerial spraying of poisons, Palisades Interstate Park authorities have introduced natural enemies of the gypsy moth to the forests. Predaceous "caterpillar hunter" beetles and tiny parasitic flies and wasps attack the caterpillars, pupae, or suede-like egg masses which sometimes cover tree trunks in autumn and winter. These enemies have been successful in reducing the annual damage to the woodlands and have spared the many "nontarget" species of insects (and thus, indirectly, the birds and frogs which eat them) which would have been poisoned by insecticide sprays.

It is in the sunnier, weedy clearings and trail borders that insects reach their greatest diversity. The wildflowers attract honeybees, bumblebees, carpenter bees, paper wasps (*Polistes*), hornets, long-horned cerambycid beetles, and syrphid or hover flies. Predaceous insects like mantids, lacewings, stink bugs, ambush bugs, and ladybird beetles visit the flowers to secure a meal. But the most popular of these flower-visiting insects are the butterflies. As many as 65 different species of butterflies are found on the Palisades. Over 50 have been recorded by this writer in Greenbrook Sanctuary alone (see Table II). One of the earliest

signs of spring is the emergence of the dark, burgundy-colored mourning cloaks from hibernation in March. The territorial males are often seen patrolling the woodland trails or resting on the ground. Sometimes an orange-brown question mark or comma butterfly or the colorful red admiral is also seen at this time, since these three species also hibernate as adult butterflies. The next butterfly to greet the spring is the tiny blue spring azure which frequents the flowers of spicebush in April. By the middle of April white European cabbage butterflies are common and falcate orange-tips flutter around bittercress plants near the cliff edge. The first tiger and spicebush swallowtails are seen soon afterwards.

Through late spring, summer, and autumn, the butterfly parade continues. Little wood satyrs, pearly eyes, and wood nymphs dance over grassy borders of forests; red-spotted purples and swallowtails frequent the shaded woods; hackberry butterflies and rarely a tawny emperor, Compton's tortoise shell, or snout butterfly visit the hackberry trees along the cliff edge; and a great variety of species takes nectar and pollen from roadside, pond edge, and meadow wildflowers: black swallowtails, great spangled fritillaries, pearl crescents, silvery checkerspots, orange and common

Caterpillar-hunter beetle larva eating gypsy moth caterpillar

TABLE II
THE BUTTERFLIES OF GREENBROOK SANCTUARY

Recorded since July, 1975 by John Serrao

The common names of the following butterflies are those that appear in *A Field Guide to the Butterflies*, by Alexander Klots. The abundance ratings given each species are in a continuum ranging from "very rare" (seen only once or twice) to "abundant."

Pearly Eye – rare July and early August

Eyed Brown – very rare (in bog, 7/29 to 8/9/81)

Little Wood Satyr – fairly common late May; very common June to early July; rare late July

Common Wood Nymph – common late June to late August

Monarch – rare June; common July; very common to abundant August to October, both on flowers and migrating overhead (larvae seen on milkweeds)

Great Spangled Fritillary – uncommon July and August

Baltimore – colony of 40 larvae found on Gerardia 5/29/83.

Silvery Checkerspot – uncommon June

Pearl Crescent – uncommon May; fairly common July and August; common September

Question Mark – rare April and August; common late May through July; uncommon September and October (larvae seen on elm, nettles)

Comma (or Hop Merchant) – rare April, May, July, and August

Mourning Cloak – very common March and April; common June and July; uncommon September and October (larvae seen on willow)

Red Admiral – rare in April and August; common in May and June; very common July; occasionally common September and October (larvae seen on nettle)

Painted Lady – rare and irregular May through September

American Painted Lady – uncommon late April to October (occasionally common September)

Buckeye – very rare (entrance road, 7/8/79)

Viceroy – very rare (entrance road, 7/28/79; 9W, 8/6/83)

Red Spotted Purple – rare June to August

Tawny Emperor – very rare (on hackberry near Picture Pt., 7/10/81)

Hackberry Butterfly – uncommon late June to August

White "M" Hairstreak – very rare (entrance road, 8/23/83 & 8/8/82)

Coral Hairstreak – rare July

Gray Hairstreak – fairly common late July to mid-September

Edward's Hairstreak – rare July

Banded Hairstreak – very common late June to early July

Striped Hairstreak – very rare (7/7/79)

American Copper – fairly common May; common July and August; uncommon September

Eastern Tailed Blue – uncommon May, July and August; fairly common September

Spring Azure – very common April, fairly common June to August

Black Swallowtail – rare June; uncommon July and August (larvae seen on Queen Anne's lace)

Tiger Swallowtail – rare April; common May and June; very common July and August (including dark-phase females); rare September

Spicebush Swallowtail – rare April; fairly common mid-May and June; common late July to mid September

Pipevine Swallowtail – rare (on entrance road thistles, 9/15-9/18/82; 4 in September 1984)

Alfalfa Butterfly (or Orange Sulphur) – uncommon July through September

Common (or Clouded) Sulphur – uncommon July through September

Little Sulphur – very rare (entrance road, summer 1975)

European Cabbage Butterfly – fairly common April through June; abundant July to October

Silver Spotted Skipper – uncommon May; fairly common July; very common August and September

Hoary Edge – common June and July

Common Sooty Wing – rare July

Sleepy Dusky Wing – common late May and early June

Horace's Dusky Wing – common late April

Juvenal's Dusky Wing – uncommon May

Wild Indigo Dusky Wing – rare September

Least Skipper – uncommon July and August (in bog)

Little Glassy Wing – uncommon late June and early July

Peck's Skipper – very common July and August

Broken Dash – uncommon July

Broad-winged Skipper – very rare (bog flowers, 7/15 & 7/30/81)

TABLE II (*Continued*)

Hobomok Skipper – common late May and early June
Zabulon Skipper – fairly common late May to August; rare September
Eastern Dun Skipper – fairly common July
Mulberry Wing – uncommon July around pond

Also recorded on Hook Mountain (by Harry Darrow), Snout Butterfly, Compton's Tortoise Shell, Falcate Orange Tip

sulphurs, two species of painted ladies, American coppers, eastern tailed blues, a half-dozen species of hairstreaks, and over 15 kinds of skippers. Occasionally a rare buckeye, viceroy, pipevine swallowtail or white-M hairstreak is also discovered sipping from a thistle or milkweed blossom. In the summer of 1983 a colony of 40 Baltimore butterfly caterpillars was found feeding on smooth false foxglove (*Gerar-* *dia flava*) in Greenbrook Sanctuary by naturalist Joan Hansen – a new record for the Palisades. The autumn migration of thousands of monarch butterflies along the cliffs and river shore brings an impressive conclusion to the butterfly season.*

*The common names of the butterflies appear in *A Field Guide to the Butterflies* by Alexander Klots in the Peterson Field Guide Series.

Mourning cloak butterfly in March

AMPHIBIANS – THE HARBINGERS OF SPRING

In mid-March when temperatures begin to moderate and the ground thaws out, the first evening rains are accompanied by the almost magical appearance of salamanders and frogs in the wet woodlands. Stimulated by the warmth and preciptitation, these primitive "gnomes of the forest" migrate to the same ancestral swamps and vernal ponds where they themselves were born as tadpoles in previous seasons. Thus begins a gradual progression from March to June of one species of amphibian after another, awakening and emerging from underground chambers or muddy pond bottoms where they spent the winter.

The first to reach their shallow woodland breeding ponds are the wood frogs. Brown with dark, raccoon-like masks, these medium-sized frogs only remain in the icy waters for one to two weeks – just long enough to mate and reproduce. The males produce a chorus of duck-like quacking sounds to attract females, which deposit large, jelly-like clumps of eggs in the water. In about three weeks the eggs hatch into tiny black tadpoles, which consume the abundant spring algae in these waters and transform into small terrestrial frogs in July.

The wood frogs are usually joined within a day or two in the vernal pools by the spotted salamanders – rubbery, 8-inch-long, black animals with yellow spots. Tight groups of 50 or more concentrate into various corners of the woodland pools, writhing and nudging each other in strange, nocturnal courtship "dances." After depositing their egg masses – similar to those of the wood frog but with larger, fewer eggs – they return to the woods for an underground, mole-like existence. The eggs hatch in about six weeks into tiny, gilled larvae which usually become salamanders by the autumn, although some may remain aquatic larvae until the following spring. The closely related Jefferson salamander, which lacks its cousin's yellow spots, has been occasionally reported from areas along the northern edge of the Palisades.

Meanwhile, in larger, more permanent bodies of water, the small salamander called the red-spotted newt is performing its underwater courtship and mating activities. Unlike the spotted salamander, newts usually form pairs rather than clusters and they remain in the water all summer. Curiously, the newt seems to skip its familiar bright

American toad

"red eft" land stage on the Palisades. Toward the end of March the spring peeper, a tiny tree frog, enters the wetlands. The males produce loud whistling sounds from large throat bubbles and an evening chorus of hundreds of peepers can be almost deafening. The peepers usually reach the peak of their breeding activity in late April, when the warmer weather stimulates the emergence of the pickerel frogs from hibernation. Decorated with dark, rectangular spots and yellowish skin beneath the hind legs, these 3-inch amphibians utter low "snoring" calls in the shallows of permanent ponds. After breeding they inhabit woodland swamps and the borders of streams and ponds.

By late April the warty American toads also enter the waters to deposit long, ribbon-like strings of eggs. Their loud calls—the most musical of any local amphibians—are long, steady trills. Active both day and night, the toads leave the water in just a few days and the eggs often hatch in only a week into tiny black tadpoles. A few weeks later, the shorelines are covered with insect-like toadlets beginning their terrestrial existence. A close relative of the American toad, Fowler's toad, has rarely been reported from the Palisades region, although its typical habitat is the sandy coastal plain where

it breeds about a month later than its cousin. It can usually be identified by its white, unspotted belly.

The gray tree frog, a larger relative of the peeper, becomes active about the beginning of May. The male's loud, melodious woodpecker-like trill comes in short bursts from the weedy shallows of permanent ponds (and even swimming pools!) during evenings and rainy days in late spring. After breeding, these masters of camouflage (they can change color from gray to brown to green in about an hour to match their backgrounds) return to their woodland homes high in the branches of trees, calling forth on damp summer nights. A more distant relative of the tree frogs, the tiny, one-inch New Jersey chorus frog, has been reported from a few areas along the western slopes of the Palisades (Closter, Northvale, N.J.). Lacking the large toe pads needed to climb, the chorus frog inhabits grassy puddles and pond edges. Its early spring mating call resembles the sound produced by running one's finger along the small teeth of a comb.

The last two frogs to breed on the Palisades are not only the largest but also the only two species to remain permanently in the ponds, even hibernating in the muddy bottoms all winter. The green frog, recognized by the prominent lateral ridge run-

Slimy salamander

ning down either side of its body, utters a short, banjo-like "plunk" in May and June, when air temperatures are regularly over 65 degrees. Our largest amphibian, the bullfrog, brings the breeding season to a close, bellowing its resounding "jug-o-rum" from late May until July near the banks of the larger ponds. Its tadpole stage lasts two years and then it takes another three years to reach its full body size of 7 or 8 inches. Both the green frog and bullfrog, as well as the American toad, are occasionally found in the marshes along the Hudson, but the brackish waters and alternate flooding and drying from the tides precludes this from being a breeding habitat for them.

There are five species of lungless salamanders on the Palisades. They "breathe" entirely through their skins and throats, which are richly supplied with blood vessels. Found in and around springs and streams are: the small, yellowish northern two-lined salamander, with one dark line running along each side of its body; the brownish northern dusky salamander; and the strikingly beautiful northern red salamander, which turns from bright red to pur-

plish as it reaches its full 6-inch size. All three of these spend the first parts of their lives as larvae on the bottom of streams, breathing with feathery external gills.

The other two lungless salamanders are completely terrestrial, even depositing their eggs on land and hatching out as miniature, air-breathing salamanders rather than as gilled larvae. One, the large slimy salamander—shiny black with white spots—inhabits moist, shaded, rocky areas, and deposits its eggs inside crevices or caves. The other, the slender red-backed salamander, is the most common Palisades species and comes with either a reddish or gray backstripe. It lives beneath logs, stones, and leaf litter, and the female suspends her cluster of about a dozen eggs inside or beneath rotting logs. She actually remains with and guards the eggs until they hatch, displaying a maternal instinct quite unusual among amphibians.*

---

*The common names of the amphibians appear in *A Field Guide to Reptiles and Amphibians of Eastern and Central North America* by Roger Conant in the Peterson Field Guide Series.

SNAKES, SKINKS, AND TURTLES – THE REPTILES

To many people the very word "snake" evokes feelings of fear or disgust and images of slimy, slithering, poisonous creatures. There are even those who refuse to walk in the woods in summer for fear of encountering one of these reptiles. Even in more southern regions of the United States where snakes are much more abundant and diversified than in New York and New Jersey, the great majority of species are harmless and secretive, and most people who walk in the woods never see one. On the Palisades there is only one dangerous species – the copperhead – and, like all snakes, this one usually does all that it can to stay out of the way of humans. In more than ten years of hiking throughout the Palisades this writer has encountered perhaps ten copperhead snakes (an average of one per year), and all have been completely nonaggressive, usually remaining perfectly still in the leaf litter where their colors are excellent camouflage. The chance of encountering a snake should definitely not prevent one from enjoying the woods and trails of the Palisades.

As a group, reptiles are not quite as cold-hardy as the amphibians. They usually wait until the warmer weather of April to fully awaken from their winter sleep. About 15 species of turtles and snakes, and even one lizard, inhabit the woods, ponds, talus, and clearings of the Palisades. The lizard – the only one in northern New Jersey – is named the five-lined skink. Scattered colonies of this fast and agile 6-inch reptile exist on the rocks of talus slopes and along the cliff edge, where they warm themselves and chase insects. Five yellowish stripes usually run down the back and the younger lizards are decorated with bright blue tails.

The eastern painted turtles are the earliest reptiles to emerge from hibernation in the muddy pond bottoms. As many as 30 of these shiny, colorful turtles can be seen sunning themselves on a single log in Greenbrook Sanctuary's pond. They share their habitats with small musk turtles or "stinkpots" and ponderous, 35-pound snapping turtles, harmless underwater but

Copperhead snake sunning on diabase ledge

short-tempered and aggressive when the females climb onto the land to look for egg-laying sites in late May and June. Turtle nests are excavated in sunny, sandy places like roadsides and those eggs which are not eaten by fox, skunk, or raccoon will hatch in September. Snappers are also known to inhabit some of the shallows and marshes of the Hudson River, like Piermont, where an occasional diamondback terrapin may also be found. This turtle—once eaten in restaurants but now legally protected—is more at home in coastal salt marshes and brackish bays.

Rarely seen around ponds, streams, and wet woodlands of the Palisades are the beautiful spotted turtle and the large, "sculptured" wood turtle. Though protected by law like the closely related bog turtle which may have once inhabited cer-

tain wetlands of the Palisades, these two species have been decreasing over the years from habitat destruction and over-collecting. The only completely terrestrial tortoise in the region is the eastern box turtle. The top of this species' shell is domed and colored with yellow or orange lines, while the bottom possesses a unique hinge, enabling the turtle to tightly close up like a box. It feeds on slugs, worms, insects, berries, and mushrooms in clearings and open woodlands.

The most commonly encountered snake on the Palisades is the black-and-yellow-striped eastern garter snake, at home both in dry, sunny woodlands and wet areas, where it feeds on amphibians and earthworms. A close relative, the large, thick-bodied northern water snake, inhabits the grassy borders of ponds, sunny swamps, and the brackish marshes of the Hudson. Its colorful reddish bands show through its dark brown skin only when the snake is wet or has just shed its skin. Large northern black racers—shiny black above and lead-gray on the belly—are occasionally seen along the Hudson's Shore Trail, around the banks of ponds, and in the more open woodlands and clearings. Colorful, slender eastern milk snakes, marked with reddish or brown blotches, inhabit woodland clearings, especially with rock walls which offer shelter and an abundant mouse population. Small, slate-gray, pencil-thin northern ring-necked snakes are sometimes uncovered beneath rocks and loose bark in open woods and on trails. Beneath debris in vacant lots, yards, and along railroad tracks lives the small northern brown snake (DeKay's snake), feeding on slugs and worms.

Large 6- or 7-foot black rat snakes inhabit the talus slopes and rocky exposures in the wilder, more secluded sections of the Palisades from Alpine northward. These powerful constrictors feed on mice and chipmunks and sometimes climb trees to prey on birds. In the same rocky woodlands lives the only poisonous snake of New Jersey's Palisades, the northern copperhead (the timber rattlesnake is gone from the New Jersey section of the Palisades but still inhabits the nearby Ramapos and Hudson Highlands, and is occasionally reported from towns like Orangetown and Clarkstown near the northwestern edge of the

Black rat snake climbing trunk of chestnut oak

Snapping turtle

Palisades). Copperheads often hibernate in the same crevices and caverns as the black snakes, and are sometimes seen basking on the same rocks in spring. Every year several of these stout, beautiful, copper-colored snakes are encountered by hikers on the Palisades without a mishap. Reluctant to move or attack, a copperhead normally tries to blend in with its surroundings to escape detection. Its fangs and venom are used almost exclusively to kill mice, shrews, and other prey rather than to bite humans. (Three other species of snakes, the eastern hog-nosed, smooth green, and eastern worm snakes, are found in the nearby Hudson Highlands and Ramapo woodlands and may occasionally wander down to the Palisades.)*

---

*The common names of the reptiles appear in *A Field Guide to Reptiles and Amphibians of Eastern and Central North America* by Roger Conant in the Peterson Field Guide Series.

BIRDWATCHING HOTSPOTS OF THE PALISADES

More people are drawn to the Palisades by birds than by any other group of animals. The ridge lies within the Atlantic Flyway, one of the major routes taken by migrating birds in spring and fall. During these seasons the woods are full of colorful songbirds searching the trees, shrubs, and leaf litter for insects and seeds as they travel to breeding or wintering areas. The shore trails, docks, and boat basins provide excellent views of waterfowl, gulls, and other birds migrating or wintering on the Hudson River. Cliff vistas offer easily accessible vantage points from which to view thousands of migrating hawks and even occasional eagles in fall. Hemlock groves hide nesting great horned owls in February, while dozens of other birds take to the thickets, clearings, ridges, slopes, and swamps to breed in summer. The cliffs themselves offer unique nesting situations for several birds. Red-tailed hawks, rock doves (pigeons), and even great horned owls are known to nest on ledges along the steep cliff face. The

Great horned owl in pine

Carolina wren, a southern bird which is very sensitive to cold weather, is uncommon in the north except for the Palisades, where it is a permanent resident of the sun-warmed cliff face and slopes.

Since 1946 the Palisades Nature Association has studied the bird populations in the 165-acre Greenbrook Sanctuary on the cliffs in Tenafly and Alpine, N.J. Professional scientists and naturalists, aided by expert amateur "birders," have maintained records of breeding birds, migrants, and winter residents there. The number of different birds recorded in the sanctuary, including those seen in the skies above and river below, is about 235. Perhaps 40 or more other species can be added from other birding "hotspots" along or below the cliffs (especially from Piermont Marsh where many shorebirds and terns can be sighted),

resulting in a conservative total of about 275 birds seen on the Palisades! (For a complete list of species, including abundance ratings and seasonal and nesting data, see Section I of Bibliography for these two references: Serrao's *Birds of Greenbrook Sanctuary* and Deed's *Birds of Rockland County and the Hudson Highlands*). The peak season is mid-May, when it is possible to see over 100 different species of birds in a single day along the Palisades. Over 90, including 22 migrating warblers, have been counted by this writer in one day in Greenbrook Sanctuary alone (see Table III). This number drops during the summer to about 80 species, including both breeding and nonbreeding summer residents (see Table VIII, page 82). The low point, of course, is mid-winter when only about 50 different species are likely to be turned up during a full day of birding (see Table IV).

Very productive birding areas exist both along the top and bottom of the Palisades. Vistas atop State Line Lookout, Tallman Mountain, High Tor, Little Tor, and in Greenbrook Sanctuary are excellent observation points for hawk and waterfowl migration, especially in autumn. The top of Hook Mountain has gained a well-deserved reputation for being one of the best and most accessible hawk-watching areas in the eastern United States. The exposed summit, which rises 730 feet above the Hudson, affords views in all directions, and migrating hawks can often be seen at close range. Every year from September to November, volunteers from local nature clubs count up to 25,000 migrating hawks of 15 different species flapping and soaring their way down from Canada and New England, westward across the Hudson past Hook Mountain to the Kittatiny ridge, then southward along the Appalachians (see Table V). The most productive hawk-watching days at Hook Mountain occur about the second or third day after the passage of a cold front, when winds from the north aid the birds in their journeys. Rising on thermal air masses and cliff updrafts, some go all the way to Central and South America for the winter. Detailed studies of these and slightly smaller migration flights at Greenbrook Sanctuary (see Table VI) over the years have provided valuable data

TABLE III
RESULTS OF 1984 BIRD COUNT
Greenbrook Sanctuary, May 19, 1984

Weather – Overcast, drizzly, cool in A.M.; clearing and warm in P.M.
Duration – 8 A.M. to 9 P.M.

NUMBER OF SPECIES – 93

Black-crowned Night-Heron
Canada Goose
Mallard Duck
Wood Duck
Turkey Vulture
Red-shouldered Hawk
Broad-winged Hawk
Osprey
American Woodcock
Spotted Sandpiper
Solitary Sandpiper
Lesser Yellowlegs
Great Black-backed Gull
Herring Gull
Ring-billed Gull
Laughing Gull
Rock Dove
Mourning Dove
Yellow-billed Cuckoo
Whip-poor-will
Common Nighthawk
Chimney Swift
Common Flicker
Pileated Woodpecker
Downy Woodpecker
Hairy Woodpecker
Great Crested Flycatcher
Eastern Phoebe
Least Flycatcher
Eastern Wood Pewee
Tree Swallow
Barn Swallow

Northern Rough-winged
 Swallow
Blue Jay
American Crow
Black-capped Chickadee
Tufted Titmouse
White-breasted Nuthatch
House Wren
Carolina Wren
Northern Mockingbird
Gray Catbird
Brown Thrasher
American Robin
Wood Thrush
Veery
Hermit Thrush
Swainson's Thrush
Gray-cheeked Thrush
Blue-gray Gnatcatcher
Ruby-crowned Kinglet
Cedar Waxwing
European Starling
Solitary Vireo
Warbling Vireo
Red-eyed Vireo
Black & White Warbler
Worm-eating Warbler
Tennessee Warbler
Nashville Warbler
Northern Parula
Magnolia Warbler

Cape May Warbler
Black-throated Blue Warbler
Yellow-rumped Warbler
Black-throated Green Warbler
Blackburnian Warbler
Chestnut-sided Warbler
Bay-breasted Warbler
Blackpoll Warbler
Ovenbird
Northern Waterthrush
Louisiana Waterthrush
Common Yellowthroat
Hooded Warbler
Wilson's Warbler
Canada Warbler
American Redstart
Red-winged Blackbird
Northern Oriole
Common Grackle
Brown-headed Cowbird
Scarlet Tanager
Northern Cardinal
Rose-breasted Grosbeak
Indigo Bunting
House Finch
American Goldfinch
Rufous-sided Towhee
White-crowned Sparrow
White-throated Sparrow
Swamp Sparrow
Lincoln's Sparrow

Postscript – The following day (May 20), 7 additional species were seen in the sanctuary: yellow and Kentucky warblers, kingbird, ruffed grouse, little blue heron, summer tanager, and red-headed woodpecker.

regarding migration routes and schedules followed by different species, the profound influence of weather variables on migration, and annual population trends.

The Piermont area is considered one of the most diversified birding areas in the Hudson Valley. These brackish, cattail-reed-Spartina grass marshes below Tallman Mountain occasionally contain secretive clapper, king, Virginia, and sora rails, American and least bitterns, common moorhens, several species of uncommon wrens and flycatchers, seaside and sharp-tailed sparrows (both of which have been known to nest here), and hundreds of swallows and laughing gulls in August. The pier which extends a mile into the river in Piermont contains open fields, mud flats, tidal canals, ditches, marshes, and a lagoon. Besides the regular waterfowl and gulls commonly associated with these habitats, the Piermont area has hosted in various seasons such rarities as red-throated loons, great cormorants, tri-colored herons, white-fronted geese, oldsquaw ducks, over 20 species of plovers and sandpipers, nine species of terns (including the rare black tern in spring), both loggerhead and northern shrikes, pipits, horned larks, grasshopper, vesper, and lark sparrows, and even an occasional bald eagle or snowy owl. Slightly farther north, the shallow Tappan Zee is

Turkey vulture

TABLE IV
RESULTS OF 1985 CHRISTMAS BIRD COUNT
Area III of Bergen County Audubon Society's Census Region
(Englewood Cliffs, Englewood, Tenafly, Cresskill, and part of Alpine)
December 21, 1985

Weather – cold (20's), calm, partly sunny, light snow cover
Duration – 8:30 A.M. to 4:30 P.M.
Sites Covered – Flat Rock Brook Nature Center, Crystal Lake, Tenafly Nature Center, Tenafly Lost Brook Preserve, Allison Park, Alpine Scout Camp (part), Greenbrook Sanctuary, Tenafly Commons (duck pond and brook), Hudson River shore path and Henry Hudson Drive between Alpine Boat Basin and Englewood.

SPECIES (60): numbers of each species seen are in parentheses.

*Horned Grebe (1)	Great Horned Owl (1)	American Robin (20)
Great Blue Heron (1)	Belted Kingfisher (1)	Mockingbird (7)
Canada Goose (40)	*Red-bellied Woodpecker (2)	Brown Thrasher (1)
Mallard Duck (414)	Downy Woodpecker (35)	*Cedar Waxwing (234)
Black Duck (14)	Hairy Woodpecker (6)	European Starling (180)
Common Goldeneye Duck (7)	Pileated Woodpecker (2)	Northern Cardinal (51)
*Bufflehead Duck (1)	Northern Flicker (2)	American Tree Sparrow (1)
*Red-breasted Merganser (4)	Blue Jay (56)	*Chipping Sparrow (1)
*Sharp-shinned Hawk (2)	American Crow (73)	Fox Sparrow (5)
Red-tailed Hawk (6)	*Fish Crow (1)	Field Sparrow (1)
American Kestrel (1)	Black-capped Chickadee (106)	Song Sparrow (11)
Ruffed Grouse (1)	Tufted Titmouse (44)	White-throated Sparrow (121)
Killdeer (1)	Red-breasted Nuthatch (2)	Dark-eyed Junco (336)
Common Snipe (1)	White-breasted Nuthatch (28)	Red-winged Blackbird (50)
*American Woodcock (1)	Brown Creeper (4)	Common Grackle (132)
Ring-billed Gull (102)	Carolina Wren (6)	Purple Finch (1)
Herring Gull (38)	Winter Wren (2)	House Finch (31)
Great Black-backed Gull (10)	Golden-crowned Kinglet (3)	*Common Redpoll (5)
Rock Dove (59)	Ruby-crowned Kinglet (1)	American Goldfinch (29)
Mourning Dove (90)	Hermit Thrush (3)	House Sparrow (47)

*(Denote uncommon or rare species, or species in unusually high numbers).

Refer to the following for Tables V through VII

BV	–	Black Vulture	**RS**	–	Red-shouldered Hawk	
TV	–	Turkey Vulture (records were not kept on this species until 1980 at Hook Mountain)	**BW**	–	Broad-winged Hawk	
			RL	–	Rough-legged Hawk	
GO	–	Goshawk	**GE**	–	Golden Eagle	
SS	–	Sharp-shinned Hawk	**BE**	–	Bald Eagle	
CH	–	Cooper's Hawk	**UE**	–	Unidentified Eagle	
RT	–	Red-tailed Hawk	**NH**	–	Northern Harrier (formerly Marsh Hawk)	

OS	–	Osprey
PG	–	Peregrine Falcon
ME	–	Merlin
AK	–	American Kestrel
UN	–	Unidentified Raptor
T	–	Total
RPH	–	Raptors per hour of observation

TABLE V
Yearly Summary of Autumn Hawk Counts at Hook Mountain, N.Y. from 1971 to 1984
Figures Supplied by Bi-State Hawk Watch Coalitition

	BV	TV	GO	SS	CH	RT	RS	BW	RL	GE	BE	UE	NH	OS	PG	ME	AK	UN	T	RPH
1971	0	–	2	2,095	37	347	88	3,295	0	5	5	0	200	256	4	7	623	103	7,067	16.4
1972	0	–	112	1,694	43	452	93	1,105	1	3	1	2	102	122	7	7	324	87	4,155	8.8
1973	0	–	87	1,932	20	462	146	7,762	2	7	3	0	162	206	2	9	354	162	11,316	20.2
1974	0	–	19	2,667	55	374	177	6,324	1	3	4	0	177	178	2	8	512	188	10,689	20.8
1975	0	–	24	6,018	52	526	184	10,585	3	4	7	0	267	180	2	13	668	185	18,718	38.2
1976	0	–	24	3,725	28	348	109	14,811	1	3	4	1	193	290	4	7	509	179	20,236	44.2
1977	0	–	28	7,070	75	334	130	6,670	3	3	4	0	270	330	9	25	764	163	15,878	45.4
1978	0	–	6	4,220	64	296	110	12,074	2	6	7	2	158	205	0	27	632	145	17,951	46.9
1979	1	–	9	4,284	62	235	134	11,175	0	5	5	0	209	273	11	17	587	145	17,151	45.5
1980	0	129	17	4,190	79	370	126	4,683	1	4	2	0	362	363	16	33	717	154	11,246	24.1
1981	0	201	22	5,067	115	297	104	18,730	0	1	5	0	236	351	6	17	622	155	25,929	64.8
1982	0	105	29	3,399	88	288	81	4,689	2	0	8	3	169	199	9	18	444	188	9,719	22.9
1983	0	111	19	3,300	80	236	102	2,158	0	3	3	0	178	198	5	24	399	111	6,927	17.9
1984	0	132	13	3,272	78	209	43	7,666	0	2	5	0	170	236	9	25	369	98	12,327	30.4

Cardinal feeding babies

TABLE VI
1979 Autumn Hawk Migration Count at Greenbrook Sanctuary
(with comparison to totals of previous years)

	TV	GO	SS	CH	RT	RS	BW	RL	GE	BE	NH	OS	PG	ME	AK	UN	Totals
9/9	–	–	11	3	1	–	145	1	–	–	3	7	–	–	1	3	175
9/11	–	–	25	2	4	1	601	–	–	1	5	9	–	–	5	1	654
9/15	–	–	132	3	1	2	859	–	–	–	3	12	–	–	6	–	1,018
9/16	–	–	85	–	–	–	4,967	–	–	–	–	10	–	–	17	–	5,079
9/17	–	–	105	1	–	1	133	–	–	–	4	5	–	–	3	–	251
9/18 & 9/20	–	–	10	–	–	–	13	–	–	–	6	8	–	–	–	1	38
9/19	–	–	116	2	–	–	162	–	–	–	3	8	–	–	9	2	302
9/23-25	–	–	63	–	–	–	13	–	–	1	–	9	–	–	15	1	102
9/26	–	–	176	4	–	1	3	–	–	–	–	6	–	–	9	–	199
10/2-6	–	–	114	4	3	–	9	–	–	–	6	25	–	2	13	–	176
10/7	–	–	26	–	–	–	–	–	–	–	2	1	–	–	6	–	35
10/8	–	–	65	–	2	2	–	–	–	–	–	6	–	–	26	–	101
10/14	7	–	129	8	7	3	–	–	–	–	5	11	–	–	20	1	191
10/15	–	–	82	2	–	–	–	–	–	–	–	2	–	1	36	1	124
10/16	–	–	100	3	10	5	1	–	1	–	–	2	1	1	17	3	144
10/17	–	–	58	2	3	1	–	–	–	–	–	3	–	1	8	–	76
10/18	–	–	12	1	–	5	–	–	1	–	–	1	1	1	2	2	26
10/20-23	–	1	12	–	3	3	2	–	–	–	1	1	–	–	10	–	34
10/24-26	5	1	33	3	19	6	–	–	–	–	6	–	–	–	6	–	79
10/29	–	1	22	1	67	1	–	–	–	–	6	–	–	–	–	–	98
10/30	6	–	35	2	62	34	–	–	–	–	1	1	–	–	2	15	158
10/31	–	1	2	2	9	2	–	–	–	–	2	–	–	–	1	–	19
11/4 & 5	2	–	3	–	7	–	–	–	–	–	1	–	–	–	1	–	14
1979 TOTALS	20	4	1,416	43	198	67	6,908	1	2	2	54	127	2	7	213	30	9,094
1978 TOTALS	45	6	1,557	41	271	101	1,215	2	1	3	38	144	0	10	270	75	3,779
1977 TOTALS	38	8	3,010	39	258	56	4,025	3	0	0	87	153	1	6	259	–	7,943
1976 TOTALS	13	3	1,142	12	129	34	7,325	0	1	3	59	137	0	5	233	–	9,155

TABLE VII
HOOK MOUNTAIN HAWK WATCH
Spring 1984

Compiled by John M. Irvine, Jr., Bi-State Hawk Watch Coalition

Here is a comparison of totals for the five years for which summaries have been made

Year	Days	Hrs.	TV	GO	SS	CH	RT	RS	BW	RL	GE	BE	NH	OS	PG	ME	AK	UN	T	RPH
1976	47	219	–	7	533	6	104	36	1,220	–	1	–	48	75	1	1	297	69	2,398	10.9
1977	26	141	–	9	305	4	26	28	961	–	1	–	22	50	2	3	86	98	1,595	11.3
1981	29	136	34	2	265	11	51	16	1,319	–	–	–	18	57	2	3	111	100	1,989	14.6
1982	14	82	36	2	105	6	28	24	526	–	–	–	11	22	0	9	116	29	914	11.1
1984	25	116	1	4	362	14	143	12	1,304	1	–	2	23	104	3	10	297	32	2,312	19.9

visited by common terns and double-crested cormorants in July and thousands of canvasbacks and other ducks in winter.

A walk along either of the two shore paths between Edgewater, N.J. and the New York state line, and between Nyack and Haverstraw can be very productive in winter. There are waterfowl in the river, red-tailed hawks soaring above, and overwintering Carolina and winter wrens, yellow-rumped warblers, gray catbirds, hermit thrushes, common flickers, northern cardinals, and various sparrows searching for insects, fruits, and seeds among the rocks on relatively warm and sunny talus slopes. Pied-billed grebes and bank swallows have been known to nest around the old claypits along the Hudson in Haverstraw. Besides plenty of migrating and overwintering ducks, geese, swans, and coots, and a great variety of songbirds in its surrounding fields, thickets, and woodlands, Rockland Lake is sometimes host to "accidental" visitors like the California gull in the late 1970s and early 1980s.

The "tank farm" wetlands along the Long Path south of Tallman Mountain is gaining a reputation as a choice area to discover red-bellied woodpeckers and unusual woodland songbirds like Brewster's and prothonotary warblers in spring. Finally, one of the most diversified areas for watching land birds is the Blauvelt State Park – Clausland Mountain region, where overgrown fields, brushlands, hardwood forests, hemlock groves, and pine-spruce plantations provide habitats for nesting broad-winged hawks, great horned owls, and both Brewster's and Lawrence's warblers; a great variety of migrating songbirds in spring and fall; overwintering boreal chickadees and finches from Canada; and even an occasional barred owl in the secluded evergreen groves. (See final chapter for travel directions to these areas)*

_____

*In this and the following sections, the common names of the birds have been accepted by the American Ornithologists Union.

PALISADES BIRDS – A SEASONAL SURVEY

The following seasonal survey provides the monthly highlights and species most likely to be seen along the Palisades.

September: The fall migration features thousands of hawks soaring westward over the cliffs (see Tables V and VI). On September 16, 1979, 5,000 broad-winged hawks were counted passing over Greenbrook Sanctuary, with 1,000 in a single rising flock, or "kettle"! Two years later at Hook Mountain, 13,000 broadwings were seen on September 20 – over 10,000 in a single hour! Smaller daily flights of ospreys (up to 50), northern harriers (marsh hawks), sharp-shinned hawks (up to 500), Cooper's hawks, American kestrels, and even an occasional bald eagle, merlin, and peregrine falcon can be seen this month. Small flocks of double-crested cormorants and common loons travel along the Hudson, great blue herons, ospreys, and sandpipers visit the ponds and

shores to feed, and hundreds of chimney swifts, common nighthawks, swallows, and blue jays migrate overhead. The woods are alive with common flickers, cedar waxwings, 25 to 30 species of warblers, thrushes, and some house wrens, ruby-throated hummingbirds, and flycatchers.

October: The broad-winged hawk migration is over, but hundreds of sharp-shinned hawks continue, and the end of the month marks the peak migration of beautiful red-tailed and red-shouldered hawks. October is also the month of waterfowl: V-shaped flight formations of Canada geese; brants and black scoters along the Hudson; mallards, black ducks, green-winged teal, and wood ducks on ponds and lakes. The shorelines and marshes are visited by marsh wrens, rusty blackbirds, common grackles, and swamp, song, and Lincoln's sparrows, and the thickets hide gray catbirds, brown thrashers, and rufous-sided

Broad-winged hawk

December through February: During the winter, the Hudson River is home to rafts of thousands of canvasback ducks, and smaller numbers of greater scaup, ruddy, bufflehead, common merganser, and common goldeneye. All these ducks are divers, disappearing completely beneath the water for their food. As many as six species of gulls can also be seen on the river in winter – the regular herring, ring-billed, and great black-backed gulls, the small, visiting Bonaparte's gulls, and the rare Iceland and glaucous gulls from the far north. Many of these same aquatic birds, plus American coots and mute and tundra swans, spend the winter on Rockland Lake.

Red-tailed hawks soar along the cliffs where they may be rarely joined by a northern goshawk or bald eagle. American goldfinches, European starlings, and red-winged blackbirds each congregate in large winter feeding flocks, while long-eared and tiny saw-whet owls hide in evergreens. Other winter visitors from the north are American tree and fox sparrows, red-breasted nuthatches, brown creepers, hermit thrushes, golden-crowned kinglets, dark-eyed juncos, white-throated sparrows, occasional flocks of American robins (from Canada), evening grosbeaks, pine siskins, and purple finches, and rarely, groups of yellow-rumped warblers, common redpolls, pine grosbeaks, and white-winged crossbills. Of course, the regular permanent residents of the Palisades also enliven the winter scene: ruffed grouse, pileated, hairy, and downy woodpeckers, eastern screech and great horned owls, mourning and rock doves, common crow, blue jay, black-capped chickadee, tufted titmouse, white-breasted nuthatch, Carolina wren, house finch, and northern cardinal.

March: By the end of winter, the great horned owls are already feeding young, rock doves (pigeons) are nesting in ledges and recesses of the steep cliff face, male red-winged blackbirds are singing in their marshy territories, and male woodcock are performing their curious courtship flights in open swamps and meadows. This month also features the return of common grackles, rusty blackbirds, brown-headed cowbirds, song sparrows, American robins, and the first red-tailed hawks from the south. Canada geese, mallards, black ducks, and wood ducks come back to the unfrozen

towhees. In the woods, winter wrens, American robins, hermit thrushes, dark-eyed juncos, and white-throated sparrows scratch for food in the leaf litter, brown creepers and yellow-bellied sapsuckers climb tree trunks, and solitary vireos, both golden and ruby-crowned kinglets, American goldfinches, and some of the later warblers – yellow-rumped, palm, Connecticut, and black-throated green – hunt for food in the trees.

November: Turkey vultures move down through the Palisades from their Bear Mountain breeding areas. A few northern harriers and red-tailed hawks still soar along the cliffs, as well as a rare northern goshawk, rough-legged hawk, and golden eagle. Migrating flocks of snow geese pass overhead, and red-winged blackbirds, brown-headed cowbirds, fox sparrows, and a few field and swamp sparrows pass through the woods. The end of the month is marked by the arrival of the winter visitants from farther north (see below).

ponds, and the first common flickers, eastern phoebes, and pine warblers are on the Palisades by the end of the month. Except for the rusty blackbirds and pine warblers, all these birds are known to breed in the Palisades region.

April: This month is the beginning of the great spring migration "push." Quiet winter woodlands suddenly become alive with transient winter wrens, brown creepers, hermit thrushes, yellow-bellied sapsuckers, golden and ruby-crowned kinglets, blue-gray gnatcatchers, solitary vireos, white-throated sparrows, and the first "waves" of early warblers: palm, black and white, northern parula, yellow, worm-eating, yellow-rumped, black-throated green, common yellow-throat, and Louisiana waterthrush. Flights of tree swallows and occasional loons and double-crested cormorants go overhead. Great blue herons, ospreys, and pied-billed grebes stop to fish at the ponds, where Canada geese, mute swans, and mallards are already incubating their eggs. Broad-winged and sharp-shinned hawks, American kestrels, and perhaps a rare bald eagle characterize a northward hawk migration that is somewhat less impressive than the autumn flights (see Table VII). By late April the brown thrasher, gray catbird, and rufous-sided towhee are singing on their breeding territories.

May: By the middle of May the spring migration along the Palisades reaches a peak (see Table III). Green-backed herons, spotted and solitary sandpipers, and belted kingfishers visit the ponds, shorelines, and mud flats. Large migrating "waves" of over 25 species of warblers, including an occasional rare prothonotary, mourning, or Kentucky warbler, literally fill the trees with their songs and agitated feeding activities. Flocks of cedar waxwings, American goldfinches, and sometimes bobolinks stop to feed in the treetops on caterpillars. The skies are full of chimney swifts and common nighthawks chasing insects, while marsh wrens hide in the reeds and several species of thrushes search for food in the dead leaves.

The permanent residents (see *Dec. through Feb.*) and earlier returning summer residents (see *Mar.* and *Apr.*) are already raising their young in the Palisades woodlands. Joining them this month are more nesting birds: broad-winged hawk, eastern kingbird, great crested flycatcher, eastern wood pewee, yellow and black-billed cuckoos, ruby-throated hummingbird, barn and

Black-capped chickadee

TABLE VIII
Comparison of Breeding Bird Censuses of 1957 and 1983 in Greenbrook Sanctuary*

Species	Number of Territorial Males 1957	1983	Species	Number of Territorial Males 1957	1983
Canada Goose	0	1	Ruby-throated Hummingbird	4	0
Mallard Duck	5	1	Pileated Woodpecker	2	2
Black Duck	1	0	Northern Flicker	12	15
Wood Duck	?	2	Hairy Woodpecker	8	5
Red-tailed Hawk	1	0	Downy Woodpecker	10	8
Red-shouldered Hawk	2	0	Eastern Kingbird	1	2
Broad-winged Hawk	1	1	Great Crested Flycatcher	15	14
American Kestrel	1	0	Eastern Phoebe	10	1
Ruffed Grouse	0	4	Eastern Wood-Pewee	14	3
American Woodcock	1	?	Northern Rough-winged Swallow	2	1
Rock Dove	0	2	Barn Swallow	0	1
Mourning Dove	1	4	Blue Jay	12	16
Black-billed Cuckoo	2	0	American Crow	?	2
Great Horned Owl	0	?	Black-capped Chickadee	13	18
			Tufted Titmouse	9	17
			White-breasted Nuthatch	5	9
			House Wren	1	0
			Carolina Wren	5	3
			Gray Catbird	15	10
			Brown Thrasher	4	5
			American Robin	10	17
			Wood Thrush	20	21
			Veery	26	5
			Starling	4	2
			Yellow-throated Vireo	8	0
			Red-eyed Vireo	27	6
			Warbling Vireo	0	1
			Black and White Warbler	24	7
			Worm-eating Warbler	11	7
			Blue-winged Warbler	8	0
			Black-throated Green Warbler	7	0
			Chestnut-sided Warbler	11	0
			Prairie Warbler	1	0
			Ovenbird	27	0
			Louisiana Waterthrush	6	0
			Common Yellowthroat	7	0
			Hooded Warbler	29	0
			American Redstart	25	0
			Red-winged Blackbird	8	11
			Northern Oriole	7	31
			Common Grackle	4	?
			Brown-headed Cowbird	9	0
			Scarlet Tanager	14	13
			Northern Cardinal	8	18
			Rose-breasted Grosbeak	0	5
			Indigo Bunting	6	8
			House Finch	0	2
			American Goldfinch	5	0
			Rufous-sided Towhee	35	10
			Field Sparrow	7	0
			Song Sparrow	2	0

*Serrao, 1985. "Decline of Forest Songbirds". *Records of New Jersey Birds,* 11(1): 5–9 (New Jersey Audubon Society)

Baby screech owl

Common flicker, mother feeding young in nest hole

tree swallows, house wren, wood thrush, veery, red-eyed (and rarely white-eyed and yellow-throated) vireo, northern oriole, scarlet tanager, rose-breasted grosbeak, indigo bunting, chipping sparrow, and the following warblers: black and white, worm-eating, blue-winged, yellow, ovenbird, Louisiana waterthrush, common yellowthroat, and American redstart (see Table VIII for Breeding Censuses).

June through August: Now, except for a few rare Acadian, yellow-bellied, and alder flycatchers and some straggling warblers, the migration is over. The 50 or 60 species of birds which remain to breed on the Palisades spend the summer busily feeding their young. A few nonbreeding summer residents also regularly hunt for food along the Hudson and the cliffs: double-crested cormorant, common tern, great egret, great blue heron, black-crowned night-heron, and osprey. In late August, the earliest fall migrants—least and olive-sided flycatchers, barn and rough-winged swallows, and a few warblers—begin to pass through the region, signalling the beginning of the great southward journey.

MAMMALS

During the summer of 1984, the headlines of some local newspapers proclaimed the appearance of coyotes in the Palisades borough of Tenafly, N.J. Frightened homeowners, some of whom claimed to have seen these large canids running around their neighborhoods, called the police and wrote letters to the newspapers appealing for advice. Local naturalists were at first dubious. Even though Tenafly contained a wild, densely forested 350-acre tract of land known as Lost Brook Preserve, and bordered still more hundreds of acres in the Palisades Interstate Park, how could wild coy-

Southern flying squirrel on black birch

Gray squirrel

otes exist so close to New York City and New Jersey's major metropolitan centers? Might not these animals be feral dogs? Nevertheless, coyotes are known to inhabit the more extensive forests of the Ramapo Mountains and Hudson Highlands only 35 miles away – this writer found a road-killed coyote on Route 9W near West Point, N.Y., in 1974. These adaptable animals could very easily travel down via the Palisades Interstate and Bergen County Park systems. Most of the sightings were confined to

homes bordering the Lost Brook Preserve, from which the so-called coyotes emerged toward dusk, but a road-killed specimen was found on the Palisades Parkway by Interstate Park employee Bob Buonocore, a seasoned outdoorsman who claimed to have no doubts about identifying the animal as a coyote. Thus, another mammal was added to the Palisades list.

Like the coyote, most of the approximately 35 species of mammals recorded on the Palisades are nocturnal and not easily observed. Their tracks in the mud and winter snow may well be the only clues to their presence in many areas. The large predators like timber wolf, mountain lion, and black bear were extirpated from the region long ago. The bobcat, porcupine, river otter, and beaver have also disappeared from the Palisades, though they still survive nearby in the more vast forests of the Highlands and Kittatinies, and may occasionally visit the Palisades (porcupines have been reported in the 1980s by rangers in both South Mt. and Clausland Mt. County Parks). Surprisingly, such wary and rarely encountered animals as the red fox and flying squirrel are still common even in the more developed sections of the Palisades.

The mammals most commonly seen by people are the ones which perform at least some of their activities in the daytime. In the oak forests are gray squirrels, which are active all year long, and noisy eastern chipmunks, which retire each winter to underground dens stocked with acorns, nuts, and seeds. The red squirrel inhabits swamps and hemlock groves where it scampers along the ground and through the trees gathering cones and gum balls. The eastern cottontail rabbit feeds on clover, weeds, twigs, and the bark of sumac, blackberry, and viburnum in forest clearings. Along the Palisades Interstate Parkway, fat woodchucks are commonly seen grazing on grass and weeds before retiring to their subterranean retreats where they spend each winter in the deep state of suspended animation known as true hibernation. Dark brown, knife-tailed muskrats feed on cattails and other water plants in the ponds, swamps, and marshes. They are sometimes seen swimming with bunches of plants trailing from their jaws. White-tailed deer are still occasionally surprised by hikers or seen in

Northern red bat roosting on tree branch

car headlights in the larger, more rugged sections of the Palisades from Alpine northward (especially the Alpine Scout Camp and the Clausland Mountain-Blauvelt Park area). A herd of 8 deer, including a newborn fawn, spent the summer of 1983 in Greenbrook Sanctuary, in Tenafly, N.J., some straying as far as the George Washington Bridge.

Toward dusk, especially over open areas like ponds and the cliff, both the little brown myotis and big brown bat, and possibly an eastern pipistrelle and silver-haired bat, are seen darting after insects in the warmer months. The beautiful red bat is unusual among bats for flying during the afternoon, especially in October and November when it migrates along the Palisades in full view of surprised hawk watch-

Star-nosed mole

Masked shrew

ers. Some apparently hibernate on the Palisades, since they are rarely seen flying on warm days in December and January.

Among the most nervously active but secretive mammals are the burrowing shrews and moles, all of which have glossy, gray fur, pointed snouts and tiny, almost invisible eyes and ears. Usually the tunnels and earth mounds are all that one ever sees of the two species of Palisades moles–the eastern mole in upland woods and the star-nose mole in the wet lowlands (even chas-

ing insect and amphibian prey underwater on occasion). Two species of shrews – the tiny masked (or Sorex) and the larger shorttail – are also found on the Palisades, but their small size and secretive, burrowing behavior generally keeps them out of sight except for an occasional view of one dashing into a hole or beneath the leaf litter or snatching seed spilled from bird feeders. Dead moles and shrews are sometimes found lying on the trails, apparently killed by predators but uneaten because of their strong musky odors.

The most common of all Palisades mammals, but rarely seen except when it enters homes, is the nocturnal white-footed mouse. Large ears and eyes, long tail, soft white belly, and reddish-brown fur (gray when young) make this a very attractive mammal. Other small rodents are the auburn-colored pine vole (or woodland mouse) in deep leaf litter and underground burrows, the meadow vole (or field mouse) in grassy runways through clearings, marshes and the Hudson River's shoreline, the nocturnal southern flying squirrel in tree cavities (or bird-nesting boxes) in the oak woods, and, in more developed sections of the Palisades, the house mouse and Norway rat. One other species, the

meadow jumping mouse, has been recorded and collected by scientists in areas surrounding the Palisades but its present status here remains uncertain. In 1981 this writer discovered a colony of eastern woodrats (*Neotoma*) (sometimes called pack rats out west) inhabiting the caves and ledges in the steep, rugged talus near Forest View, north of Alpine, N.J. (see page 37). Subsequent explorations and live-trapping studies have shown this colony – at the time the only one verified to exist in the state (a second one has since been discovered in Morris County) – to be quite healthy and possibly even expanding southward in other talus regions below the cliffs in Alpine.

The remaining mammals are almost strictly nocturnal, mainly carnivorous species. The opossum, this country's only marsupial (its young are suckled in a pouch), emerges at night to hunt for small rodents, birds, insects, and fruits along streams, swamps, and brushy areas. Both the raccoon and striped skunk are becoming increasingly well known to residents along the Palisades as they adapt their feeding and denning activities to yards, buildings, and storm sewers. The red fox raises its pups each spring mainly in natural cavities on

Young white-footed mouse

Opossum with ten babies

talus slopes and rock-strewn ridges. About the end of April and beginning of May, the young pups are sometimes seen around their dens late in the day by hikers. The grounds around the den are often littered with the remains of their prey: mostly rabbit fur and feet and bird feathers, but this writer has found a snapping turtle shell, a skunk tail, and even the skull of a house cat. The gray fox is rarer and more secretive than its relative, and, like the long-tailed weasel and mink, it is usually restricted to the wilder, more secluded sections of the Palisades. Certainly the most unusual and surprising mammal of the Palisades region is the harbor seal. This animal rarely enters the Hudson River and swims northward, to the great delight of any hikers fortunate enough to observe it from the shores or cliff tops.*

---

*The common names of these mammals appear in *A Field Guide to the Mammals* by Burt and Grossenheider in the Peterson Field Guide Series.

Chapter VI

Modern Problems and Solutions

NATURAL SUCCESSION

Like all wild areas, the Palisades is not without its share of problems. Some are rooted in artificial situations arising from human "progress," while others are entirely of natural origin. For example, the inevitable process of plant succession has caused the surrounding forests to gradually reclaim the abandoned gardens, fields, and fire openings which existed along the Palisades before the Park Commission acquired these areas starting in the early 1900s. As these open and brushy areas disappear, there is a decline in the wildlife dependent on these habitats for food and homes: woodchucks, cottontails, field mice, field sparrows, blue-winged and chestnut-sided warblers, house wrens, bluebirds, milk snakes, and butterflies. Likewise, populations of wood frogs and spotted salamanders are declining in some areas as the shallow woodland swamps and vernal pools in which they breed gradually fill in with dead leaves and other organic matter and become terrestrial habitats.

To counteract these natural processes to some extent, the Park Commission and Palisades Nature Association have cooperated on several projects in Greenbrook Sanctuary to increase the diversity of habitats and wildlife along the Palisades. Several former vernal ponds have been dredged and restored with the egg masses of the amphibians which once breeded there each spring. In 1981, adult wood frogs deposited eggs in these pools on their own for the first time in 15 years, and over the next few years their populations thrived and multiplied. This project was so successful that other regional nature centers are now copying it. A few small tracts of woods still in the early stages of plant succession have been cut and planted with native grasses and wildflowers. Already these new meadows have attracted numerous butterflies, bees, and other pollinating insects; flocks of migrating songbirds; milk snakes and mantids; and nesting house wrens after long absences.

To make the Palisades attractive to an even greater variety of wildlife, a five-acre pond and small adjoining sphagnum bog were created in the sanctuary by the Park Commission and Nature Association in the early 1950s. Typical bog plants like Atlantic white cedar, leatherleaf, wild cranberry, white arum, and insectivorous pitcher plants and sundews were planted in the sphagnum moss, where they still thrive today. The Greenbrook pond immediately became a prime habitat for bullfrogs, painted and snapping turtles, water snakes, ducks, geese, kingfishers, red-wings, migrating herons and ospreys, and muskrats. In the mid-1970s a second pond—smaller but more densely wooded—was created by Park employee Fred Corring at the Park's New Jersey maintenance headquarters in Alpine by damming a stream and flooding a sweetgum swamp. In late March this pond attracts hundreds of breeding wood frogs and spring peepers, and nesting mallards and wood ducks.

Wood frog migrating to breeding pool in March

POLLUTION AND POISONS

Among the most distressing man-made problems affecting the Palisades have been air pollution and the use of persistent poisons in the environment (see page 15). Lichens have suffered great reductions in both species diversity and abundance in the 20th century because of the air pollution spreading from automobile smog and industrial emissions. This has been especially severe in the southern sections of the Palisades. North of the New York state line and farther away from the main sources of pollutants, the growth of lichens on rocks and tree trunks is much more noticeable.

More recently, two species of birds which once thrilled many a hiker and bird watcher along the Palisades have disappeared because of pesticides. Until the late 1950s, five or six pairs of peregrine falcons, or duck hawks – the world's fastest flying predators – nested atop the steep cliffs from Englewood, N.J. to Haverstraw, N.Y. Here they dived on pigeons, shorebirds, and ducks at speeds estimated to exceed 150 miles per hour. The widespread use of the insecticide DDT in the United States following World War II quickly brought the entire population of peregrine falcons in the eastern United States to complete extinction by about 1960. The poison, which accumulated in the fatty tissues of the birds from eating contaminated prey, affected the reproductive functions of the falcons and caused them to lay thin-shelled eggs. The eggs cracked beneath the weight of the incubating parents and complete reproductive failure resulted. The Palisades represented one of the last remaining breeding areas of the peregrines in the eastern United States, but these cliff eyries are now empty too.

DDT was also partly responsible for the

disappearance by the early 1960s of the northern bald eagles which regularly wintered below the cliffs and fished in the Hudson River from ice floes. From one of Greenbrook Sanctuary's cliff vistas, named "Bald Eagle Point," it was not unusual to see five or six eagles patrolling the river on a mid-winter day in the 1950s. Sightings of this majestic raptor then became extremely rare for about two decades, but began to be reported regularly again below the Palisades and Highlands in the early 1980s. Now the Interstate Park has created a bald eagle wintering sanctuary on Iona Island just a few miles north of the Palisades and at least a half-dozen eagles were seen there during the winter of 1985. Perhaps these birds are recovering now that DDT has been banned since 1972 in the United States. Recent successes at reintroducing the peregrine falcon to former breeding areas in New Jersey, New York, and other eastern states may also bring this bird back to its home on the Palisades cliffs. Indeed, sightings of this exciting raptor along the ridge have increased in the 1980s and they now actually nest (1983, 1984, and 1985) on a few nearby bridges in New York City!

THE SONGBIRD DECLINES

More mysterious has been the decrease since the 1960s of several species of woodland songbirds which, according to intensive surveys conducted by the Palisades Nature Association since 1946, were once among the Palisades' most common nesting birds (see Table VIII). The eastern wood pewee, veery, red-eyed vireo, and several woodland warblers (hooded, black and white, black-throated green, ovenbird, and American redstart)—all long-distance migrant, forest birds—have drastically declined along the Palisades since the 1950s, when censuses uncovered from 10 to 30 nesting pairs of each of these species per 100 acres of forest. Some species, like the hooded warbler, have disappeared completely during the breeding season! On the other hand, chickadees, titmice, cardinals, woodpeckers, and other birds which either don't migrate at all or else travel just short distances each fall, have remained stable or increased during this same period. These same trends have been observed and reported in various forest preserves throughout the eastern United States.

Fragmentation of their woodland breeding grounds is sometimes cited as the possible cause of these declines. Since the 1950s, as the Palisades region became more developed, forests which were once vast and contiguous were broken down into separate parcels interrupted by housing developments, golf courses, and roads. This resulted in increased human disturbance, predation by blue jays, crows, and cats, and parasitism by cowbirds to the more sensitive species of small birds which once nested safely deep within forest interiors. However, since the downward trend has been observed simultaneously in many vast, undisturbed forests from Minnesota to New York and south to Maryland, a more regional or global factor must also be responsible. A likely cause for the decline of these birds is the destruction of their wintering grounds in tropical America, where forests are being reduced by tens of thousands of square miles each year. Since the species which show the greatest declines are those which spend at least half the year in the tropics, this seems a logical explanation. Those species which reside in North American woodlands throughout the year, and thus escape this extensive deforestation, have maintained steady numbers or even increased. No matter how many sanctuaries are preserved for these migrating woodland birds in their North American nesting grounds, their continued decline is likely unless similar large preserves are set aside in their tropical wintering areas of Central and South America.

Veery thrush, a songbird declining in the eastern U.S.

LOSS OF LAND

Large predatory mammals have been gone from the Palisades for many years. The last mountain lion in the New York City region was reportedly shot in the Palisades at Clinton Point (Englewood Cliffs) in 1856. The black bear disappeared near the turn of the century, and the bobcat more recently. As business and housing developments continue to gobble up large tracts of unprotected forest, other large mammals such as deer, and wilder ones such as the gray fox, have also been forced to retreat to more undisturbed refuges. This has been occurring with alarming frequency along the Palisades since the post-World War II "housing boom," especially in the sections near the George Washington Bridge connecting the Palisades "bedroom communities" to the offices and businesses in New York City. In the beginning of the 1980s alone, several hundred acres of forest from Englewood to Alpine were being converted into homes. The white-tailed deer, common in these areas as recently as the 1960s, is now hardly ever seen south of northern Alpine.

One of the most controversial proposed developments is Norwood Easthill Associate's plan to convert 150 acres of Palisades forest in the Norwood section of the Greater New York Boy Scout Camp into 112 single-family lots and 40 townhouses. The densely wooded tract, which lies on the western backslope of the Palisades adjoining 850 more acres of Scout Camp lands in Alpine, boasts herds of deer, nesting red-tailed hawks and great horned owls, cascading mountain streams, mature oak/beech/maple forests, and some of the largest yellow birches, bitternut hickories, and tulip trees in New Jersey. The Scouts claim to need the $3.6 million from the sale of the Norwood tract to maintain the rest of their land in Alpine. Most of the land was given to the Scouts in 1942 by John D. Rockefeller. Although an attempt in 1983 by the Palisades Interstate Park Commission to claim the land (based upon the original intention and wording of the Rockefeller deed) failed in court, the Norwood Easthill Watch environmental group continues to fight the proposed development to win legal protection for the land.

From 1900 to the 1950s the Interstate

Park preserved over 6,000 acres of the Palisades in New York and New Jersey, but only rarely in recent years has the momentum of land development been checked. Beginning in the mid-1960s the Rockland County Park Commission has preserved 1,000 acres of the Palisades in New York. In 1976 Tenafly's "East Hill," almost 300 acres of forest atop the Palisades, was saved from being converted into a massive housing development. Through the efforts of local citizens, who were able to raise the $9 million needed to acquire the land (including $3 million from the state's Green Acres fund and a half million from the Palisades Interstate Park Commission), this forest is now being preserved in its natural state as "Lost Brook Preserve" (see last chapter). In February, 1981, Continental Group, the former owner of the mills at Piermont, donated the pier to the village of Piermont and about 70 acres of marsh to the Nature Conservancy to be preserved as wildlife habitat. (The major central portion of the marsh was already owned and protected by the Interstate Park.) In October, 1982, the entire 934-acre Piermont Marsh was formally designated a Federal Estuarine Sanctuary, along with three other Hudson River marshes farther north. These valuable wetlands will now be preserved for scientific research, environmental education, and recreational activities such as fishing and bird watching (see last chapter).

Reference has already been made to the appearance of the Palisades south of the Palisades Interstate Park in Fort Lee. The 18-mile stretch of the cliffs from Edgewater south to Jersey City not only lacks the 300 to 500-foot height of the Palisades in New Jersey's more northern regions, but it is also farther inland from the Hudson River. Thus, it doesn't possess the same sublime beauty and magnificent cliff-river contrast of the famous stretch of the Palisades from Fort Lee into New York state. Extension of the river shore by as much as 1,000 feet of fill for oil tanks, warehouses, and other developments has further separated the cliffs from the Hudson River in some areas. For the most part, the Palisades here has become defaced with billboards, grafitti, and garbage, and views both from and of (from across the river) the cliffs are obscured by high-rise apartments and other buildings. Communities are also cut off from the riverfront by private holdings.

Beginning in the 1980s, however, these municipalities (Edgewater, North Bergen, West New York, Weehawken, Hoboken, Jersey City, etc.) have been considering massive comprehensive and coordinated

White-tailed deer, now endangered on N.J. Palisades

plans to clean up both the riverfront and the cliffs, and to prepare regulations in light of intense pressure to develop what's left of this increasingly valuable real estate. The state of New Jersey has already mandated a continuous public walkway along the Hudson River, with guaranteed public access to the riverfront in every municipality. Other proposals include restrictions against further building on top of or against the cliffs to protect views; the construction of marinas, shops, restaurants, and housing; and a modern public transit system to avoid congestion in this projected pedestrian-oriented "riverfront city." Any parcels of undeveloped natural lands that are left would be preserved as parks. In 1983, the North Bergen Action Group took a giant step in this direction by leasing for one dollar per year from Hudson County, a 6½-acre woodland along the face and top of the Palisades. The Group plans to create interpretive trails and to preserve the area as a wildlife sanctuary.

EDUCATION AND PRESERVATION

To encourage this sort of environmental action and thinking in both young and old, several municipal nature centers and the Park's own Greenbrook Sanctuary conduct year-round educational programs about the ecology, natural history, and significance of the Palisades region. The main goal is to foster a knowledge and appreciation of the natural wonders and complex inter-relationships in this environment. As increasing amounts of land are lost to development, the few remaining wild areas like the Palisades are becoming even more valuable as outdoor learning centers and natural "oases" for wildlife. And, as more and more of the millions of people living minutes away from the Palisades look no farther than its spectacular cliffs and quiet woodland trails as their own refuges from urban noise, stress, and pollution, the twin missions of preservation and environmental education become all the more important. Hopefully, the users of these lands will respect and appreciate their worth so that the waterfalls, ancient trees, wildflowers, and animals of the wild Palisades will remain for future generations to enjoy.

Red fox pup in den, Greenbrook Sanctuary, N.J.

Chapter VII

A Palisades Tour Guide

In this final chapter we sample the great variety of recreational opportunities available along the Palisades: bicycle paths, hiking trails, nature centers, wildlife preserves, scenic vistas, and state, county, and town parks. The "tour" begins at the southern end of the Palisades Interstate Park in Fort Lee, N.J. (south of here the Palisades is almost entirely "developed" with factories, warehouses, high-rise apartments, and other housing projects) and works its way northward along the ridge to the end of the Palisades in Mount Ivy, N.Y.

Each site includes location and travel directions, a brief background, facilities, and highlights – scenic, geological, plant, animal, or otherwise. Some of these places are undoubtedly familiar to the reader, but others represent more secret, out-of-the-way, little "wildernesses" which are surprisingly accessible yet still primeval. This is an invitation to explore all of these places and discover the many natural wonders which exist just minutes away from the great metropolis of New York and New Jersey.

PALISADES INTERSTATE PARK – N.J. SECTION

– New Jersey section = about 2,500 acres.

Headquarters – former Oltman House (moved there in 1953), Alpine, N.J. (Box 155, 07620).

Phone – (201) 768-1360.

Directions – Exit 2 off Palisades Interstate Parkway to Headquarters.

Background – see Chapter II.

Schedule – Headquarters open Monday to Friday, all year, 8:30-4:30 (except holidays) closed noon-1p.m.. Police Dept. open every day, 24 hours/day.

Facilities – offices, information about Park, Greenbrook Sanctuary, Boat Basins, permits, etc.

Activities and Regulations (from Brochure and Map of N.J. section of Park):

Animals – Pets are not permitted in picnic areas, developed areas, or on paved surfaces. Properly leashed, they may be taken on the trails.

Bicycling/Jogging – Bicyclists and joggers are not permitted on the Parkway, either Approach Road, or the Henry Hudson Drive between Edgewater and Englewood. They may use the Drive between Englewood and Alpine only on weekends and holidays until noon (from April 15 to November 1) and all day from November 1 to April 15 (weather permitting).

Boating – Two marinas accommodate 252 boats for a season running from May 1

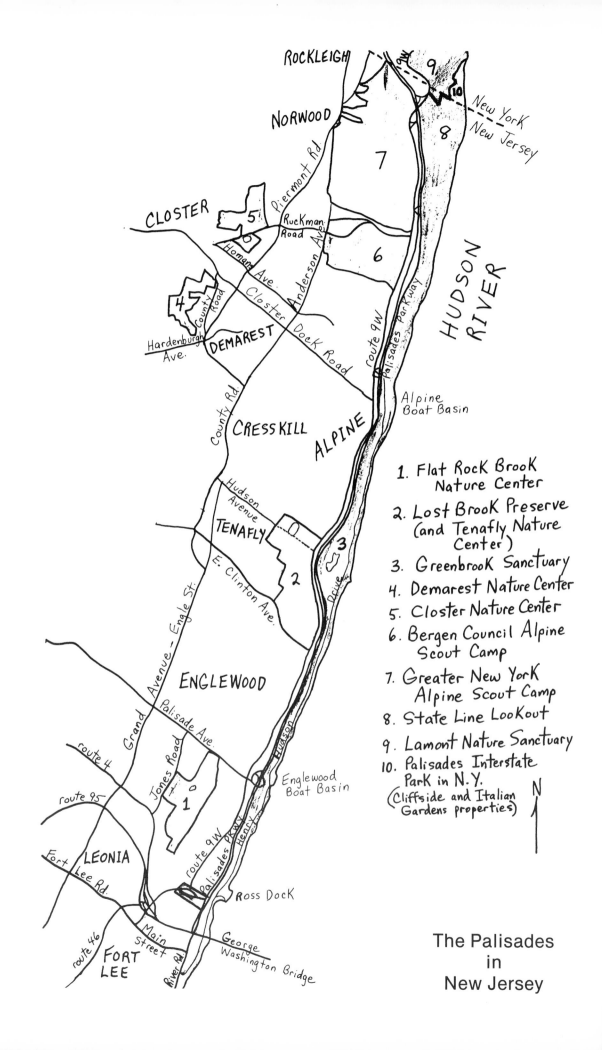

ROCKLEIGH

9

10

New York
New Jersey

NORWOOD

8

7

Piermont Rd.

CLOSTER

5

Ruckman
Road

Anderson Ave.

HUDSON RIVER

6

Homan Ave.

Closter Dock Road

route 9W

Palisades Parkway

4

County Road

DEMAREST

Hardenburgh Ave.

County Rd.

CRESSKILL

ALPINE

Alpine
Boat Basin

Hudson Avenue

TENAFLY

3

2

E. Clinton Ave.

1. Flat Rock Brook
Nature Center
2. Lost Brook Preserve
(and Tenafly Nature
Center)
3. Greenbrook Sanctuary
4. Demarest Nature Center
5. Closter Nature Center
6. Bergen Council Alpine
Scout Camp
7. Greater New York
Alpine Scout Camp
8. State Line Lookout
9. Lamont Nature Sanctuary
10. Palisades Interstate
Park in N.Y.
(Cliffside and Italian
Gardens properties)

Grand Avenue - Engle St.

ENGLEWOOD

Hudson

Palisade Ave.

route 4

Jones Road

1

Englewood
Boat Basin

route 95

N

route 9W

Palisades Pkwy

Henry

LEONIA

Fort Lee Rd.

Ross Dock

route 46

Main Street

George Washington Bridge

FORT LEE

River Rd.

The Palisades
in
New Jersey

96

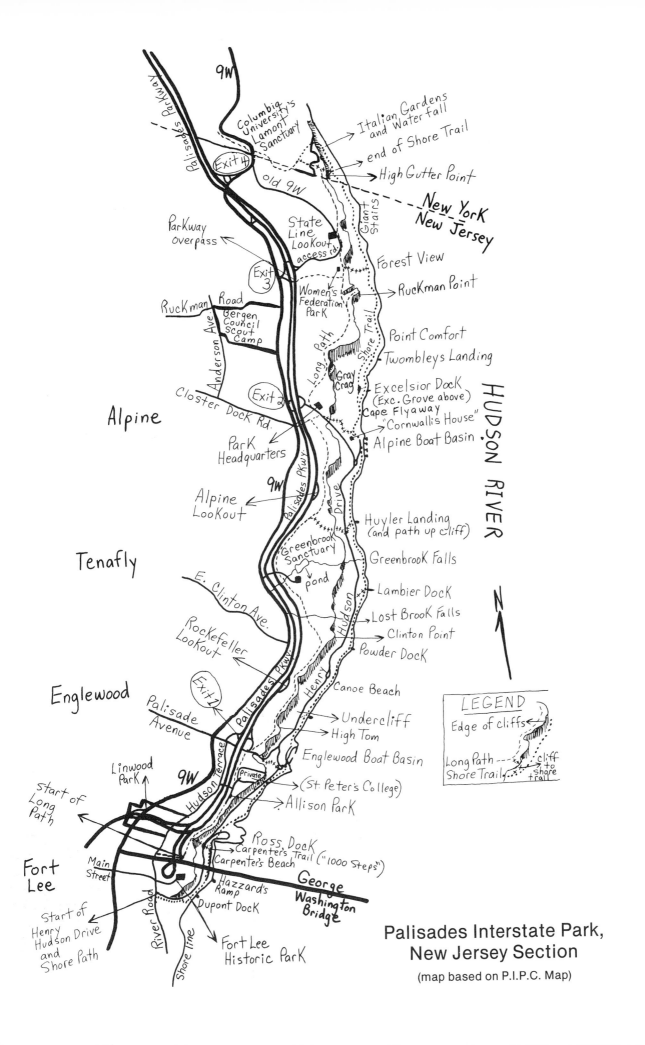

9W

Columbia University's Lamont Sanctuary

Italian Gardens and Water fall

end of Shore Trail

High Gutter Point

Palisades Parkway

Exit 4

old 9W

New York
New Jersey

Parkway overpass

State Line Lookout access rd.

Giant Stairs

Forest View

Exit 3

Women's Federation Park

Ruckman Point

Ruckman Road

Bergen Council Scout Camp

Point Comfort

Twombleys Landing

Anderson Ave.

Long Path

Shore Trail

Gray Crag

Excelsior Dock (Exc. Grove above)

Closter Dock Rd.

Exit 2

Alpine

Cape Flyaway

"Cornwallis House"

Alpine Boat Basin

HUDSON RIVER

Park Headquarters

9W

Palisades Pkwy.

Drive

Alpine Lookout

Huyler Landing (and path up cliff)

Greenbrook Sanctuary

Greenbrook Falls

Tenafly

pond

Lambier Dock

E. Clinton Ave.

Hudson

Lost Brook Falls

Rockefeller Lookout

Clinton Point

Powder Dock

N

Englewood

Exit 1

Palisades Pkwy.

Canoe Beach

Palisade Avenue

Henry

Undercliff

High Tom

LEGEND
Edge of cliffs

Englewood Boat Basin

Hudson Terrace

Long Path
Shore Trail

cliff to shore trail

Linwood Park

9W

private

(St. Peter's College)

start of Long Path

Allison Park

Fort Lee

Ross Dock

Carpenter's Trail ("1000 Steps")

Carpenter's Beach

Main Street

Hazzard's Ramp

George Washington Bridge

start of Henry Hudson Drive and Shore Path

River Road

Dupont Dock

Shore line

Fort Lee Historic Park

Palisades Interstate Park, New Jersey Section

(map based on P.I.P.C. Map)

97

to November 1. Rates are based on the size of the boat and include electricity and water. Gas is sold at both basins and transient slips are available for a nightly fee. Boats on trailers may be launched from Hazzard's Ramp in the Ross Dock Area and car-top boats must be launched from Bloomers Beach in the Englewood Area. Inflatable boats of any kind may not be launched from within Park boundaries.

Cross-Country Skiing – see State Line Lookout.

Fishing/Crabbing – In season and in accordance with the N.J. Fish and Game Code, fishing and crabbing are permitted from the seawalls, docks, and shoreline. As the Hudson River is considered tidal water, no licenses are required. Species caught in the River include striped bass, catfish, white perch, tommycod, shad, eels, and blue-claw crabs.

Hiking – see Palisades Hiking Trails.

Permits – Permits are required for 1) picnics or outings involving over 50 people, 2) buses, 3) commercial photography or filming, 4) facility rentals, 5) educational research, and 6) the bringing of alcohol in bulk. Permits must be obtained in advance from Park Headquarters during regular business hours.

Picnicking – Four areas along the River offer parking, picnic tables, restrooms, and pay phones. Barbequeing in grills (NO GROUND FIRES AT ANY TIME) is permitted only in these four sites and not in Fort Lee Historic Park or State Line Lookout. Areas cannot be reserved and please remember to bring your own grills and charcoal.

Special Events – Many cultural, historical, environmental, educational, and recreational programs take place at various sites within the Park. For a bi-monthly Calendar of Events, please contact Park Headquarters.

PALISADES HIKING TRAILS

The best way to experience the forests, wildlife, scenery, and primitive atmosphere of the Palisades is by walking through it. Fortunately, there exist two superb trails (both on the National Recreational Trails register since 1971) which take the hiker along the two extremes of the unique character of the Palisades. The *Shore Trail* (marked with white blazes) runs along the Hudson River at the bottom of the cliffs for the entire length of the New Jersey section of the Interstate Park. The *Long Path* (marked with blue blazes) traverses the top of the ridge over the entire 35-mile distance of the Palisades from Fort Lee to Mount Ivy. Though generally separated by hundreds of feet, the two trails are connected periodically via steep trails (marked with blue and white squares) with stone steps

and switchbacks winding between the top and bottom of the Palisades. By sampling both these trails, the hiker has the opportunity to experience and contrast the full range of Palisades flora, fauna, and habitats, to study the different geological features on the top and bottom of the cliffs, and to enjoy the unparalleled scenic vistas afforded from each vantage point. Hikers must be off the trails by dark.

These trails are maintained by the New York-New Jersey Trail Conference, a non-profit federation of over 60 hiking and outdoor clubs comprising nearly 3000 individuals. Formed in 1920, the Conference's volunteers maintain 700 miles of trails in the New York-New Jersey metropolitan area and promote conservation, outdoor education, and land preservation.

THE LONG PATH

—over 200 miles long, extending northward from the George Washington Bridge in Fort Lee, N.J., across the length of the Palisades, into New York State's Ramapo Mountains and Hudson Highlands (Harriman State Park), Shawangunk Mountains, and Catskill Mountain Preserve, currently ending at Windham, N.Y.

Directions—the Path begins at the New Jersey side of the G.W. Bridge, at the Bridge's north pedestrian walkway on Hudson Terrace (see **Fort Lee Historic Park* for directions by bus or car). Cars may be parked at the Historic Park or on Hudson Terrace. The trailhead is designated by three *blue blazes* on a large rock at the stairway to the north walkway over the Palisades Interstate Parkway. After climbing the steps toward the Hudson River, the Path turns left atop the cliffs and parallels the river. The Path can also be reached at many points along its length, including several side trails ascending the cliffs from the river in New Jersey (see below and also **Shore Trail*), and :

—from Hudson Terrace and Route 9W: near **Allison Park*; or near the entrance road to **Greenbrook Sanctuary*; or the tunnel from Closter Dock Road beneath the Parkway; or at the Park's **Alpine Headquarters*; or the pedestrian overpass across Parkway to **Women's Federation Monument*.

—other access points along the Palisades: **State Line Lookout*; parking pullover on 9W at **Lamont Sanctuary*; **Tallman Mountain Park*; village of Piermont; **Tackamack Park* in Orangetown; Nyack, N.Y. (intersection of Route 59 and Waldron Ave.); pullovers on Route 9W north of Christian Herald Road beneath **Hook Mountain*; from northeastern part of **Rockland Lake State Park*; at Long Clove (9W junction with Route 304); South Mountain Road below **High Tor*; Central Highway atop **South Mountain*; and in Mount Ivy, the end of the Palisades.

—from the Palisades Interstate Parkway, the Long Path can be reached from both Rockefeller and Alpine Lookouts, but cars may be parked here for only 20 minutes.

Background—as far back as 1931, Vincent Schaefer of Schenectady's Mohawk Valley Hiking Club proposed a con-

---

Note: Under the Shore Trail and Long Path, sections marked with double asterisks ** are discussed in more detail in separate sections to follow.

Frozen waterfall near "Gray Crag," Alpine, N.J.

tinuous New York State "Long Path" similar to Vermont's Long Trail. After the construction of the Palisades Interstate Parkway in the late 1950s, the increased accessibility of the cliffs (now all in public ownership) renewed interest in the project, and the work began in the early 1960s. Plans are under way to extend the Path from its current end in the Catskills to the Adirondack Mountains.

Highlights–Generally sticking to the height of the land through which it passes, the Long Path enables hikers from the New York–New Jersey metropolis to escape into the woods and enjoy the views and atmosphere of nearby cliffs and mountains. It traverses the entire Palisades ridge for about 35 miles from Fort Lee, N.J. to Mount Ivy, N.Y., where the ridge dips beneath the ground. During this route the Path descends the occasional gaps or "cloves" in the Palisades; ascends the summits to open vistas offering splendid views of the Hudson River, New York City, Westchester, and the Hackensack Valley; passes abandoned ruins of former cliff-top estates; enters ancient forests of upland oak/hickory or lowland beech/birch/maple/hemlock; crosses cascading mountain streams and waterfalls; and runs through many of the ridge-top parks preserved by the Palisades Interstate Park Commission and Rockland County Park Commission.

More specific points of interest (in order, starting from the south end, with approximate mileages from the start noted) are as follows:
(See Bibliography for *N.Y. Walk Book* and *Guide to Long Path,* both by N.Y.-N.J. Trail Conference, which give more detailed directions and mileages for the Long Path.)

1) *First 8 miles*: this section atop the Palisades is generally level, except for several stream valleys in the rugged Greenbrook Sanctuary area. Also, the Path runs through the narrow strip of Palisades Interstate Park land between the cliff edge and the Palisades Parkway, so the hiker is rarely beyond sight or sound of traffic. Nevertheless, there are many excellent views, and several interesting ruins of former estates.

–the woodland is mostly young, second-growth, dry upland forest, dominated by red, white, black, scarlet, and chestnut oaks, pignut hickory, black birch, with many small hackberry trees, some sweet-gums, white ashes, good-sized black cherry trees, and lots of blackhaw viburnum in the understory.

–¼ mile–Carpenters' Trail ("1000 Stairs") descends cliffs to **Ross Dock* recreation area on river.

–½ mile–Coytesville Park, with an old mounted cannon on the cliffs.

–ornamental Austrian pines, forsythia, lilac.

–1.2 mile–entrance to **Allison Park,* beyond which are St. Peter's College, St. Michael's Villa, and the site of the former Palisades Mountain House which burned down in 1884.

–2 mi.–Palisade Ave. and a stairway trail descending to **Englewood Boat Basin* on the river.

–Path then passes former Dana estate and High Tom rock promontory and gorge (overlooking **Undercliff Picnic Area*).

–3 mi.–**Rockefeller Lookout* off Palisades Parkway (400 feet high).

–stone ruins of former Cadgene estate, then Clinton Point vista (4 mi.).

–5 mi.–**Greenbrook Sanctuary* entrance road where cars can park.

–Path skirts sanctuary fence and dips into several stream valleys dissecting the sanctuary.

–5½ mi.–intersection of *red-blazed* old Huyler Road which descends to river (may have been used by British under Cornwallis in 1776–see page 20).

–6 mi.–**Alpine Lookout* off Palisades Parkway–fine views.

–ruins of Zabriskie estate and several other former estates, then tunnel (left) leading under Parkway to Route 9W at Closter Dock Road. (7½ mi.).

–intersection with **Henry Hudson Drive* (path passes underneath through a tunnel)–on the other side is a trail which descends to **Alpine Boat Basin* on the river.

–8 mi. **Headquarters* of Palisades Interstate Park in N.J.

2) *Miles 8 to 12*: This section features wilder forests, more spectacular cliff scenery, and the highest, steepest sections of the Palisades in New Jersey.

–beyond the Headquarters building are the ruins and exotic trees (huge Norway spruces, Austrian pines, Port Oxford cedars, a magnolia, and a giant ginkgo) of the former Ringling estate (of circus fame).

–after a fairly mature forest with big red oaks, sweetgums, sugar maples, pignut and bitternut hickories, and a few hemlocks, the Path reaches Gray Crag, the largest separated section of rock on the Palisades (300 feet long by 10 to 20 feet wide), with a deep canyon between it and the rest of the cliffs.

–slightly farther is a 300-foot waterfall over the cliffs (dry in summer but beautifully frozen with ice and windswept, snow-covered hemlocks in winter): from the cliff project picturesque dead cedars.

–next follows a recently burned area in stages of early forest succession (sumac, aspen, gray birch).

–9½ mi. – Ruckman Road (abandoned here) ends at cliffs, 520 feet high – a former pitching place (see page 24) with great views.

–10 mi. – abandoned buildings, foundations, and many ornamental trees and shrubs (cedars, yews, rhododendrons) of former Burnett estate; a trail leads from here westward out to Parkway overpass to 9W and the **Alpine Scout Camp*. Just past the Burnett estate is the **Women's Federation Monument* and castle at cliff edge.

–Path descends into ravine where another trail joins leading down to the river and **Forest View* through a primeval forest.

–Path climbs from ravine to **State Line Lookout* area on "Old 9W," 532 feet high (10½ mi.).

Palisades, looking north from State Line Lookout

State Line Lookout, 530 feet above Hudson

entrance to Lamont-Doherty Geological Observatory.

3) *Miles 12 to 22½:* this section features a county park, town park, several parks in the Interstate Park system, some walking on streets, and the region of the Palisades which temporarily bends inland away from the Hudson River.

–from Lamont Observatory, the Path follows 9W north, goes into woods, and out onto 9W again to reach Oak Tree Road in hamlet of Palisades, N.Y. To the right, the road leads to Sneden's Landing (see page 21).

–13mi.– parking lot at south end of **Tallman Mountain State Park* and bike path; Path turns east off 9W into lot and shortly turns left (north) into woods and passes the Park's "oil tank ponds," earthen berms, with spring wildflowers and amphibians galore.

–14 mi.– **Tallman Park's* picnic area; cross traffic circle, ascend through woods to upper picnic area and descend steeply to **Piermont Marsh* (15 mi.).

–after crossing Sparkill Creek (which flows through the deep Palisades Gap considered by many geologists to be the former Hudson River course – see page 12), the Path climbs out of Piermont Village via roads and steps (follow blue blazes along roadsides), crosses 9W, follows Highland Ave. north, turns left uphill to Rockland Cemetery on slopes of Mt. Nebo, and finally enters the wild forests of **Clausland Mountain County Park* (17 mi.), then crosses Clausland Mountain Road into **Tackamack Park* (18 mi.), then enters **Blauvelt State Park* (19 mi.) with its former concrete rifle range walls and tunnels, pine plantations, and old fields.

–from Blauvelt Park, the Path crosses Tweed Blvd., passes a water tank, talus slope (20 mi.), and descends past Nyack College.

–the remaining 2 miles to Christian Herald Road and Route 9W are over streets and past homes (follow blue blazes).

4) *Miles 22½ to 28½:* the six-mile length of the **Hook Mountain ridge.*

102

–11½ mi.– State Line monument at fence marking the N.Y. State line; Path goes through fence at cliff edge to High Gutter Point (another former pitching place): more steep cliff-edge steps here, with spectacular views of Piermont Marsh, Hook Mountain, Lamont Observatory, Tappan Zee; here are rock pillars and extremely steep cliff overhangs.

–Path descends into **Lamont Sanctuary,* with beautiful hemlock ravine, stream, and waterfall; here the **Shore Trail* ascends from river and ends at its junction with the Long Path.

–Path crosses stream (side trail descends to Italian Garden site on river), bears left, finally leaving Sanctuary at Route 9W and

-Path follows 9W north from Christian Herald Rd. for a short distance before turning right into woods and passing some big sugar maples, white oaks, and tulip trees (and red trilliums in spring) along the low, level trail; the Path then climbs up **Hook Mountain* (23½) with its superb views (729 feet) and autumn hawk migration flights.

-after another 2 miles along the ridge, the Path descends steeply to Rockland Landing Road (25½): left leads to **Rockland Lake State Park*; right leads down to **Nyack Shore Path* along river.

-Path ascends again from this gap, past a family cemetery, then soon descends to Trough Hollow which also connects Rockland Lake with the river (see page 19).

-Path ascends ridge again and, for next 2 miles, crosses knolls, passes former quarry with good views, then finally descends steeply through hemlock, striped maple, black birch, mountain laurel, and ferns, over a railroad tunnel and power line to reach Route 9W and Long Clove, a natural gap in the Palisades.

5) *Mile 28½ to end of Palisades:* for the final 6½ miles of its length, the Palisades ridge bends westward away from the Hudson River and climbs to High Tor, its highest point at 832 feet, then Little Tor and South Mountain before it dips beneath the ground at Mt. Ivy.

-from Long Clove, the Path crosses 9W and follows little-used roads past an apple orchard and a large quarry; after over a mile on roads, it climbs **High Tor* very steeply opposite the quarry's entrance road. From the bare summit are unparalleled views. The Path then descends the other side of High Tor to a fire road which continues to Central Highway (33 mi.) marking the end of **High Tor State Park*; about a mile before this junction, however, a white-blazed path leads right to the top of Little Tor (710 feet) and a road leads left down to the State Park's recreation area.

-across Central Highway (along which cars can be parked in pullovers near the crest) the Path enters **South Mountain County Park*. For the final 2-mile length of the Palisades the Path runs through mostly young, second-growth oak woods with lots of red cedar and grassy openings. After skirting the edge of the old Gurnee Quarry, the hiker can look ahead and see the Palisades sink beneath the ground at Mount Ivy, with the Ramapo Mountains in the background. The Path descends from the quarry to Routes 45 and 202 near the Palisades Interstate Parkway.

THE SHORE TRAIL

-about 13 miles long, in Palisades Interstate Park, N.J. section.

Location-along the Hudson River shore, from Fort Lee, N.J. north to the New York State line, shortly beyond which it climbs into **Lamont Sanctuary* and joins the Long Path.

Directions-south end of this *white-dotted* trail is at southern end of **Henry Hudson Drive,* where it curves up to meet River Road and Hudson Terrace just downhill (south) of **Fort Lee Historic Park.*

-cars can be parked either at Historic Park or along Hudson Terrace near entrance to the Drive.

-also can be reached from **Englewood* and **Alpine Boat Basins,* **Ross Dock,* and several trails connecting it to the **Long Path* on top of the cliffs (see below).

Note: Under the Shore Trail and Long Path, sections marked with double asterisks ** are discussed in more detail in separate sections to follow.

Background – trail completed in early years of Park; later designated a National Recreational Trail (1971).

Highlights – an extremely interesting and beautiful trail, mostly level, which features tidal waters of Hudson River, unbelievably steep cliffs of the Palisades, rugged talus slopes with huge boulders, ancient shadowy slope forests, spring wildflowers covering the rocks, roaring waterfalls, steep-sided ravines and gaps in the Palisades, and the weather-worn ruins of abandoned bathhouses, beaches, piers, and shelters. The Path generally follows the level of the river shore but occasionally it ascends slightly higher to a terrace which enters the shade of the ancient forests sloping down from the cliffs. The trail continually offers two extremes: on one side, the dark, dense, almost primeval forests sloping down from the cliffs; on the other, the open, sunny, airy feeling of the river – gently lapping waves, algae-covered rocks, noisy gulls, salty breezes.

– more specific points of interest (in order, starting from south end – with approximate mileages noted) are as follows:

1) *First 3 miles*: Descend from road via steps to shore; pass excellent examples of red sandstone exposure along beach. Near this site was found in 1910 the fossils of crocodile-like phytosaur (see page 7). The trail passes some catalpa trees, remains of DuPont Dock, **Hazzards* boat launching ramp beneath G.W. Bridge, former beaches at Hazzards and then Carpenters' (1 mile) below former quarry (bought by Park in its first year, 1900).

– Carpenters' Trail ("1000 Steps") – stone stairway ascends the cliffs to top along steep sides of old quarry, reaching Long Path, with great views.

– **Ross Dock* – recreation area immediately beyond Carpenters' Trail.

– lots of black locust, Japanese honeysuckle, wine raspberry, black and sweet cherries, ailanthus along trail here.

– **Englewood-Bloomers* recreation center and Boat Basin (2½ miles).

– road from Boat Basin up to 9W, or hiking trail with winding steps to top along a waterfall, to reach Long Path.

2) *Miles 3 to 6:* This section contains many flat blocks of diabase fashioned into picnic tables and seats. The trail is generally wide, open, level, bordered by lush growth of Japanese honeysuckle, poison ivy (in seawall), and trees associated with open clearings (ailanthus, black cherry, sumac, sassafras, apple, and especially black locust). Also, lots of basswood grows here, and field mice scurry beneath the honeysuckle. Overwintering sparrows, juncos, hermit thrushes, and other songbirds feed on seeds and fruits.

– **Undercliff* – dock and ruins of bathhouse along broad, grassy expanse on shore; picnic area and old cemetery on Drive above trail.

– High Tom is name given to cliff point above.

– Canoe Beach (former campgrounds, now a picnic area), then former Powder Dock (4½ miles), with Clinton Point outcrop on cliffs above.

– Lost Brook, which emerges from **Greenbrook Sanctuary* and **Lost Brook Preserve* on top of Palisades.

– Old Lambier Dock (5½ miles) – good views northward from end; Old Lambier Road once climbed from here up the cliffs through a narrow ravine into Tenafly (see page 22). Road now closed above Henry Hudson Drive. Continue about ½ mile to the Falls.

3) *Miles 6 to 8:* Greenbrook Falls – a magnificent, 250-foot cascade in spring and after heavy rains, and an impressive mass of ice in winter; falls from **Greenbrook Sanctuary* through a steep hemlock gorge.

– former site of Huyler House, then Huyler Road and Landing (6½ miles) – road supposedly taken by Lord Cornwallis and British troops to scale cliffs in 1776 (see page 20), then a busy river landing. Road is marked in *red* and ascends cliffs on outskirts of Greenbrook Sanctuary to intersect Long Path on top. Lots of "escaped" Japanese maples and some large oaks and sugar maples flank the old road.

–for the remaining 1½ miles to the Alpine Boat Basin, the trail periodically leaves the shore and ascends slightly to a higher level within the cool, mature forest. Stone steps aid the short ascents and descents. Along this stretch are old slope forests with big white pines, red oaks, tulip trees, black oaks, hemlocks, sugar maples, black birches, and huge chestnut oaks growing right atop rock ledges. There are also dense stands of mountain laurel and lots of spring wildflowers (especially Solomon's seal).

–**Alpine Boat Basin** (8 miles)– Alpine Approach Road leads from here up to Route 9W and Closter Dock Road, past the **Park Headquarters.**

–an old trail (claimed by some to have been the one used by the British under Cornwallis in 1776) may be used by hikers to ascend cliffs to Long Path.

4) *Miles 8 to 10½*: the 2½ miles from Alpine to Forest View feature more splendid cove and slope forests, with big sugar maples, black birches, hemlocks, black and red oaks, tulip trees, waterfalls, spring wildflowers in profusion (especially rue anemone, rock cress, Dutchman's breeches, columbine, early saxifrage, early meadow rue, spring beauty), dense thickets of mountain laurel, lots of ferns, and some red elderberry, bladdernut, and maple-leaf viburnum in the shade. Autumn colors in these forests rival those of New England. There are even some "escaped" Japanese maples beneath the big trees. From the Boat Basin, the trail ascends into the mature forest again behind the ruins of former Riverview bathhouse, and after about ¼ mile, a side path leads right down to the river to an old colonial fishing hamlet (Cape Flyaway) where remains of an Indian camp (oyster shells) were found.

–after another ¼ mile the trail forks into two levels: lower level passes old Excelsior Dock (and a stairway up to Excelsior Grove picnic area on the upper level), then Twombley's Landing (another ancient Indian campsite where weapon points and oyster shell heaps were uncovered dating back over 7,000 years), and lots of bram-

bles, weeds, seaside goldenrod, Japanese honeysuckle, poison ivy, some bayberry, "pioneer" trees on the broad, sunny lower level.

–the upper level passes through old-growth forests and Excelsior Grove picnic area.

–at Point Comfort (about 1¼ miles from Boat Basin) the two levels rejoin–here the most dramatic cliff scenery begins, continuing almost to the end: sheer, 500-foot cliffs rise up from broad, grassy Shore Trail, with vertical fractures and columns very evident, as well as "Indian Head" profile of rock north of Forest View.

–in the talus forest above the path (10 miles) grow many good-sized Canadian white birches, at the southern limit of their range (except for higher Appalachian Mountains) and the only ones in the eastern part of New Jersey.

Greenbrook Falls in spring

105

–apple trees (beautiful in April), black locusts, red cedars also line the trail; red-tailed hawks and rock doves nest on ledges in the steep cliff face; black racer snakes are occasionally seen.

–**Forest View**–former recreation center, and site of the most rugged, primeval Palisades forests (see separate section).

–side trail with stone steps ascends cliffs here to meet Long Path; **Women's Federation Monument** is at top, and trails lead out to Route 9W, or north to State Line Lookout.

5) *Mile 10½ to end*: This is the most rugged section of the trail, but with some of the most striking cliff scenery. Enormous fallen diabase blocks extend from the river to the steep, 500-foot cliff face for some distance, making walking difficult; caves and crevices are home for one of New Jersey's only colonies of eastern woodrats (see page 37), as well as black rat snakes, 5-lined skinks, copperheads.

–Shore Trail splits into upper and lower level again for short distance, rejoining at stone stairway.

–princess trees and black birches common in talus, with box elder along the shore.

–after less than a mile of rugged talus, the trail becomes the "Giant Stairs" and descends to the shore.

–after passing the New York State line, the trail forks left up a trail to High Gutter Point at top of cliffs in **Lamont Sanctuary** area, just north of **State Line Lookout**. It joins the Long Path up here, which leads out to Route 9W.

–beyond the ascending trail, an extension of the Shore Trail leads along the river shortly to the Park's recently acquired Italian Garden ruins beneath a waterfall (see State Line Lookout section).

PALISADES INTERSTATE PARKWAY

–38 miles: 12 in New Jersey along the top of the Palisades, and then curving away from the Hudson River upon entering New York State for another 26 miles; extending from western end of George Washington Bridge in Fort Lee, N.J. (Bergen County) northward through Rockland County, N.Y. and into Orange County, N.Y., ending at Bear Mountain. The N.J. section is patrolled by Palisades Interstate Park Police, the N.Y. section by N.Y. State Troopers.

Directions–(N.J. section) accessible at south end from George Washington Bridge, or from Routes 4, 46, 80, and 95; access from Route 9W (which parallels the Parkway in New Jersey) at Palisade Ave. in Englewood (Exit 1), Alpine Approach Road (Exit 2), Boy Scout Camp Alpine (Exit 3), and south of N.Y. State border (Exit 4).

Background–(see Chapter II for detailed background and history)–the Palisades Interstate Park accepted a 700-acre gift of land atop the Palisades from John D. Rockefeller in 1935. This made it possible to seriously consider the Parkway plan, since 90% of the needed land was now owned by the Park. In 1946 both New York and New Jersey appropriated funds, and construction began the following year. In 1957, the New Jersey section was completed, as was 21 miles in New York. The following year all 38 miles were finished.

Facilities and Features–two one-way routes separated by a wooded island 30 to 300 feet wide, with large trees, ornamental evergreens, and flowering shrubs and trees.

–very pleasant, scenic route atop the Palisades in New Jersey, with no billboards, advertising, or commercial traffic allowed.

–gas stations near Exits 1 (both sides of Parkway) and south of Exit 5 (in center of Parkway).

–*scenic vistas (20-minute parking) at: Rockefeller Lookout (north of Exit 1)–opened in 1955 to honor John D. Rockefeller, who gave so much land, funds, guidance, and leadership to preservation of the Palisades; excellent views of cliffs, river, Bronx, northern tip of Manhattan (Spuyten Duyvil), G.W. Bridge, skyscrapers of N.Y.

–Alpine Lookout (south of Exit 2)–views of Yonkers, Westchester, cliffs, etc.

–State Line Lookout (see separate section).

–easy access to: Park facilities along Hudson River and Henry Hudson Drive (from Exits 1 and 2); Park's N.J. Headquarters (Exit 2); Alpine Scout Camp and Women's Federation Monument (Exit 3); Lamont Sanctuary and Tallman Mountain State Park (Exit 4); Blauvelt State and Clausland Mountain County Parks (from Route 303 at Exits 5 and 6); High Tor State Park (from Route 202 at Exit 12).

Note - a single asterisk * denotes the special features or main highlights for each area.

HENRY HUDSON DRIVE

–part of Palisades Interstate Park.

Location–8-mile drive from Edgewater, N.J. north to Alpine, N.J., halfway between the Hudson River and the top of the cliffs.

Directions–access at south end from River Road in Fort Lee; or, 3 miles farther north from Palisade Ave. in Englewood (Exit 1 of Palisades Interstate Parkway–Red and Tan bus stops at Palisade Ave. and Route 9W); access at north end from Alpine Approach Road (Exit 2 of Parkway–Red and Tan bus stops at Closter Dock Road and Route 9W).

Background–Built in 1916, this road connected the two ferries at Englewood (from Dyckman St., New York City) and Alpine Landings (from Yonkers, N.Y.). It was once used by millions of people from both states to visit the Palisades Interstate Park's beaches, camps, and recreational centers when the Hudson River was still swimmable (see page 28). Now it is used mainly to travel between the two Boat Basins and as a scenic alternative to Route 9W.

Schedule–open daily (weather permitting) from April to November, no fee.

Hardwood forest on slopes below Drive, Alpine, N.J.

–during this time bicyclists and joggers may use the road (between Englewood and Alpine only) only on weekends and holidays until noon. At all other times between April and Nov. the road is open to vehicular traffic only. From Nov. to April 15, bicyclists and joggers may use the drive all day.

Facilities and Natural Highlights – access to Englewood and Alpine Boat Basins (picnic areas, playgrounds, rest rooms, water, fishing, hiking on Shore Trail) and Ross Dock and Undercliff Picnic Areas.

–wonderfully scenic drive, with the Hudson River below and the cliffs of the Palisades rising straight up from the road.

–ancient slope forests, rugged talus slopes with huge tulip trees and exotic princess trees (Royal Paulownias) at bottom of slopes.

–many spring wildflowers on the slopes: wild pinks, columbine, Dutchman's breeches, early meadow rue, early saxifrage, etc.

–Greenbrook Falls is a very impressive waterfall which cascades over 250 feet from Greenbrook Sanctuary to the Hudson River.

–*interesting geological scenery: "contact zones" where the Palisades diabase of the cliffs meets the lower layers of red sandstone and shale (see pages 9 and 10).

–challenging course for runners and bikers.

–*one of the best areas to view a great variety and high numbers of overwintering songbirds feeding on seeds, wild grapes, and other fruits along the sheltered, sun-warmed slopes.

FORT LEE HISTORIC PARK

–34 acres, part of the Palisades Interstate Park.

Location – on top of Palisades, ¼ mile south of George Washington Bridge, off Hudson Terrace in Fort Lee, N.J.

Phone – (201) 461–3956.

Directions – by bus (or foot): from New York City's Port Authority George Washington Bridge Bus Terminal, cross the G.W. Bridge to Bridge Plaza in Fort Lee; walk 2 blocks east to Hudson Terrace, then south along Hudson Terrace to Park entrance.

–by car (from New York City): over G.W. Bridge upper level, take "Fort Lee"/ Lemoine exit, make sharp right down hill and right turn at bottom of hill onto Hudson Terrace (beneath Bridge) – one block to Park.

–from north, take Palisades Parkway to Hudson Terrace exit (beyond Exit 1). OR – take 9W to Hudson Terrace (turn left at Palisade Ave. off 9W).

–from west, take I-95 east to Fort Lee/ Palisades Parkway exit; continue on South Marginal Rd. 5 blocks, turn right onto Hudson Terrace; Park entrance is about 50 feet on left.

Background – This is the site where George Washington and his army helplessly watched the American troops surrender to the British at Fort Washington directly across the river in 1776. This "Point Bluff" redoubt had been built to guard the Hudson Valley from the British, but the Americans were forced to retreat from here on Nov. 20 when Lord Cornwallis crossed over from Yonkers and marched south across the Palisades toward Fort Lee (see page 20). A small tract on top of the cliffs here was given to the Park in 1911 by Dr. James Douglass of N.Y.C., but most of the historic site was slated to be developed into apartment houses in 1952. Various parcels were acquired by the Palisades Interstate Park via the Rockefeller Fund and state Green Acres from 1956 to 1965 and made into the historic park. The 1776 earthworks have

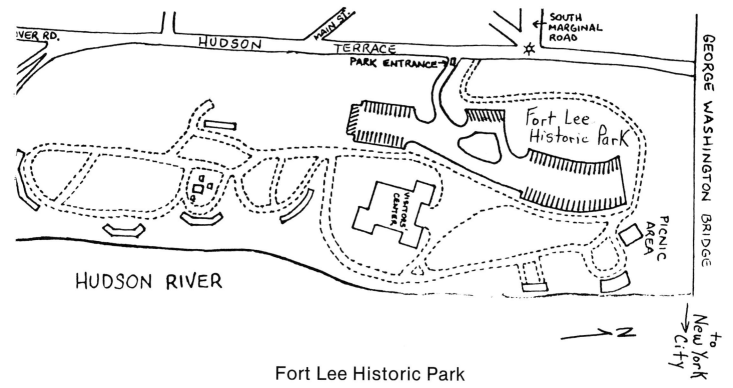

Fort Lee Historic Park

(Map supplied by Palisades Interstate Park Commission)

been recreated and the Museum was opened in 1976.

Schedule – Park open every day, 8 A.M. to dusk.

– Visitors' Center (Museum) open: Jan. & Feb. – call for winter schedule; March 1 to Memorial Day – Wed. to Sun., 10 A.M. to 5 P.M.; Memorial Day to Labor Day – daily, 10 A.M. to 5 P.M.; Labor Day to Dec. 31 – Wed. to Sun., 10 A.M. to 5 P.M.

– nominal parking fee from April through October.

Facilities and Features – two-story Visitors' Center/Museum with information desk, exhibits, film, 200-seat auditorium; paved walking paths, reconstructed gun batteries, 18th Century soldiers' hut, rest rooms, water, souvenir stand, and observation deck.

– *special events, guided tours and educational programs ("Living History" program for classes studying American Revolution) by reservation; point of departure for Boy Scouts' "Palisades Historic Trails" educational hiking program; facility rental for group meetings, programs, concerts (used by 4,500 people in 1984).

– excellent views of George Washington Bridge and New York skyline.

ROSS DOCK

– part of the Palisades Interstate Park.

Location – Just north of George Washington Bridge, on Hudson River in Fort Lee, N.J.

Directions – a short walk north of G.W. Bridge, either along the Shore Trail or via Carpenters' Trail (1000 stone steps connecting the Long Path on top of the Palisades with the Shore Trail).

-by car take Henry Hudson Drive at its south end.

Background – above Ross Dock is the former Carpenter Brothers' Quarry which was responsible for some of the greatest destruction to the cliffs and talus slopes. This was the first area acquired by the new Palisades Interstate Park Commission in 1900, via a gift from J. P. Morgan (see page 26).

-Ross Dock, which was used to load the quarried trap rock onto boats, was soon developed into a major Park recreational facility, with fireplaces, grills, a picnic area, refreshment stand, rest rooms, parking, a bathing beach, and a group campground (completed 1931); during World War II the camp colony was closed, as was the bathing beach soon afterwards.

Schedule – open mid-April through October, 8 A.M. to dusk; nominal parking fee.

Facilities and Natural Highlights – *large picnic grounds, fishing, playgrounds, rest rooms, basketball court, public phone, water.

-excellent views of George Washington Bridge just south of dock.

-hiking on Shore Trail north to Englewood Boat Basin and beyond, and south to its start.

-Carpenters' Trail ("1000 Stairs") leads up to top of cliffs and the Long Path, passing walls of the old Carpenter Brothers' Quarry.

-Hazzard's Boat Launching Ramp – formerly the heavily-used "Hazzard's Beach," closed by World War II because of pollution and closing of ferry from 158 St. in New York City.

-Hazzard's Ramp is on Hudson River just south of George Washington Bridge; open daily mid-April through October, 8 A.M. to dusk, for boat launching and parking (cars with boat trailers only); nominal parking fee (season's pass available).

ALLISON PARK

-about 7 acres, part of the Palisades Interstate Park.

Location – on top of the Palisades, 1¼ miles north of George Washington Bridge, beside Palisades Interstate Parkway in Englewood Cliffs, N.J.

Directions – by foot via Long Path along top of Palisades.

-by car from Hudson Terrace, via tunnel beneath Palisades Parkway, about half-mile south of Exit 1 ("Palisade Ave.") and Bus Stop.

Background – part of former estate of William Allison (born in Undercliff 1849, died 1924), built here after Palisades Mountain House Resort burned down in 1884. (see page 24) Part of the former estate grounds also includes St. Michael's Villa, formerly an orphanage of the Sisters of St. Joseph of Newark. St. Peter's College is also adjacent to the Park. Besides the Palisades Interstate Park Headquarters in Alpine (the former Oltman House), these are the only buildings between the cliffs and Route 9W which were not demolished when the top of the Palisades came into Park ownership. The Allison estate gave much land to the Interstate Park throughout the first half of the 20th century, including this Park in 1967.

Schedule – open every day, dawn to dusk, no fee.

Facilities and Natural Highlights – paved walking paths, rest rooms, water, benches, parking, overlooks.

-scenic views of the Hudson River and New York.

-*beautifully landscaped estate, with ornamental yews, cedars, pines, rhododendron, forsythia, cherries, birches, and Andromeda on the grounds surrounding the old estate buildings.

-*Linwood Park* is another part of the former Allison estate given to the Interstate Park. Located west of Hudson Terrace, just north of the George Washington Bridge, the open expanse of grass once featured an ice-skating pond and basketball courts, but now just has benches and paved paths (and sledding in winter).

ENGLEWOOD BOAT BASIN AND PICNIC AREA

-part of Palisades Interstate Park.

Location-on the Hudson River, about 2 miles north of the George Washington Bridge, in Englewood Cliffs, N.J.

Directions-Exit 1 ("Palisade Ave.") of Palisades Parkway-follow road down to river; or directly from Henry Hudson Drive from Alpine or Edgewater.

-Red and Tan bus stops at Palisade Ave. and Route 9W.

-by foot, via Shore Trail which enters the site; hikers can descend to Boat Basin from top of cliffs via Palisade Ave. or stairway path.

Background-formerly the site of a fishing village (an extension of Undercliff); the shore here was filled in shortly after 1900, and the area became the Park's first recreation center accessible by ferry, from Dyckman Street in New York City across the river. There was formerly a bathing beach here, as well as bathhouses at the north end ("Bloomer's Beach") and a campground and gas station.

Schedule-open every day, dawn to dusk.

-nominal parking fee from April through October.

Facilities and Natural Highlights-*picnic areas, playground, parking, seasonal refreshment stand, rest rooms, public phone, water, fishing, boat basin (contact Park regarding fees for seasonal or daily stall rentals, mooring rentals).

-hiking along Shore Trail, north toward Alpine Boat Basin or south toward Ross Dock.

-both road and stairway path wind up to the top of the cliffs to meet the Long Path, Palisade Ave., and Route 9W.

-fairly mature slope forest extends up the cliffs, with big tulip trees and sycamores.

UNDERCLIFF PICNIC AREA

-part of Palisades Interstate Park.

Location-along Henry Hudson Drive, just above the river; just north of Englewood Boat Basin, in Englewood Cliffs, N.J.

Directions-by car via Henry Hudson Drive, reached directly via Palisade Ave. in Englewood.

Background-site of the Undercliff Vil-

111

lage (fishing, farming, quarrying, ship building) for well over 100 years (William Allison born here 1849). Park acquired it 1905 (see page 19).

–formerly a major Park recreational center, with parking lot, picnic area, pavilion, grills, refreshment stand, playground, rest rooms, and a large bathhouse and bathing beach. Only the picnic area remains, the other facilities abandoned when the river became polluted after World War II.

Schedule–open noon to dusk, weekends and holidays from late May to Labor Day (Sundays only, in early May).

–nominal parking fee.

Facilities and Natural Highlights–picnic area, fishing, rest rooms, water, hiking on Shore Trail along river.

–*old cemetery of Van Wagener family and others who once lived in Undercliff Village, with headstones dating back to early 19th century (see page 19).

–abandoned bathhouse (on river below picnic area) is situated on broad, grassy expanse with big willows, sycamores, and horse chestnuts.

–forest extending up slopes to cliffs is comprised of huge tulip trees, sycamores, maples, sweetgums, with some very large European sweet cherry trees planted there long ago.

FLAT ROCK BROOK CENTER FOR ENVIRONMENTAL STUDIES

– 150 acres: 75 owned by city of Englewood, with 75 contiguous acres of privately owned Allison Woods Park.

Location–on western edge of top of Palisades, at east end (top) of Van Nostrand Ave. in Englewood, N.J. (443 Van Nostrand Ave., 07631);

Phone–(201) 567-1265.

Directions–from Englewood, turn south off Palisade Ave. onto Jones Road, then east (left) onto Van Nostrand, which ends at Center.

–also accessible from Route 4 (Jones Road exit), Route 80 (Broad Ave. exit, north to Van Nostrand), or Palisades Interstate Parkway (Palisade Ave. exit).

–N.J. Transport Buses stop at Van Nostrand and Broad Avenues.

Background–parking area was site of former quarry.

–75 acres set aside by Trust of William Allison in 1927 to be preserved as woods

for public use; remaining 75 acres purchased bit by bit in late 1960s and early 1970s by city of Englewood, with both private donations and New Jersey state Green Acres funds. Nonprofit Flat Rock Brook Nature Association established in 1974 to manage land, and provide educational and recreational programs for public. In 1980 an award-winning solar-heated interpretive building was completed.

Schedule–land open to public all year, dawn to dusk, no fee.

–building open 9AM to 5PM weekdays.

Facilities and Natural Highlights–parking, rest rooms, exhibits, office, classroom, kitchen, Jones Road picnic area.

–weekend nature walks, field trips, evening slide programs, annual Nature Day, and other special events for public.

–*well developed curriculum and courses for visiting school classes and scouts conducted by trained guides and staff; afterschool classes all year.

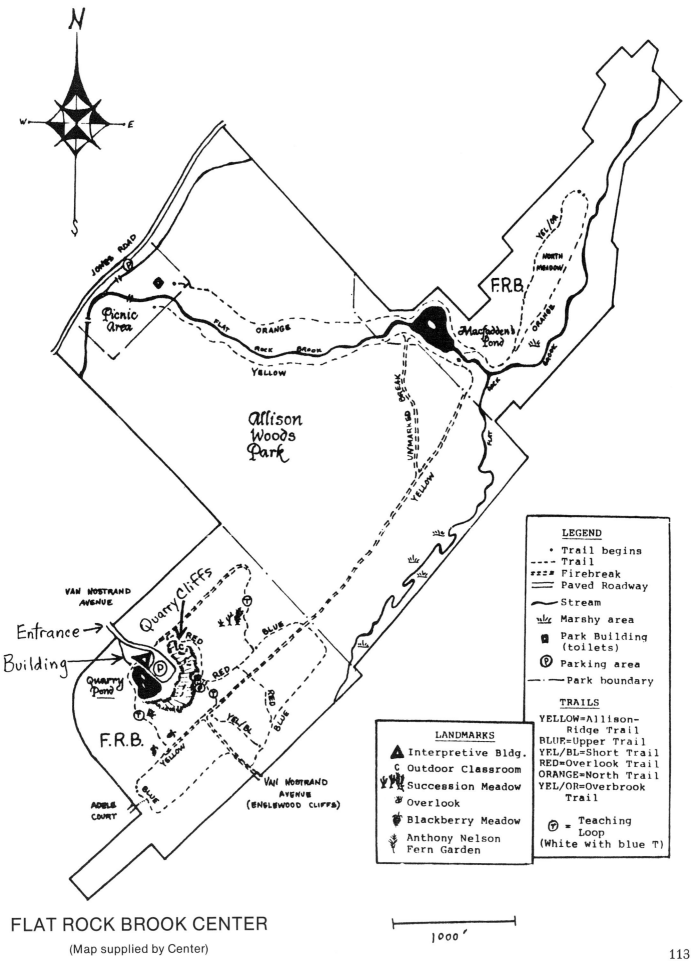

FLAT ROCK BROOK CENTER

(Map supplied by Center)

–summer nature courses for children; trail-guide training sessions.

–newsletter and special outings for members.

–diabase quarry cliffs with lookout to western New Jersey.

–overgrown meadows, two small ponds, beautiful cascading stream (Flat Rock Brook), large yellow birches (rare on Palisades), mature upland oak forests and some lower slope tulip tree/sweetgum forests.

–several hiking trails into different habitats.

–muskrats, herons, bullfrogs, painted turtles, nesting great horned owls, winter sparrows.

TENAFLY'S LOST BROOK PRESERVE AND NATURE CENTER

–380 acres: 16.5 owned by Palisades Interstate Park, the rest owned by Borough of Tenafly (including 50-acre Tenafly Nature Center).

Location–on top of Palisades, 4 miles north of George Washington Bridge, off west side of Route 9W, extending from East Clinton Ave. north to Montammy Country Club, and bordered on west by residences on western back slope of Palisades, in Tenafly, N.J. 07670.

Phone–(Nature Center)–(201) 568-6093

Directions–buses (Red and Tan) stop along 9W at East Clinton Ave. and one mile farther north opposite Greenbrook Sanctuary entrance. Trails enter Preserve at both stops.

–very limited parking along entrance road to Greenbrook off east side of 9W, 5 miles north of G.W. Bridge; also, a few small pull-overs on East Clinton Ave. along south side of Preserve and along Route 9W.

–Nature Center reached by turning north off Clinton Ave. onto Engle Street, then turning right (east) at end of Engle onto Hudson Ave.–Center is at top of hill.

Background–former private land in 18th and 19th centuries, including the Lambier estate which still exists on Old Hudson Avenue (formerly Lambier Road). In 1960, 50 acres were set aside by Borough of Tenafly on its quickly-developing "East Hill," and the Tenafly Nature Association was formed to manage it as a sanctuary and educational center. Six years later an interpretive building was completed. An additional 45 acres on the East Hill had already been donated to Tenafly in 1948 and 1950 by the Rockefeller family for park use. Meanwhile, another 300 acres of privately owned forest behind the Nature Center was slated to become massive housing and industrial developments, first by its individual owner, then by Centex Company. All proposals were rejected by Tenafly Planning Board. By 1976, Tenafly's citizens raised 9.3 million dollars (including 3 million from the state's Green Acres Fund and a half million from the Palisades Interstate Park) to purchase the "Green Acres" or "East Hill" tract, and it is now one consolidated 380-acre tract called "Lost Brook Preserve" (named after one of its streams which flows out of the Preserve, beneath Route 9W, into Greenbrook Sanctuary and over the cliffs, getting temporarily "lost" in the talus slope before reemerging above the Henry Hudson Drive). The Preserve includes 16.5 acres along 9W given to the Palisades Interstate Park in return for its contribution. Trails are maintained by local boy scout troops and explorer posts.

Schedule–trails in Preserve are open to public every day, dawn to dusk, no fee.–Nature Center is restricted to Members and Tenafly residents, every day; Building–9 A.M. to 5 P.M.; grounds– dawn to dusk

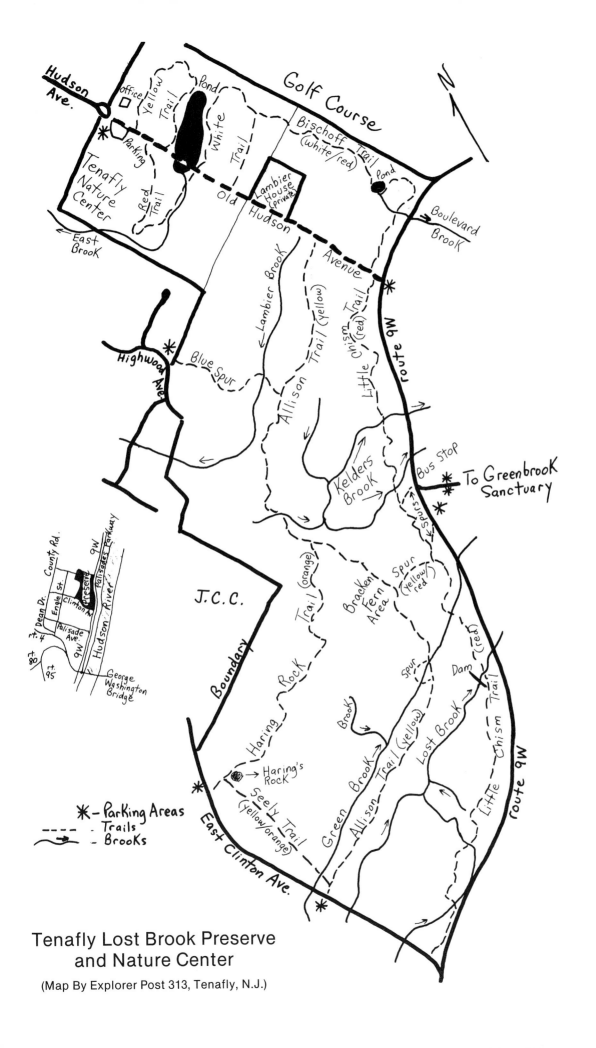

N

Hudson Ave.

Golf Course

office

Yellow Trail

Pond

White Trail

Bischoff Trail (white/red)

Pond

Parking

Old Hudson

Lambier House (private)

Boulevard Brook

Tenafly Nature Center

Red Trail

Avenue

East Brook

Lambier Brook

Allison Trail (yellow)

Little Chism Trail (red)

Route 9W

Blue Spur

Highwood Ave.

Kelders Brook

Bus Stop

To Greenbrook Sanctuary

Spurs

County Rd.

9W

Palisades Parkway

Preserve

J.C.C.

Haring Rock Trail (orange)

Bracken Fern Area

Spur (yellow/red)

Dean Dr.

Eagle St.

Clinton Av.

Palisade Ave.

Hudson River

rt. 4

rt. 80

rt. 95

9W

George Washington Bridge

Boundary

Spur

Dam

(red)

Lost Brook

Little Chism Trail

Route 9W

Brook

Haring's Rock

Green Brook

Allison Trail (yellow)

✳ - Parking Areas

--- - Trails

→ - Brooks

Seely Trail (yellow/orange)

East Clinton Ave.

Tenafly Lost Brook Preserve and Nature Center

(Map By Explorer Post 313, Tenafly, N.J.)

Facilities and Natural Highlights – Nature Center offers indoor and outdoor exhibits, live animals, nature walks, field trips, well developed curriculum for local school classes, summer nature courses, classroom, office, rest rooms.

–beautiful Nature Center pond with abundant plants and animals: bullfrogs, spring peepers, turtles, muskrats, nesting wood ducks, red-winged blackbirds, transient herons.

–*Preserve features hundreds of acres of undisturbed, little-used forests, with some huge trees (sweetgum, white oak, tuliptree), lots of fragrant pink azalea and highbush blueberry in spring and sweet pepperbush in summer.

–generally flat land with many temporary swamps and vernal ponds (breeding wood frogs and spring peepers), several slow-moving streams (some of which flow into Greenbrook Sanctuary and over the cliffs), lots of red maple, sweetgum, red oak, scar-

let oak; many spring wildflowers (Canada Mayflower, wood anemone, jack-in-pulpit, etc.).

–several dense swamp thickets of buttonbush, blueberry, chokeberry, pepperbush, especially along the streams.

–interesting "barrens" covered with bracken ferns.

–red fox, pileated woodpecker, great horned owl, broad-winged hawk, ovenbird, veery, many other animals raise young here; goshawk winters; coyotes reported in both 1984 and 1985.

–several hiking trails, including the Allison (yellow) and Little Chism (red) Trails, each of which extends entire 1.5 mile length of Preserve north and south.

–trail leads from East Clinton Ave. for short distance to Haring's Rock, largest sandstone glacial erratic in region (see page 11).

GREENBROOK SANCTUARY

–165 acres within Palisades Interstate Park but set aside and maintained as a special-use nature preserve.

Location – on top of Palisades, off Route 9W, in Tenafly and Alpine, N.J., 5 miles north of George Washington Bridge, P.O. Box 155, Alpine, N.J. 07620.

Phone – (201) 768-1360.

Directions – entrance is one mile north of East Clinton Ave. (Tenafly) on Route 9W – reached from Palisades Interstate Parkway, Exit 1 (go 3 miles north on 9W) or Exit 2 (go 3 miles south on 9W).

–Buses (Red and Tan) stop at sanctuary's entrance road on Route 9W.

Background – northern end of sanctuary includes part of Huyler Road, or Lower Closter Road, which local historians claim was used by British troops under Lord Cornwallis in 1776 to scale the cliffs from the Hudson River; road was later used as a main thoroughfare for passengers and goods travelling from western valleys across the Palisades to the river dock (see page 22).

–northern part of sanctuary also site of former Jay and Jeffry estates in 19th century (foundations still there with old plantings, see page 23).

–center of sanctuary crossed by Old Lambier Road which enters from Lost Brook Preserve across Route 9W and then de-

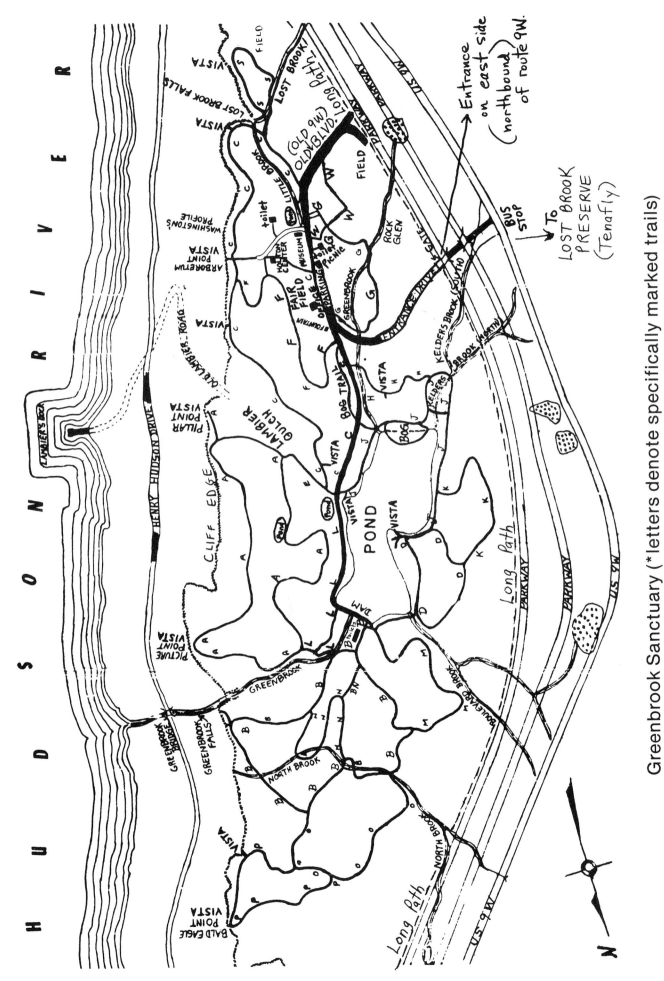

Greenbrook Sanctuary (*letters denote specifically marked trails)

(Map from Palisades Nature Association)

117

scends cliffs through ravine to Old Lambier Dock on river – used to ship produce in 19th century (see page 22).

–land was acquired by Palisades Interstate Park in 1917 when it was considered the wildest, most rugged, and largest (½ mile wide) section of Park in New Jersey. At that time, Sylvan Blvd. (old 9W) went through the sanctuary, with drivers of Model "T's" stopping for short walks to see the cliffs and falls – road was abandoned in 1929 when 9W was moved west.

–southern end of sanctuary was used by Civilian Conservation Corps in 1933 as a base camp, then in 1945 by Army as bomb demolition site.

–tract was set aside by Park in 1946 as nature sanctuary, and private, nonprofit Palisades Nature Association given permission to maintain it and develop trails, educational programs, field research.

–5-acre pond completed 1956, fence built around sanctuary 1959, naturalist's office completed 1976.

Red fox pup near den, Greenbrook Sanctuary, N.J.

Schedule – open every day, dawn to dusk to members of the Palisades Nature Association and their guests, and to groups of adults and school children by appointment (contact above address for membership information).

Facilities and Natural Highlights – small museum, office, library, parking lot, picnic area, pavilion, drinking fountain, outhouses, 6½ miles of trails, no phone.

–*5-acre pond, 5 streams, waterfalls (including Greenbrook Falls, the largest stream cascading over the Palisades), small sphagnum bog with pitcher plants, sundews, white cedar, leatherleaf.

–spectacular vistas 300–400 feet above Hudson, along 1¼ mile of cliff edge.

–two old historic roads (see above Background).

–mature forests of upland mixed oak, hemlock groves, tulip tree coves, beech-birch-maple slopes, red maple-sweetgum swamps.

–many 200 to 250-year-old trees, 130-foot-tall tulip trees.

–hundreds of wildflowers, including rare yellow lady slipper, coralroot, rattlesnake

master, harebell, lizard's tail, and more common wild pink, columbine, may apple, butterfly weed, Canada and Turk's cap lilies.

–over 25 herptiles, including copperhead, 5-lined skink, northern red salamander, good breeding populations of wood frog, spotted salamander.

–25 mammals, including starnose mole, red bat, southern flying squirrel, red fox.

–55 butterflies recorded, including rare pipevine swallowtail, Baltimore, white "M" hairstreak (see page 66).

–235 bird species on list: nesting great horned owls, ruffed grouse, pileated woodpeckers, scarlet tanagers, indigo buntings, worm-eating warblers, Carolina wrens, wood ducks; thousands of migrating hawks in autumn (see page 78); excellent warbler migration in spring, with rare yellow-throated, prothonotary, Kentucky warblers seen; 93 different species of birds seen on one day in May 1984; good views of waterfowl on river and migrating overhead, herons and ducks on pond, 4 species of owls in winter.

–*professional full-time naturalist and weekend assistant conduct nature and ecology programs for members and guests every Saturday of the year, most Sundays, and evenings and early mornings in spring; periodic field trips; visiting school classes and adult groups by appointment.

–complete booklets of flora, fauna, habitats, and reprints of articles from scientific journals and magazines about the sanctuary's studies.

–breeding bird censuses, hawk counts, wildflower surveys.

–quarterly Members' Bulletin, annual meetings.

–habitat improvement projects (restoring vernal ponds for breeding amphibians, creating meadows, etc.).

DEMAREST NATURE CENTER

–55 acres owned by borough of Demarest, N.J. and leased to Demarest Nature Center Association.

Location – in lowland at base of western slope of Palisades; between County and Columbus Roads, Demarest, N.J. (P.O. Box 41, 07627).

Directions – County Road to Hardenburg Ave., turn west over railroad tracks, then right turn onto road which passes Wakelee Field and ends at Demarest Swim Club parking lot; or, main entrance is on Columbus Road, which can also be reached via Hardenburg Ave.

Background – in 1972 borough-owned land was leased to Demarest Nature Center Association.

Schedule – open to public every day, dawn to dusk; no fee.

Facilities and Natural Highlights – hiking trails, including 1½-mile jogging trail with various exercise stations.

–footbridges over Tenakill Brook; small ponds (ice-skating in winter).

–*open meadows, thickets, and mature mixed oak/beech/hickory forests with huge, ancient trees and spring wildflowers.

–adjacent children's playgrounds and ball fields.

–monthly programs and community events for adults and children and summer nature course for children.

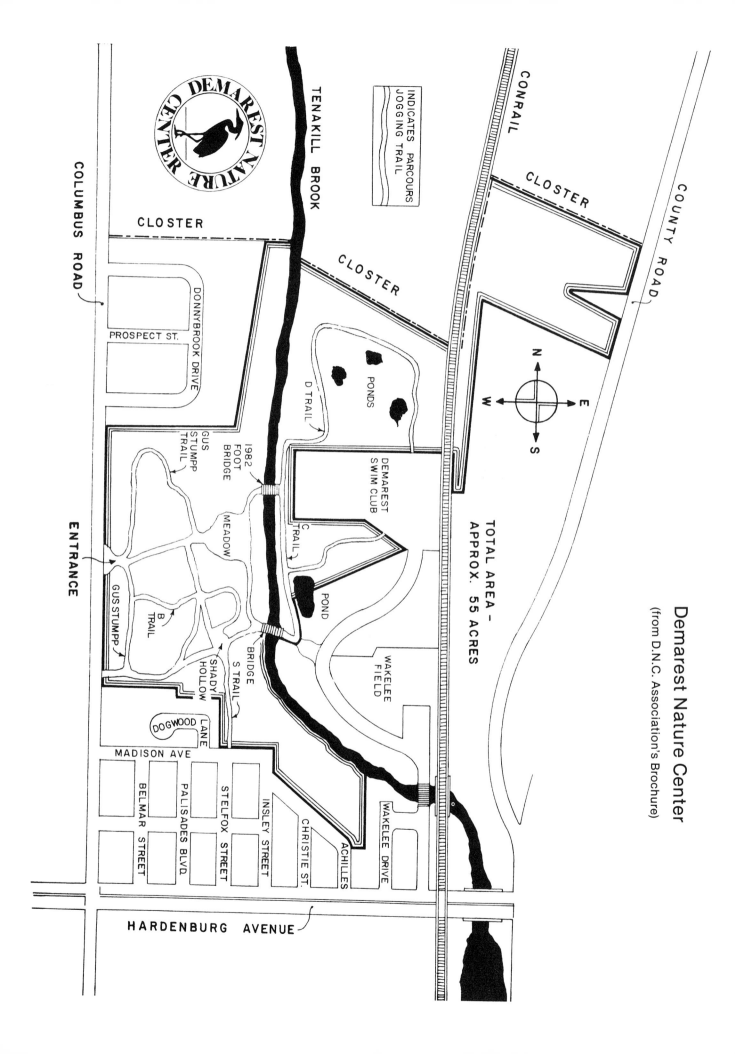

Demarest Nature Center

(from D.N.C. Association's Brochure)

CLOSTER NATURE CENTER

–135 acres owned by Borough of Closter, N.J. and leased to Closter Nature Center Association.

Location–in lowland at base of western slope of Palisades; off both sides of Ruckman Road (extending north to Norwood line) in Closter, N.J. (P.O. Box 80, 07624).

Phone–(201) 768-1668.

Directions–from Piermont Road (reached via Closter Dock Road from 9W), turn west on Ruckman Road and proceed to Nature Center Pond and Cabin.

Background–In 1962 Closter Nature Association was formed and the borough leased it 80 acres of woodland to be used as a nature center. A building was erected in 1967 beside Ruckman Pond. Seventy additional acres adjacent to Nature Center were acquired by Closter in 1960s via federal and state Green Acres programs and over the years some of this was added to the Nature Center's leasehold. An additional 45 acres was added in 1985.

Schedule–grounds open to public every day, dawn to dusk; no fee.

Facilities and Natural Highlights–building open during special events and programs.

–pond (ice-skating, fishing), parking lot.

–*hiking trails through extensive second-growth, lowland, red maple swamp forests, with much highbush blueberry, spicebush, elm, pin oak, shagbark hickory, rare club mosses and black ash trees.

–vernal ponds with lots of breeding wood frogs, spring peepers; occasional deer.

–monthly evening programs and slide shows, periodic nature walks, 5-week summer program for children.

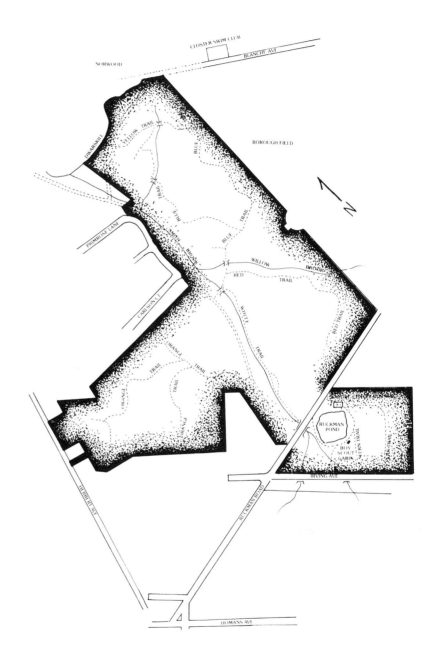

Closter Nature Center
(Map supplied by C.N.C. Association)

ALPINE BOAT BASIN AND PICNIC AREA

—part of the Palisades Interstate Park.

Location—on Hudson River about 8 miles north of George Washington Bridge in Alpine, N.J.

Directions—Exit 2 ("Alpine Approach Road") off Palisades Interstate Parkway (or directly from Route 9W), proceed east to river down Henry Hudson Drive; or drive north on Henry Hudson Drive from Englewood.

—bus (Red and Tan) stops along 9W at Closter Dock Road, just south of Alpine Approach Road.

—for hikers, Shore Trail enters Boat Basin, and Long Path connects via trail descending cliffs.

Copperhead snake—note heat-sensitive pit between eye & nostril

—*Background*—formerly Closter Landing, with Old Closter Dock Road possibly used by the British troops under Cornwallis to ascend cliffs in 1776; also a former ferry landing from Yonkers and a Park bathing beach, with bathhouse, grills, pavilion, etc. until pollution of river closed beach after World War II (see Chapter II).

—Blackledge-Kearny House ("Cornwallis Headquarters") was original headquarters of Palisades Interstate Park Commission, and was site of dedication ceremonies of N.J. section of Park on Sept. 27, 1909. House originally served as riverside inn for fishermen, steamboat captains and crews, farmers from valleys beyond cliffs.

Schedule—open every day, dawn to dusk.

—nominal parking fee from April through October.

Facilities and Natural Highlights— picnic areas, playground, rest rooms, parking, fishing, water, seasonal refreshments, special events, (Summer Outdoor Concerts), boat basin (contact Park regarding fees for seasonal or daily stall rentals).

—Alpine Pavilion available for group rentals.

—Blackledge-Kearny House ("Cornwallis Headquarters") supposedly built 1750, enlarged by Kearny family in 19th century and restored by Park in 1934—believed by some to have been used by British Lord Cornwallis on Nov. 20, 1776 (see page 20).

—*fine views of red sandstone underlying Palisades and outstanding cliff scenery, autumn foliage of slope forests.

—hiking along Shore Trail south toward Tenafly and Englewood, or north to most magnificent cliff scenery, old-growth slope forests, waterfalls, talus, spring wildflowers, and beautiful shoreline.

BOY SCOUT CAMP, BERGEN COUNTY COUNCIL

–about 350 acres, owned by New Jersey leased to Palisades Interstate Park.

Location–in Alpine, N.J.: on western edge of summit of Palisades, and extending westward down its backslope; about 9 miles north of George Washington Bridge between Route 9W and Anderson Ave., and extending from the Park's maintenance building (south of which is another 200 acres of undeveloped Bergen County-owned woods) northward to the 1,000-acre N.Y. City Alpine Scout Camp, just north of Ruckman Rd.

–contact Boy Scouts of America, 1060 Main St., River Edge, N.J. 07661.

Phone–(201) 342-8600.

Directions–Route 9W to Closter Dock Road (about 7 miles north of G. W. Bridge), drive down Road for 2 miles to Piermont Rd., turn right and go 1 mile to Ruckman Rd., turn right and follow Ruckman ½ mile to entrance. (Piermont Rd. can be easily reached from the N.J. towns west of 9W also).

Background–New Jersey leased the land to the Palisades Interstate Park in 1963; the Park in turn leases it to the Boy Scouts of America, Bergen County Council, for their camping and outdoor education programs.

Schedule–open for the use of Bergen County Boy Scouts.

Facilities and Natural Highlights–5 campsites with lean-tos, 5 tent sites, outdoor privies, ranger's cabin with water.

–"Palisades Historic Trails" booklet guides scouts along both the Long Path and Shore Trail from their starts in Fort Lee north to Women's Federation Park (where a blue and white cliff-to-shore trail connects the two paths), then continuing out across the pedestrian overpass to 9W, south to Ruckman Rd., and ending at the Scout Camp's Ranger Cabin; the booklet interprets the scenery and human history encountered along the bottom and top of the Palisades.

–350 acres of woods and swamps with two major streams, hiking trails.

–mostly level, second-growth woods with some old stone walls, lots of spring wildflowers, and some mature oak/beech/tulip tree forests including a few very large trees (up to 11 feet in circumference).

–*one of last holdouts in New Jersey section of Palisades for herds of white-tailed deer because of large, contiguous acreage (350 acres, plus 200 more of County woods, and 1,000 more of New York Scout Camp forests).

–Ruckman Road is near the northern boundary of the Camp, beyond which is the Greater New York Camp Alpine; large overgrown field along road has many interesting shrubs, pioneer trees, wildflowers, birds.

BOY SCOUT CAMP, GREATER NEW YORK COUNCIL

–1,000 acres, owned by Greater New York Council of Boy Scouts of America.

Location–on western edge of summit of Palisades, and extending westward down its backslope, in Alpine and Norwood, N.J.; about 10 miles north of George Washington Bridge, between Route 9W and Piermont Road, and extending north to south from Exit 4 of Palisades Parkway to

123

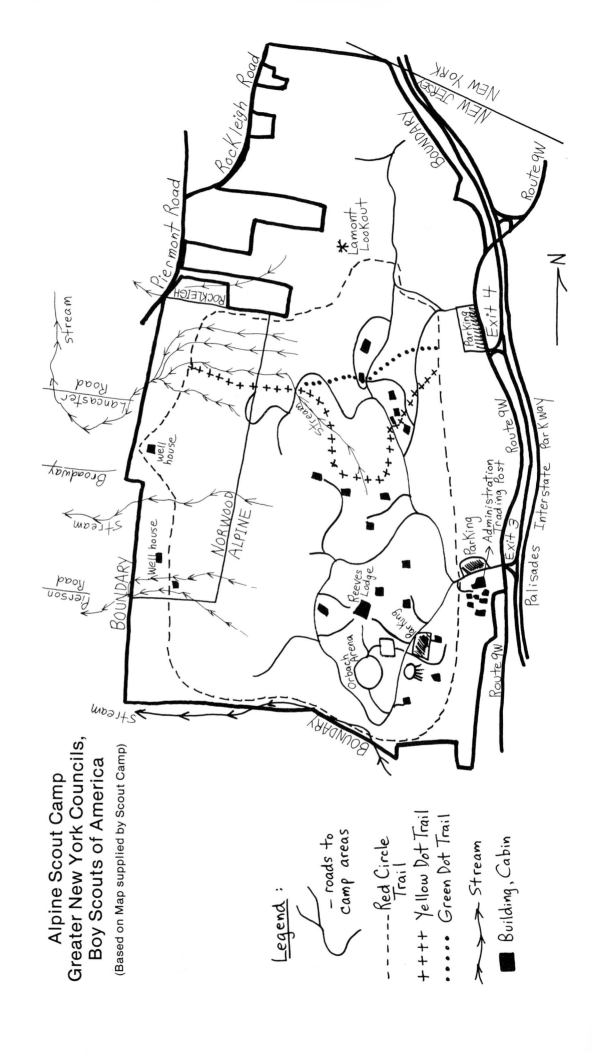

Alpine Scout Camp
Greater New York Councils,
Boy Scouts of America

(Based on Map supplied by Scout Camp)

Legend :

⌐ – roads to camp areas

- - - - Red Circle Trail

+ + + + Yellow Dot Trail

• • • • Green Dot Trail

↝ Stream

■ Building, Cabin

border of Bergen County Scout Camp near Ruckman Road.

–contact Greater New York Councils, Boy Scouts of America, 345 Hudson St., New York, N.Y. 10014.

Phone – (201) 768-1910 in Alpine; (212) 242-1100 in New York (camping services).

Directions – entrance is on Route 9W, near Exit 3 of Palisades Parkway; Red and Tan bus stops at entrance.

Background – 711 acres of the land were donated to the Scouts by J. D. Rockefeller family in 1942. About 1980, controversy arose over Scout's decision to sell 151 acres on its steep western slope in Norwood for $3.5 million to a developer for townhouses and single family residences. The Scouts claimed to need the income to maintain their other 850 acres in Alpine. The Palisades Interstate Park Commission intervened in 1984, arguing that, in the 1942 deed, Rockefeller intended that the Scouts offer the land free to the Park before selling it off, but the State Superior Court upheld the Scouts' claim that this intention applied only to the Alpine acreage. The Norwood Easthill Watch group was formed by local residents to fight the sale and development on environmental grounds, and, as of 1985, the case is still in litigation.

Schedule – call above numbers to receive information and permission regarding public access.

Facilities and Natural Highlights – campsites, lean-tos, shelters, cabins, store, trading post, water, picnic area, phone – used by thousands of boy scouts from New York City.

–some scenic vistas along western rim of summit, with rock outcrops affording views of western valley.

–hiking trails through some open, young woods (near campsites) and *old, mature forests (especially along stream in northwestern corner in Norwood section) of beech/oak/hickory/sugar maple/tulip tree, with some beautiful hemlock groves, enormous tulip trees (over 15 feet in circumference and 120 feet tall), some of the largest yellow birches (7 feet in circumference) and bitternut hickories (9 feet in circumference) in New Jersey. This western section was added to the state of New Jersey's prestigious Natural Areas Registry in 1985.

–beautiful mountain streams, some swamps with skunk cabbage.

–nesting great horned owls, red-tailed hawks, ruffed grouse, veeries, worm-eating warblers, and some of the last remaining gray foxes and herds of white-tailed deer in New Jersey section of the Palisades.

WOMEN'S FEDERATION MONUMENT

–part of Palisades Interstate Park.

Location – on top of Palisades, about a mile south of the New York state line, in Alpine, N.J.; extending from Palisades Parkway to cliff edge.

Directions – Palisades Parkway to Exit 2, go north on 9W for 2 miles (or, Exit 3, drive south a short distance); park in pullover on east side of 9W, from which a pedestrian overpass crosses the Palisades Parkway and leads to the cliff edge.

–bus (Red and Tan) stops on 9W at Boy Scout Camp a short distance north of overpass.

–hikers can reach it via Long Path on top of Palisades, or from Shore Trail via path ascending cliffs to the Park's "castle."

Background – one of the first sections of the cliff summit acquired by Palisades Interstate Park, in 1909; memorial castle built at cliff edge in 1929 to commemorate the New Jersey Federation of Women's Clubs

Hardwoods and hemlocks on slope of Palisades, near Women's Federation Monument

which were the impetus behind the formation of the PIPC in 1900 (see page 26).

Schedule – open every day, dawn to dusk, no fee.

Facilities and Natural Highlights – stone castle at cliff edge (see page 26).

–*magnificent 500-foot-high views of river, cliffs, New York (Yonkers and Hastings-on-Hudson), migrating hawks in autumn.

–ruins and old gardens of former Burnett Estate, with ornamental yews, cedars, rhododendrons, pines, flowers.

–hackberry trees, red cedars, fire cherries, blackhaws grow from rocks on cliff edge, with columbine, pussytoes and other wildflowers.

–young forest of mixed oak/pignut hickory on summit.

–5-lined skinks (lizards) and black rat snakes hide among rocks and indigo buntings nest here in summer.

–hiking north and south on Long Path on top of Palisades – leads to State Line Lookout slightly north of here.

–*trail leads from the top down to Forest View on the river, via steep series of stone steps, through beautiful hemlock ravine and slope forest of huge red oaks, tulip trees, black birches, sugar maples, white ashes, beeches, with red elderberry, lots of ferns and wildflowers (Dutchman's breeches, early saxifrage, sweet cicely, partridge berry, pink lady slipper, wood betony, herb Robert, jack-in-pulpit), and interesting geological scenery (see *Forest View*).

FOREST VIEW

–part of the Palisades Interstate Park.

Location – at base of the cliffs along the Hudson River in Alpine, N.J., about 2½ miles north of Alpine Boat Basin.

Directions – Shore Trail, north from Alpine Boat Basin or south from New York State line; or via trail descending cliffs from Women's Federation Monument (see that section for directions).

Background – formerly site of fishermen's homes and farmland on wide shorefront, before days of the Park. Park transformed area into a major recreational center, with ball field, picnic areas, fire places, pavilion, canoeing, camping, boat basin, office, rest rooms, etc. – reached by ferry from Yonkers in summer. It was abandoned after Hudson became polluted following World War II, and now it is used by hikers on Shore Trail who occasionally stop at the few remaining stone picnic tables or take trail up cliffs to Women's Federation Monument.

Schedule – open every day, dawn to dusk, no fee.

Facilities and Natural Highlights – stone picnic tables, old pier.

–*perhaps wildest, most scenic section of Palisades in New Jersey: unbelievable views of steep cliffs, especially from old dock at low tide, looking north to "Indian Head" rock face and south to Ruckman Point.

–hiking along Shore Trail north to its end at New York state line, or south to Alpine Boat Basin, past the steepest and most dramatic cliffs; hiking up to summit along steep, wild trail to Women's Federation Monument (see page 28).

–*ancient, mature slope forests of black birch, sugar maple, hemlock, white oak, white pine, red oak, tulip tree, with some huge specimens.

–*extensive stand of white birches (paper birches) just south of trail ascending cliffs – the only location in New Jersey outside of the northwestern mountains.

–shoreline overgrown with blackberry, raspberry, multiflora rose, Japanese honeysuckle, poison ivy, burdock, milkweed, with some huge apple trees, willows, and box elders (ash-leaf maples) near pier, and big princess trees (Royal Paulownias) on talus among witch hazel and red elderberry.

–*extensive talus area ¼-mile north, with enormous blocks of diabase covering many acres from river shore upward to lower cliff face: lots of princess trees and black birches grow among these rocks, black rat snakes, 5-lined skinks, and giant millipedes live on ledges and in crevices, and one of New Jersey's only colonies of eastern woodrats hide in recesses and caves here (see page 37); giant algae-covered rocks, tidal currents of

Nest of red-eyed vireo

Hudson, Spartina grass, crab and clam shells, gulls, and salty aroma is reminiscent of coastal New England.

–on densely-forested slopes: nesting Carolina wrens, worm-eating warblers, scarlet tanagers, pileated woodpeckers, veeries, red-eyed vireos; cerulean warblers seen here occasionally in summer.

–along river: gulls, black-crowned night herons, kingfishers, and many overwintering ducks.

–along overgrown shore: nesting yellowthroats, blue-winged warblers, yellow warblers, indigo buntings, and rare white-eyed vireos.

STATE LINE LOOKOUT

–255 acres, part of the Palisades Interstate Park, N.J. section.

Location – on top of Palisades, just south of New Jersey–New York state line, extending from Parkway to cliff edge, and including 20 acres across the line in New York State adjoining Lamont Sanctuary.

Phone (Lookout Inn) – (201) 768-5062.

Directions – Palisades Parkway to turn-off road, 2 miles north of Exit 2 (near Exit 3) – road (Old 9W) leads to parking lots.

–or, from Route 9W, park at pull-over near Lamont Geological Observatory (just north of Parkway Exit 4) and walk along the wide road (Old 9W) to Lookout.

–Long Path also enters Lookout area.

Background – northwestern section ("Skunk Hollow") formerly a community of free blacks from early 1800s to early 1900s (see page 24).

–original lunch stand building and bridle paths completed in 1930s during Depression.

–Sylvan Blvd. (Old 9W) formerly passed right along cliff edge here until Parkway was built and 9W moved westward.

–several miles of marked cross-country ski trails have recently been added.

Schedule – grounds open every day, dawn to dusk, no fee.

–Inn open every day 10 A.M. until dark.

Looking down to Hudson River through gap in cliffs, State Line Lookout

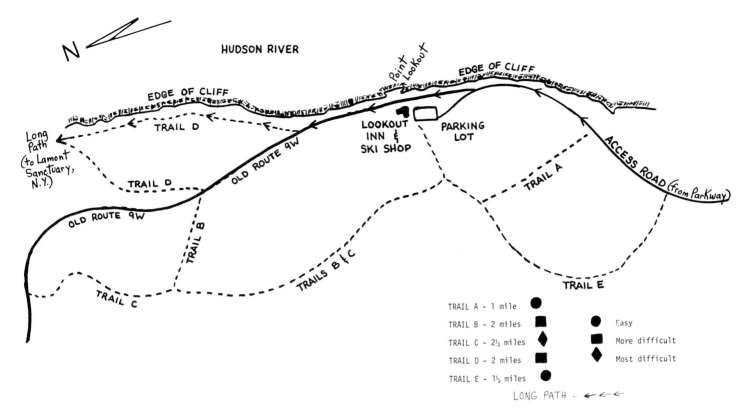

Cross-Country Ski Trails
State Line Lookout

(Map supplied by Palisades Interstate Park Commission)

Facilities and Natural Highlights –
Lookout Inn with hot and cold refreshments, rest rooms, public phone, ski rentals, parking lot, lookout telescopes, outdoor art/craft/antique shows.

–magnificent views of river, talus below, cliffs, New York (Hastings-on-Hudson, Dobbs Ferry).

–*highest point on Palisades in New Jersey (530 feet) with some sheer drops of about 300 feet – very breath-taking vistas.

–Long Path enters here shortly after it leaves Women's Federation Monument, and then it proceeds to a fence where a monument (set in 1882) marks the state line – beyond fence is the former Lydia Lawrence estate ("Cliffside") given to Park early 1900s. Here the Path passes some unbelievable cliff scenery, with extremely steep overhangs, views north to Lamont Observatory, Piermont Marsh, and Hook

Mountain. Long Path then descends into a ravine (where it meets the end of the Shore Trail) with old hemlocks and northern hardwoods, and into Lamont Sanctuary. (Path eventually leaves here to meet 9W.)

–another trail intercepts Long Path in Lamont Sanctuary and descends down to river shore and Park's "Italian Gardens" property (former Tonetti estate), with old marble statuary, columns, ruins of pergola, grotto, and a pool at bottom of waterfall which cascades from Lamont Sanctuary.

–other trails in State Line area west of cliff edge visit forests of oak and hemlock, with some unusually large hop hornbeam trees.

–cliff edge near Lookout has 5-lined skinks among the rocks and stone walls; also black rat snakes; good vantage point to observe autumn hawk migration across Hudson and along Palisades.

129

LAMONT NATURE SANCTUARY

–23 acres, owned by Columbia University.

Location – on top of Palisades, just north of New Jersey-New York state line, in Palisades, N.Y.; bordered on south by Palisades Interstate Park (State Line Lookout), on north by Columbia University's Lamont-Doherty Geological Observatory, on west by Route 9W, and on east by Interstate Park's cliff-top and Italian Garden properties: contact Lamont-Doherty Geol. Observatory, Security Office, Rm. 205, Geophysics Bldg., Palisades, N.Y. 10964.

Phone – (914) 359-2900, ext. 260.

Directions – Palisades Parkway to Exit 4, drive north on Route 9W for ¼ mile and park on right side, in small pull-over beside chain and boulders; enter woods via blue-blazed Long Path just before Guard Booth at Columbia Observatory entrance road.

–or park at State Line Lookout and walk in via Long Path.

–Red and Tan bus stops along 9W at N.Y.-N.J. state line near entrance.

Background – former estate of Dr. John Torrey (after whom the Torrey Botanical Club in New York City is named), who lived there 1854 to 1865. He was succeeded as owner by financier Thomas Lamont, whose wife left the land to her sons, Corliss and Austin, in 1953, to be maintained as a natural area. In 1954 the Rockland County Audubon Society was named by the sons as custodian of the property. The land was deeded to the Nature Conservancy in 1969, and leased a year later to Columbia University for research and education. It was finally transferred to Columbia in 1977.

Schedule – hikers may enter via Long Path.

–open dawn to dusk, March 15 to November 30, to faculty, staff, and students of Columbia University; outside groups and individuals may obtain permission from University Information and Visitor Service or from Lamont Observatory (see above address and phone).

Facilities and Natural Highlights – spectacular, steep cliffs, magnificent views across river and northward to Piermont Marsh and Hook Mountain and Tappan Zee Bridge, from both Interstate Park and Columbia University properties.

–*trails through deep hemlock ravine beside a mountain stream which forms a sensational series of cascades down the cliffs to the Hudson River, first falling to the Palisades Interstate Park's "Italian Gardens" property.

–Long Path leaves State Line Lookout area and enters Interstate Park's N.Y. section passing through a fence marking the State Line; Lamont Sanctuary is then entered via a series of steep stone steps into the ravine; then it crosses the stream and leaves the Sanctuary to reach Route 9W.

–another trail leads down to the bottom of the waterfall and the river.

–very large hemlocks, estimated to be 300 years old (but stricken with heavy infestation of scale insects in 1984 – see page 41); huge white ashes, white oaks, beeches, black birches, red oaks, black oaks, sugar maples, white pines, and some sycamores and tulip trees.

–rocky slopes covered with three species of evergreen ferns (polypody, Christmas, marginal wood), herb Robert, other wildflowers.

–black rat snakes, dusky salamanders, many birds in winter including occasional goshawks and bald eagles.

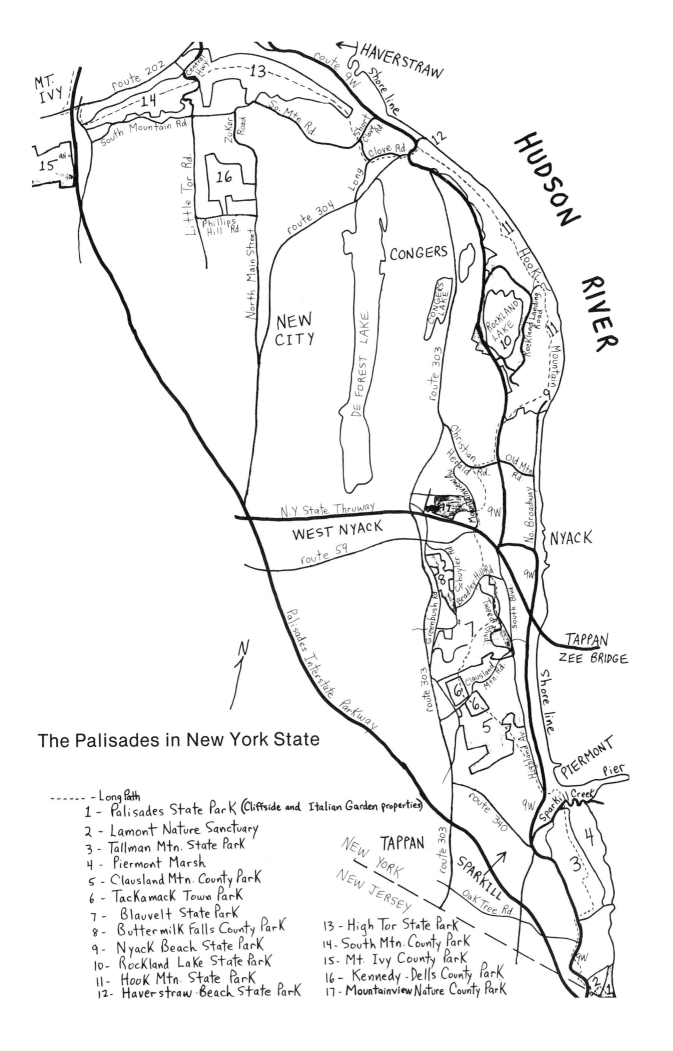

The Palisades in New York State

------ - Long Path

1 - Palisades State Park (Cliffside and Italian Garden properties)
2 - Lamont Nature Sanctuary
3 - Tallman Mtn. State Park
4 - Piermont Marsh
5 - Clausland Mtn. County Park
6 - Tackamack Town Park
7 - Blauvelt State Park
8 - Buttermilk Falls County Park
9 - Nyack Beach State Park
10 - Rockland Lake State Park
11 - Hook Mtn. State Park
12 - Haverstraw Beach State Park
13 - High Tor State Park
14 - South Mtn. County Park
15 - Mt. Ivy County Park
16 - Kennedy-Dells County Park
17 - Mountainview Nature County Park

Lamont Nature Sanctuary
(Adapted from pamphlet supplied by LDGO)

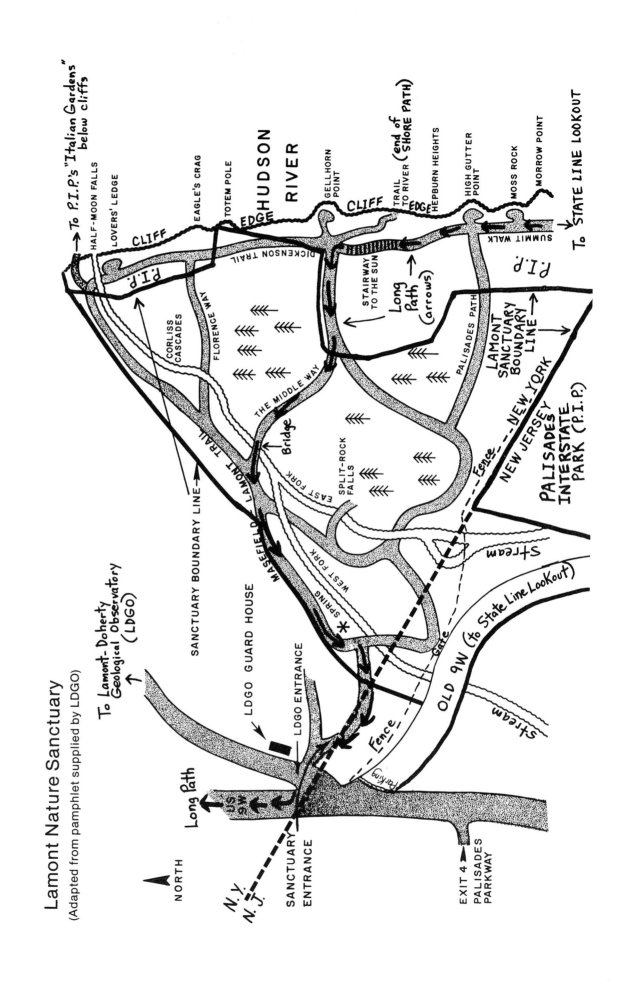

TALLMAN MOUNTAIN STATE PARK

–687 acres in the Palisades Interstate Park, N.Y. section.

Location–about a mile stretch on top of the Palisades, in hamlets of Palisades and Sparkill, N.Y. (town of Orangetown); extending from Route 9W down into the Piermont Marsh in the Hudson River, and from the end of the "mountain" (where it descends steeply to the Sparkill Gap and Creek) southward almost to Oak Tree Road.

Phone–(914) 359-0544.

Directions–entrance is on Route 9W, near intersection of Route 340, 2 miles north of Palisades Parkway Exit 4.

–can also be entered by foot via Long Path, either from the south where it re-enters woods on 9W opposite Golf Driving Range (a parking lot is provided here), or from north at base of Tallman Mountain near Piermont Marsh (parking here also).

–bike path also enters Park at each of the two above parking areas.

–Red and Tan bus stops on 9W in Sparkill, N.Y.

Background–cliff area was once threatened with quarrying but 164 acres were acquired by the Park in 1928 from Standard Trap Rock Co. of Sparkill with money donated by Commissioners Rockefeller, Perkins, and Harriman.

–another 540 acres, including 175 in the Piermont Marsh below, were planned as an oil tank "farm" in 1923 by the Standard Oil Co., and many oil-seepage ditches with earthen berms were created. These became woodland ponds after the land was acquired by the Park in 1942. It is now one of the most heavily used and developed of the Interstate Parks on the Palisades.

Schedule–open all year, 8 A.M. to dark except summer, when it closes 4:30 P.M.

Spring peeper

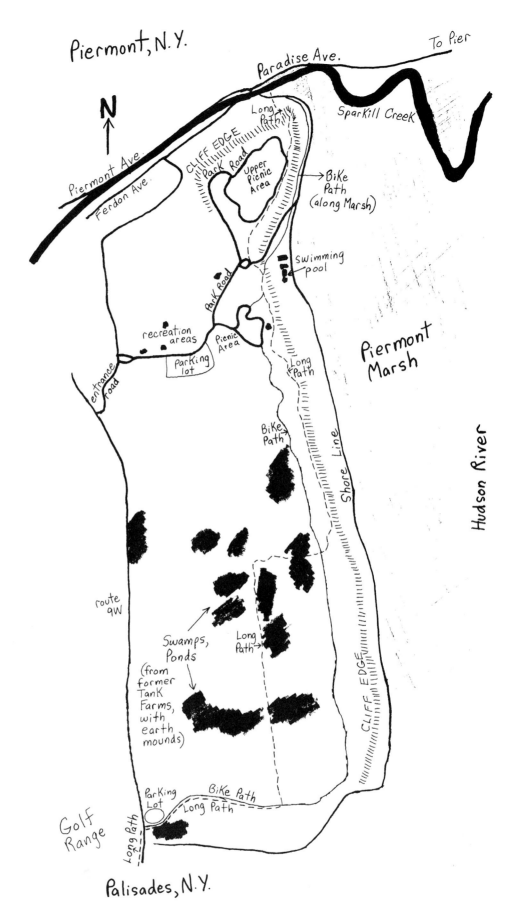

Tallman Mountain State Park
and
Piermont Marsh

134

weekdays and 7:30 weekends and holidays. Nominal parking fee in summer.

Facilities and Natural Highlights – picnic areas, tennis courts (summer only), handball, playground, refreshment stand (summer), swimming pool and bathhouse (minimal fee; summer – 10 to 6 weekdays, 9 to 7 weekends and holidays).

– beautiful views from top of the Mountain of Sparkill Gap (see page 12) and Piermont Marsh (see separate section) on river below; and of Hook Mountain and Tappan Zee to the north.

– hiking along the Long Path which descends the Mountain steeply to the Piermont Marsh.

– bike path also descends more gradually to the bottom.

– easy access to Piermont Marsh for great bird watching (see separate section for details, as well as page 75).

– forests on top of broad summit of Mountain are mature mixed oak, with 300-year-old white oaks.

– forests in lower, wetter areas west of cliff edge have big tulip trees, elms, shagbark hickories, red maples, sweetgums, tupelos, beeches.

– forests on talus slopes below Mountain have big chestnut oaks, sugar maples, hemlocks, black birches, black locusts, with large cottonwoods at base of Mountain along river.

– *woodlands, swamps, and talus slopes are covered with spring wildflowers: Dutchman's breeches, coltsfoot, spring beauty, Canada Mayflower, wood anemone, trout lily, spicebush, skunk cabbage, many others – seen on both Long Path and bike path.

– *ponds from former tank farms are now the most extensive swamps on top of Palisades: breeding wood frogs, spring peepers, other amphibians; turtles, garter snakes, red-bellied woodpeckers, many migrating warblers, including rare prothonotary.

PIERMONT MARSH

– 940 acres, owned mostly by Palisades Interstate Park Commission (870 acres), with remainder owned by New York State Dept. of Environmental Conservation and Village of Piermont, N.Y.

Location – in the tidal shallows of the Hudson River just south of the Erie Pier in Village of Piermont, and extending south for 1½ miles to Sneden's Landing; west shore formed by 150-foot cliffs and talus of Tallman Mountain.

Directions – park at Tallman Mountain State Park (see previous section) and take Long Path or bike path down the Mountain to the river. The bike path follows the edge of the marsh.

– or, take Route 9W into Piermont, turn east on Piermont Ave., then right onto Par-

adise Ave. which leads to paperboard factory; park here and walk along the mile-long Erie Pier which is the northern border of the marsh.

– best way to explore marsh is by canoe, launched from pier or in Sparkill Creek which flows into marsh.

Background – (see chapters on Post-Revolutionary Developments, Hudson River, Bird-watching Hotspots, and Modern Problems).

– one mile-long Erie Pier built 1841 as eastern terminus of Erie Railroad – passengers and freight switched from train to boat bound for New York City; it was also a thriving landing for ferries and day-liners. The Pier was abandoned 20 years later after Jersey City became eastern terminus; now

135

shallows south of pier have reverted to marsh rich in plant and animal life. Pier owned by Village.

-in October 1982, the National Oceanic and Atmospheric Administration's Office of Coastal Zone Management (U.S. Dept. of Commerce) formally designated Piermont Marsh as part of a Federal Hudson River Estuarine Sanctuary, to be administered by NYSDEC in cooperation with PIPC, as a center for research and education. The major portion (870 acres) of the marsh was already owned by the Interstate Park; another 70 acres in northern end between Creek and Pier was donated to Village of Piermont by Continental Group, Inc. (owner of the paper factory), then transferred to Nature Conservancy. In 1982, Nature Conservancy transferred it to NYSDEC.

Schedule – open every day, dawn to dusk, no fee.

Facilities and Natural Highlights – (see also Tallman Mountain section)

-parking lot at end of pier for 40 cars; fishing, boat launching from pier, as well as great views of Hook Mountain to the north and the New Jersey Palisades to the south.

-marsh is northern most locality in New York state for salt marsh plants (see page 15); salinity of water may be as high as 12 parts per thousand. Fiddler crabs, diamondback terrapins occasionally seen.

-one of Hudson's most productive fishery areas and spawning habitats for striped bass, herring, shad, etc.

-swamp rose mallow, seaside goldenrod, 4 species of Spartina grass, cattails, reeds, wild rice, water parsnip, indigo bush; big cottonwoods along west shore (bike path); lots of white mulberries along Pier (loaded with fruit in early summer).

-*a walk along the pier or a canoe trip into the marsh is a great opportunity to see a variety of birds at all seasons: mudflats along the Sparkill Creek have ducks, shorebirds, herons, gulls; open fields and "dumps" have killdeer, horned larks, sparrows, even a rare snowy owl in winter; reeds hide marsh wrens, bitterns, gallinules, rails, sparrows; river shallows have ducks, grebes, cormorants, loons, terns, gulls; woods below Tallman Mountain have warblers, flycatchers, vireos, etc.; skies overhead have migrating swallows, martins, hawks, even eagles.

CLAUSLAND MOUNTAIN COUNTY PARK

-513 acres, part of Rockland County (N.Y.) Park system.

Location – a portion of the Palisades ridge which temporarily moves inland from the Hudson River north of the Sparkill Gap before returning to the river in Nyack as Hook Mountain.

-in Orangeburg, N.Y. (town of Orangetown), bordered on north by Clausland Mountain Road, east by Tweed Blvd., south by Kings Highway, and west by Greenbush Road.

Directions – Palisades Interstate Parkway to Exit 5, then take Route 303 north

about one mile to Greenbush Road, turn right and drive about one mile to Clausland Mountain Road, turn right and drive to top of hill to parking lot of Orangetown's Tackamack Park – enter Clausland Mountain Park on south side of road after passing through south section of Tackamack Park.

-or continue on Clausland Mountain Road to Tweed Blvd., turn right and travel to Park sign off road.

-Long Path enters Park from south after it leaves Rockland Cemetery and Mt. Nebo.

Background – named after the Indian, Jans Claus, whose Indian name was Tack-

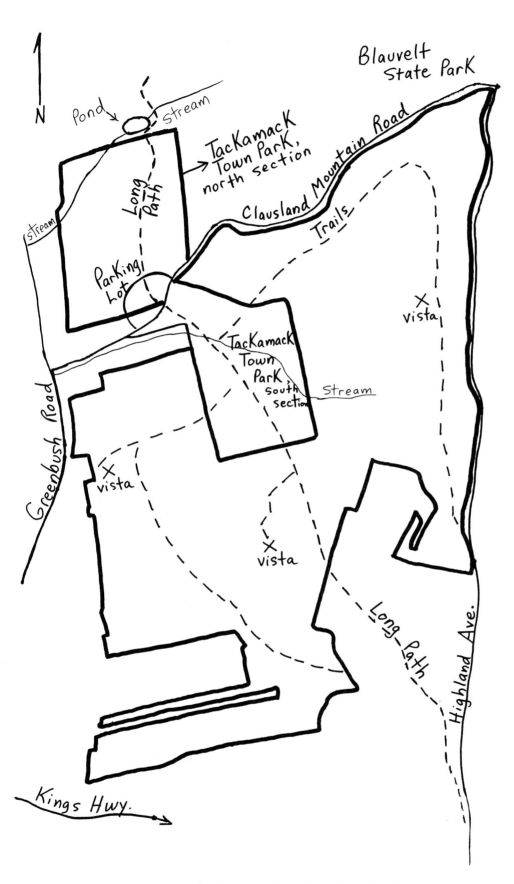

N

Pond

Stream

Tackamack Town Park, north section

Blauvelt State Park

Clausland Mountain Road

Long Path

Stream

Stream

Trails

Parking Lot

X
vista

Tackamack Town Park south section

Stream

Greenbush Road

X
vista

X
vista

Long Path

Highland Ave.

Kings Hwy.

Clausland Mountain County Park

(Based on Map prepared by Rockland County Planning Board for Rockland County
Park Commission's 1985 Brochure)

amack. Aided by County funds, a federal grant, and local donations, including Rockland County artists who donated their works to save the "Mountain," the County purchased the land in 1969, with three small adjoining tracts acquired in 1981.

Schedule – open every day, 8 A.M. to dusk, no fee.

Facilities and Natural Highlights – passive, undisturbed, rugged woodlands bisected by Long Path and two side trails.

–some scenic vistas from hilltops.

–*very wild, densely forested and hilly terrain with splendid, steep ravines, brooks, deep hemlock valleys, some small woodland ponds, skunk cabbage swamps; very large birches (both black and yellow species), sugar maples, beeches, and hemlocks; lots of spring woodland wildflowers; great horned owls, white-tailed deer, pileated woodpeckers, with reports of porcupines, barred owls, and timber rattlesnakes (all rare in this region).

–*large trees, deep valleys, and big moss-covered logs convey impression of wild, northern forest.

TACKAMACK TOWN PARK

–105 acres owned by Orangetown, N.Y.

Location – in Blauvelt, N.Y., between Blauvelt State Park on north and Clausland Mountain Park on south; divided into sections on either side of Clausland Mountain Road.

Directions – see Clausland Mountain County Park.

Background – named after Indian, Jans Claus, whose Indian name was Tackamack.

Schedule – open every day during daylight hours, no fee.

Facilities and Natural Highlights – Long Path traverses both sections, entering south from Clausland Mountain County Park and leaving north into Blauvelt State Park.

–steep stream valley on south side of Clausland Mountain Road, with big hemlocks, black and yellow birches, maples, and hickories.

–on north side, beyond parking lot, the forest begins as a young, second-growth woods with aspen, gray birch, cherry, and some big hackberry trees, then changes into a more mature forest with some big beech trees along the brook and water impoundment.

–park had nesting Lawrence's and Brewster's warblers in 1981, plus yellow-throated vireos, broad-winged hawks.

–*white-tailed deer, red fox, pileated woodpecker, and many other species of wildlife are associated with this wild, large tract of contiguous forest (105 acres plus 590 adjoining acres of Blauvelt State Park and 513 acres of Clausland Mountain County Park).

BLAUVELT STATE PARK

–590 acres in the Palisades Interstate Park, N.Y. section.

Location – part of the Palisades ridge which temporarily moves inland from the Hudson River above Piermont and the

Sparkill Gap before returning again to the river in Nyack as Hook Mountain.

–in Blauvelt, N.Y. (town of Orangetown): north of Clausland Mountain Road (and the county park), bordered on west by

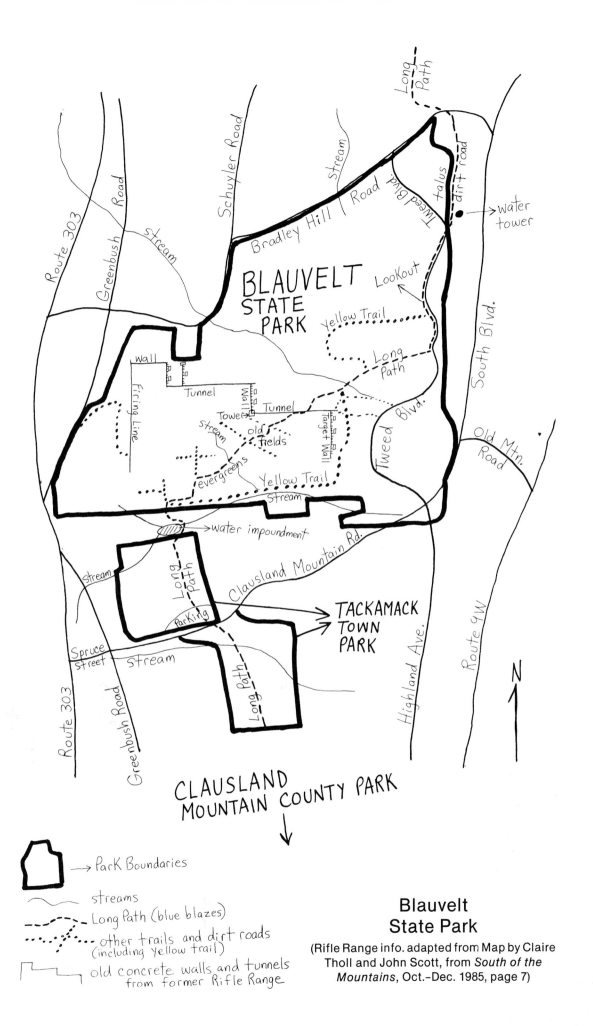

Long Path

Long Path

Schuyler Road

Stream

Route 303

Greenbush Road

stream

Bradley Hill Road

Stream

Tweed Blvd.

talus

dirt road

→ water tower

BLAUVELT STATE PARK

Lookout

Yellow Trail

Long Path

South Blvd.

Wall

Tunnel

Firing Line

Wall

Tunnel

Tower

old fields

stream

Target Wall

Tweed Blvd.

Old Mtn. Road

evergreens

Yellow Trail

Stream

Stream

→ water impoundment

Long Path

Parking

Clausland Mountain Rd.

stream

TACKAMACK TOWN PARK

Highland Ave.

Route 9W

Spruce Street

Stream

Long Path

N

CLAUSLAND
MOUNTAIN COUNTY PARK
↓

Route 303

Greenbush Road

→ Park Boundaries

streams

Long Path (blue blazes)

other trails and dirt roads
(including Yellow trail)

old concrete walls and tunnels
from former Rifle Range

**Blauvelt
State Park**

(Rifle Range info. adapted from Map by Claire
Tholl and John Scott, from *South of the
Mountains*, Oct.–Dec. 1985, page 7)

Greenbush Road (next to Route 303), on north by Nyack College grounds.

Directions – park in lot off Clausland Mountain Road in Tackamack Park (see Clausland Park section).

– or, enter from Tweed Blvd. near Park's north end (parking pullovers near summit of road).

– Long Path enters from Tackamack Park in south and from Nyack College in north, near Route 59 and the N.Y. State Thruway.

Background – part of tract formerly owned by Stephen Bradley family, whose estate gave 212 acres to Park in 1911.

– part of the area was also once the property of the Blauvelt family. In this area, the Blauvelt Rifle Range was built in 1911 for the New York State National Guard, to replace their range in Creedmoor, Long Island. Targets were supported on high concrete walls, with long, connecting, safety tunnels (one with ventilation slits). There were also square concrete storage rooms, a mess hall, headquarters, and an observation "tower" with interconnecting rooms (at the end of the longest tunnel). This "Camp Bluefields" was abandoned less than 3 years later and transferred to the Park by New York because it was dangerous to

nearby communities within range of the rifles (bullets hit homes).

– area rented by YWCA 1913 to 1918, then used as a state-run Camp for military training (ages 16–19), then as an Army training ground during World War II.

Schedule – open every day, dawn to dusk, no fee.

Facilities and Natural Highlights – (undeveloped) – fine views from high points off Tweed Blvd. (640 feet) of both Hudson River and Palisades, and of Hackensack Valley and Lake Tappan.

– interesting remains of former rifle range (explore with caution – crumbly concrete and broken glass).

– many hiking, cross-country ski, and bridle paths in all directions including the blue-blazed Long Path which traverses most of the Park and the yellow-blazed "Piermont Trail".

– *much of the Park is undisturbed, mature forest (with hundreds of more contiguous acres in Clausland Mountain County Park and Tackamack Town Park): huge black birches, mockernut and pignut hickories, and white, red, and black oaks on upland ridges; dense old hemlock groves in deep

Opossum

stream valleys and ravines, with big syca-mores, beeches, elms, tulip trees, and maples associated with some immense hemlocks (which may be succumbing to the Fiorinia Scale insect – see page 41).

−talus forests at north end near water tank and Nyack College: basswood, elms, big white ashes, bladdernut, red elderberry, many spring wildflowers like bloodroot, wild ginger, and Dutchman's breeches.

−*beautiful fragrant evergreen plantations:

red and white pine, Norway spruce, and many birds during winter.

−overgrown brushlands and fields of "Camp Bluefields" with old apple trees, red cedar, aspen, gray birch, multiflora rose, cherry, sassafras, blackberry, sumac, and many birds at all seasons feasting on fruits and seeds.

−many uncommon animals including herds of deer and even an occasional porcupine in the wild forests.

BUTTERMILK FALLS COUNTY PARK

−72 acres, part of Rockland County (N.Y.) Park system.

Location – a portion of the Palisades ridge which temporarily leaves the Hudson River and moves inland north of Sparkill Gap before returning to the river in Nyack as Hook Mountain.

−north of Blauvelt State Park, divided in half by town lines of Orangetown and Clarkstown (Central Nyack), N.Y. – bordered on west by Greenbush Road, on north by Route 59, and on east by Schuyler Ave.

Directions – from Route 59 (Exit 11 on N.Y. State Thruway), turn south on Greenbush Road, continue past Rockland Center for the Arts. Park is on east side of road, with parking at entrance. A second proposed entrance is on Schuyler Ave.: take Route 303 to Bradley Road, turn left, then left on Schuyler and go half-mile to future parking area.

Background – deep gorge and waterfall have been locally famous natural attractions for decades but not purchased by County until 1976–77, with additional acquisitions in 1981, and plans for another 91 acres in the near future, so the Park will be connected to Blauvelt State Park (PIP) and the Long Path.

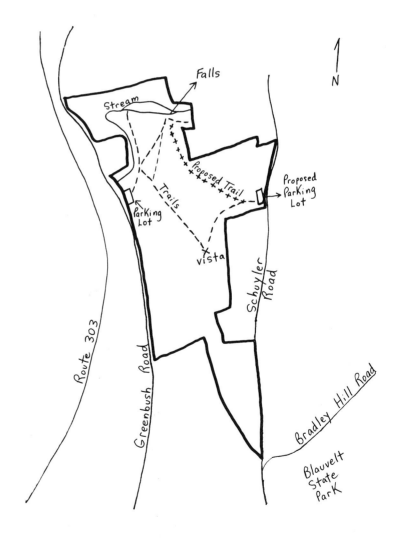

Buttermilk Falls County Park

(Based on Map prepared by Rockland County Planning Board for Rockland County Park Commission's 1985 Brochure)

141

Schedule – open every day, 8 A.M. to sunset, no fee.

Facilities and Natural Highlights – picnicking and hiking.

– (Long Path crosses proposed eastern addition to Park after it leaves Blauvelt State Park.)

– trails lead from parking area up to the top of the Falls.

– trails also lead southward from parking area to scenic vista at large flat rocks, with views of the Ramapos (west), South Mountain (north) and New Jersey (south).

– *probably the most beautiful waterfall and mountain-like forest ravine on the Palisades, very reminiscent of the Adirondack Mountains of New York or the White Mountains of New Hampshire. After a rainfall the top of the waterfall is a roaring cascade over bare diabase rock, through a steep-sided gorge of big hemlocks, with some towering beech, sugar maple, black birch, big chestnut oaks, and even yellow birch, striped maple.

– talus slope south of waterfall has some very large white and black oaks, and a massive white pine (9 feet around its trunk) closer to the stream at its lower reaches.

MOUNTAINVIEW NATURE COUNTY PARK

– 73 acres in the Rockland County (N.Y.) Park System.

Location – Central Nyack, N.Y.; a portion of the Palisades ridge which temporarily leaves the Hudson River and moves inland north of the Sparkill Gap before returning to the river in Nyack as Hook Mountain.

– bordered on south by New York State Thruway, on east by Mountainview Avenue, and on west by Strawberry Hill Road.

Directions – from Route 59 (Exit 11 on Thruway), turn north on Mountainview Ave. – Park entrance is about ¼ mile, on left, near crest of hill. A second entrance is at Strawberry Hill Road, reached from north end of Greenbush Road.

Background – The area was acquired by Rockland County in 1979 as a result of a gift from the Winston Perry family, which donated the County's 50% share of acquisition cost.

Schedule – open every day, 8 A.M. to sunset, no fee.

Facilities and Natural Highlights – undeveloped – parking lot planned.

– several unmarked trails lead up to 475-foot vistas of the Tappan Zee Bridge and Thruway, easily reached from eastern side.

– one trail completely traverses the Park east to west, sloping very steeply down to Strawberry Hill Road, losing almost 400 feet in altitude.

– most of the Park is young, second-growth woods, composed of mixed oak, pignut hickory, lots of blackhaw, wineberry, and dense tangles of Japanese honeysuckle. It is very brushy, with a dense shrub layer.

– on western slopes, there are some large trees in wetter areas near a stream: shagbark hickory, red maple, white ash, big musclewoods, and a black walnut.

– large red cedars and rock walls near western end indicate former clearings.

– white-tailed deer and ruffed grouse frequent heavy brush (browse & cover).

NYACK BEACH STATE PARK AND NYACK SHORE PATH

–part of Palisades Interstate Park, N.Y. section (Nyack Beach is 61 acres). (may soon be incorporated into Hook Mountain State Park)

Location–along the Hudson River beneath Hook Mountain, in village of Upper Nyack, N.Y.

Phone–(914) 358-1316.

Directions–Route 9W to Christian Herald Road (gas station at corner), turn east toward river, descend hill; at North Midland Ave., the road turns right and then makes a quick left, continuing down the hill as Old Mountain Road. At end of road, make left on North Broadway and take it right into Park.

–from Nyack, Park can be reached directly from North Broadway.

–Bus stop at Christian Herald Road and 9W.

–from north, hikers and bikers can take Shore Path from Haverstraw.

Background–acquired by Park with its Hook Mountain purchases during the height of quarrying in the first two decades of the 20th Century.

–on river shore between Nyack and Haverstraw were once busy landings for steamboats and ferries, the docks dating back as far as the early 1700s (Slaughter's Landing, for example); in 1860, Trough Hollow carried a cog railway which transported ice from Rockland Lake's Ice Houses to the river dock (see page 22).

–(see Hook Mountain State Park for history of Park acquiring the quarries above Nyack Shore Path.)

Schedule–open every day; nominal parking fee from Memorial Day to October only (daily from mid-June to Labor Day, weekends and holidays otherwise).

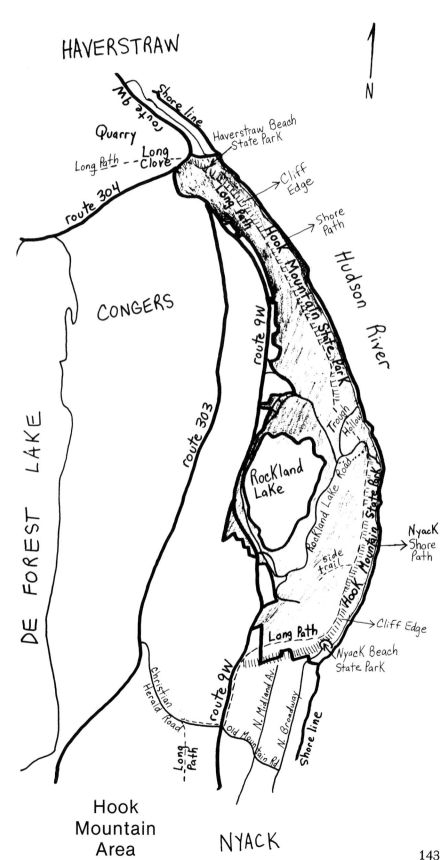

Facilities and Natural Highlights – picnic areas, ball fields, fishing, boat launching, cross-country skiing.

– *beautiful, level Shore Path for 5½ miles from Nyack Beach north to Haverstraw Beach, for hiking, running, biking; several side trails connect path up to Hook Mountain, Rockland Lake, and Long Clove on 9W.

– Path passes dramatic remains of several former quarries on Hook Mountain, as well as old landings, former Park buildings, recreation fields beneath quarries, and former structures used to transport ice from Rockland Lake (on other side of Hook Mountain) down to Hudson River.

– great views along Path of Hudson River, Tappan Zee, Westchester.

– interesting geological formations: red sandstone outcrops near Nyack Beach, and "contact zone" between sandstone and diabase near Haverstraw Beach.

– sharp eyes may discover some ancient Indian oyster shell middens above the Path.

– fine, old cove forests sloping down from Hook Mountain to Shore Path: big hemlocks, tulip trees, sugar maples, flowering dogwoods, with many wildflowers including wild ginger, the rare climbing fumitory (Allegheny vine), and maidenhair fern.

– rockier slopes have mature typical Palisades talus forests: black birch, hop hornbeam, basswood, white ash, black locust, princess tree (Paulownia), chestnut oak, flowering dogwood, witch hazel, red elderberry, bladdernut, rare round-leaf dogwood, and lots of ferns (3 common evergreen species – polypody, Christmas, marginal wood – plus some very rare maidenhair spleenwort fern in sandstone outcrops); also some yellow birch and lots of striped maple (near southern limit of its range except in higher Appalachian Mountains).

– lots of spring wildflowers along the talus: Dutchman's breeches, early saxifrage, columbine, rock cress, herb Robert.

– in more open, disturbed areas like the old quarries: "pioneer trees" like white ash, black locust, ailanthus, aspen, fire cherry, and staghorn sumac, and "weeds" like tartarian honeysuckle, multiflora rose, cocklebur, pennyroyal, and unusual feverwort ("wild coffee") and black swallow-wort vine.

– one quarry, a former Park recreation site, has an attractive plantation of white pines and Norway spruces.

– along the wet shore itself are elm, red maple, hackberry, box elder (ash-leaf maple), huge willows, cottonwood, and indigo bush.

HOOK MOUNTAIN STATE PARK

– 676 acres in the Palisades Interstate Park, N.Y. section.

Location – almost 7 continuous miles of river front, cliff slopes, and summit in Upper Nyack, N.Y., where the Palisades returns to the Hudson River shore as the 730-foot precipice, Hook Mountain.

– extends northward from Upper Nyack along the river almost to the Long Clove, the natural fault in the Palisades at the south end of Haverstraw where Hook Mountain ends.

– bordered on west by Rockland Lake State Park and Route 9W, on east by Hudson River, with Nyack Beach State Park in south and Haverstraw Beach State Park in north.

Directions – Route 9W north to Upper Nyack, pass Christian Herald Road (gas station on right) and proceed uphill to one of

144

several parking pullovers along 9W. Enter woods on east side of 9W at Long Path (blue blazes near telephone pole and guard rail); Long Path leads to open summit of Hook Mountain in about 20 minutes (rocky and steep in places). The Long Path continues along the entire 6-mile summit, descending temporarily after about 3 miles to Rockland Lake Road which leads to the Lake; then climbing up and down again shortly afterwards to "Trough Hollow," a gap connecting Rockland Lake to the Landing on the river; then climbing again and descending finally to Long Clove (near Route 304) at the end of Hook Mountain.

–9W can be reached from Exit 11 of N.Y. State Thruway in Nyack.

–Hook Mountain can also be climbed via Long Path from Rockland Landing Road, after parking in Rockland Lake State Park (North section), or from the Nyack Shore Path (see separate section).

–Red and Tan bus stops at Route 9W and Christian Herald Road.

Background – Hook Mountain's summit once was a beacon for river boats, and the shore along its base contained several busy landings. In 1872, a large stone crusher was erected at the south end of the Mountain, with several others added below the ridge by the turn of the century. Sections of the cliffs were being destroyed before the Palisades Interstate Park began purchasing the land in 1911. That year the Park bought the Manhattan Trap Rock Co.'s quarry at the south end of the Hook and opened the shore for recreation. In 1914 the Park purchased the properties of the Clinton Point Stone Co. and took, via condemnation proceedings, the Congers estate quarry at the north end of the Mountain. In 1917 the New York Trap Rock Co.'s quarry at Rockland Landing was also bought by the Park.

Schedule – open every day, dawn to dusk, no fee.

Facilities and Natural Highlights – Long Path traverses entire ridge, with side trails descending to recreational facilities at Rockland

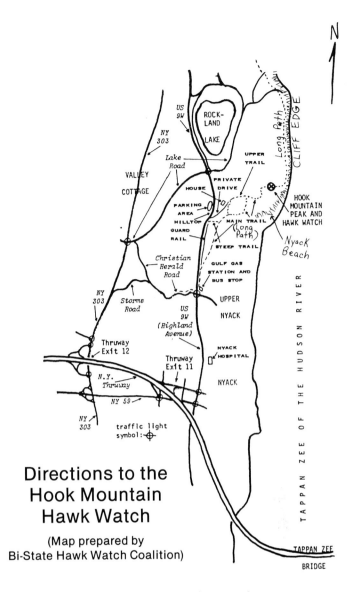

Directions to the Hook Mountain Hawk Watch

(Map prepared by Bi-State Hawk Watch Coalition)

Lake to the west, and Nyack Beach to south (and Nyack Shore Path – see separate section).

–summits afford breath-taking views in all directions: north to Haverstraw Bay; across the river to Ossining and Croton-on-Hudson; south along the Palisades past Piermont Marsh and into New Jersey; and west to Rockland, Swartout, and Congers Lakes, Hackensack Valley, and the Ramapo Mountains; also dramatic (and dangerous) views from top edges of old quarries.

–*main summit is a nationally renowned hawk watching site, with local Audubon birding chapters and nature clubs stationed there every autumn (since 1971) from September to early November, and in more recent years again from March to end of May. They keep track of thousands of migrating hawks, falcons, ospreys, vul-

Sulphur polypore, or "chicken mushroom"

–rare plants also grow on exposed summit: prickly pear cactus, yellow corydalis, prickly ash, choke cherry, scrub oak, currant; also, lots of boulder lichens, columbine, rue anemone, Dutchman's breeches, rock cress, polypody fern.

–uncommon butterflies, including falcate orange-tip, snout, Compton's tortoise shell, and hackberry butterflies.

–forests along the ridge: young, second-growth white ash, pignut hickory, sassafras, black cherry, red, black, and chestnut oaks, basswood, flowering dogwood, blackhaw, red cedar, hackberry, some pitch pine and shadbush; smaller plants include Solomon's seal, spring beauty, wild leek, bladdernut, gray dogwood.

–at base of Mountain (south end) off 9W are some huge trees (white oak, sugar maple, tulip tree) and lowland flowers like red trillium.

–a few beautiful open expanses, or "balds" along the ridge-top, with red cedar, pitch pine, haircap moss, several lichens (including British soldiers)–very reminiscent of N.J. Pine Barrens.

tures, and eagles, especially in autumn following winds from the north, which the raptors use in soaring southward for the winter (see pages 74 and 79). Hawks are attracted to the updrafts and thermals rising from steep Hook Mountain as they cross the river. Thousands of broad-winged hawks can be seen on a few days (even in a single hour!) in mid-September if weather conditions are right, and hundreds on many other days, often at very close range. A dozen different species can be seen in a day.

–in valleys and ravines on either side of ridge, and in "cloves" and "hollows" interrupting the 6-mile ridge: sugar maple, black birch, flowering dogwood, hop hornbeam, mountain laurel, with some dense hemlock groves and lots of spring wildflowers.

–"dark pond" on summit where trail descends to Rockland Lake: surrounded by young hemlocks, tupelos, red maples, striped maples, winterberry; egg masses of wood frogs and spotted salamanders in spring.

ROCKLAND LAKE STATE PARK

–1,079 acres in the Palisades Interstate Park, N.Y. section.

Location–in Rockland Lake and Congers, N.Y. (town of Clarkstown), below the

western slopes of Hook Mountain which is the Park's eastern boundary (separating it from the Hudson River); bordered on west by Route 9W (except for small section of Park on western side of 9W).

146

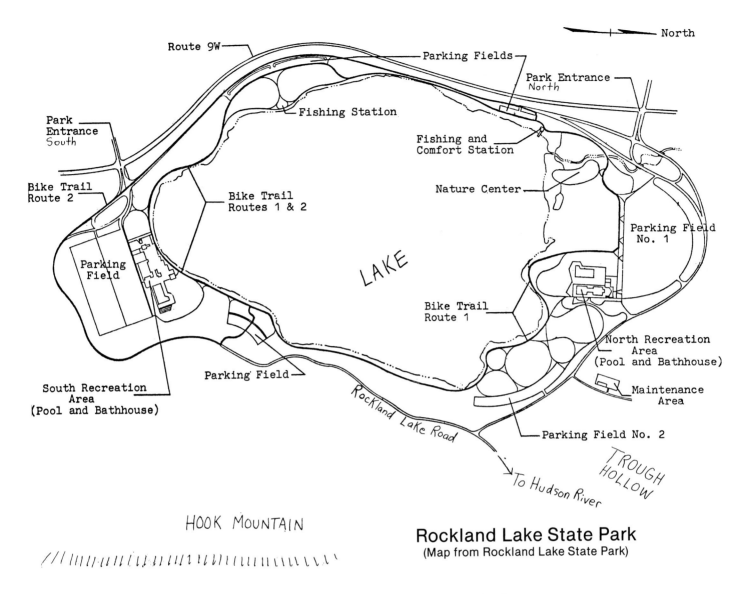

North

Route 9W

Parking Fields

Park Entrance
North

Fishing Station

Fishing and
Comfort Station

Park
Entrance
South

Nature Center

Bike Trail
Route 2

Bike Trail
Routes 1 & 2

Parking Field
No. 1

LAKE

Parking
Field

Bike Trail
Route 1

North Recreation
Area
(Pool and Bathhouse)

Maintenance
Area

Parking Field

South Recreation
Area
(Pool and Bathhouse)

Rockland Lake Road

Parking Field No. 2

To Hudson River

TROUGH
HOLLOW

HOOK MOUNTAIN

Rockland Lake State Park
(Map from Rockland Lake State Park)

Phone – North section: (914) 268-3020. South section: (914) 268-7598.

Directions – Route 9W directly to both north and south entrances.

– hikers can enter from top of Hook Mountain via side roads linking the Long Path with the Lake (Rockland Lake Road, Trough Hollow).

– the Nyack Shore Path along the Hudson River also connects with side roads across the ridge to the Lake.

Background – Rockland Lake was formerly the site of a major ice-harvesting industry, from 1831 to 1924, when mechanical refrigeration caused the closing of the huge ice houses. Ice from the crystal-clear, spring-fed Lake was in great demand in New York, and the Knickerbocker Ice

Company employed thousands of men to cut the ice and transport it to the river landing through Trough Hollow via a cog railway, which replaced the old escalator-like chutes in the 1850s. A spur line of the West Shore Railroad also ran to the ice houses (see page 22).

– after the end of the ice industry, Rockland Lake became a popular private recreation area, with swimming and ice-skating. In 1958, Rockefeller, Harriman, and Perkins contributed their own money to purchase for the Park the 256-acre Lake and 225 acres of adjoining upland. An additional 288 acres were acquired that year with New York State matching funds, and by 1959 the new State Park included 771 acres. A Nature Center was created in 1965. The State Park immediately became one of the Interstate Park's most popular and heavily used areas with a great variety of activities.

Schedule – hiking trails, exercise trails, picnic areas, ball fields open all year, dawn to dusk; other activities, see below.

– nominal parking fee daily mid-June to Labor Day (also, South section, weekends from Memorial Day to mid-June).

Facilities and Natural Highlights – huge parking lots, many picnic areas, 3-mile jogging, biking, and exercise trail around Lake, basketball courts at both ends, softball field (South), ice-skating, cross-country skiing, sledding.

– refreshment stands at each end, open in summer (one at North end is also open from April to December, dawn to dusk).

– tennis courts (North), open in summer, small fee.

– fishing station (North), April to December, daily June through Sept., weekends and holidays otherwise.

– rowboat rentals (North), April to December.

– swimming pool and bathhouse at each end, open every day in summer, minimal fee.

– golf course at each end, open April to November (South) or December (North) – inquire about rates, hours, lessons, cart rentals.

– *Nature Center (North end) open May through October, 9 A.M. to 5 P.M., (daily in summer; closed Tues. and Wed. in spring and fall), no fee: interpretive boardwalk trail through 20-acre woodland swamp and lake-side bog, with observation deck on Lake; self-guiding Braille Trail; interpretive building, school programs (call (914) 268-7428), guided tours, live animals (native reptiles, amphibians, fish, mammals) in fine displays.

– access to Nyack Shore Path along Hudson River, as well as Long Path atop Hook Mountain, from Rockland Lake Road and Trough Hollow.

– interesting wetland vegetation in Nature Center area: red maple, ash, sycamore, poison sumac (rare in region), sweet pepperbush, highbush blueberry, swamp azalea, a large Atlantic white cedar (the only one native in the region).

– *wide variety of habitats makes Rockland Lake Park interesting to botanists and ornithologists alike: upland ridge and slope forests of Hook Mountain; open meadows and fields around lake; golf courses; thickets of shrubs and brambles; the lake surface itself, which contains lots of ruddy ducks, geese, mute swans, coots, canvasbacks, scaup, mergansers, etc. in winter. Nesting birds in the park include wood ducks, phoebes, tree swallows, barn swallows, orioles, many red-winged blackbirds and yellow warblers, and many other species. There are also lots of migrating songbirds in surrounding forests and fields, including bluebirds, red-headed woodpeckers, meadowlarks, savannah sparrows, etc.

HAVERSTRAW BEACH STATE PARK

– 73 acres in the Palisades Interstate Park, N.Y. section (may soon be incorporated into Hook Mountain State Park).

Location – along the Hudson River at the former Waldberg Landing, where the Long Clove interrupts the Palisades ridge at the north end of Hook Mountain, at the southern boundary of Haverstraw, N.Y.

Directions – Route 9W north from Rockland Lake, pass Route 304 intersection and then look for the large conveyor from the Haverstraw quarry which passes over 9W toward the river; make next right turn over the railroad tracks, descend hill and turn right on road which goes south along the river past the piles of crushed stone and then past a small settlement before ending at Haverstraw

Beach State Park (at a barricade where the Nyack Shore Path ends).

–by foot or bike via Shore Path from Nyack.

–or, hikers can descend Hook Mountain to the Long Clove (near junction of Routes 9W and 304) and take the wood road which descends through tunnel beneath railroad tracks and ends at Shore Path.

Background – formerly a thriving settlement known as Waldberg or Snedekers Landing.

–acquired by Park with its Hook Mountain purchases (see that section) and made into a recreational center with swimming, picnicking, etc; abandoned after Hudson River became polluted, now almost unused.

Schedule – open every day, dawn to dusk, no fee.

Facilities and Natural Highlights – undeveloped: see Nyack Beach and Shore Path section for information about scenery, forests, flora, geology, and side trails of Shore Path which runs along river for 5½ miles from here south to Nyack Beach State Park.

HIGH TOR STATE PARK

–565 acres in Palisades Interstate Park, N.Y. section.

Location – along the summit and southern flanks of the Palisades where the ridge (here called "South Mountain") finally bends inland (west) away from the Hudson River as High Tor (830 feet) and Little Tor (710 feet) in Haverstraw and New City, N.Y. (town of Clarkstown).

–bordered on southeast end by one remaining quarry on Palisades at Short Clove Road; on northwest end by Central Highway and South Mountain County Park; along north flank by private land sloping down from the ridge top toward Route 202; and along the south flank by South Mountain Road (New City).

Phone – (914) 634-8074.

Directions – turn west off 9W onto Short Clove Road which passes the quarry and becomes South Mountain Road – Park entrance is on right side after about 2 miles.

–or, South Mountain Road can also be reached from its west end at Route 45 near Pomona; or by travelling west on Route 202 from Haverstraw then south along Central Highway, which climbs the ridge and intersects South Mountain Road.

–hikers can reach the summits of High Tor and Little Tor via the Long Path which traverses the entire ridge: the Path is reached from a Park road in the State Park which leads up to it; or from a parking area near the crest of Central Highway, which is crossed by the Long Path (walk east from parking area); or from a small parking area on Short Clove Road just beyond the quarry, where the Long Path crosses the road and ascends the steep mountain.

Background – the top of High Tor is the highest, boldest precipice in the Palisades region, and was once used as a lookout and signal point by colonists during the Revolution. More recently, an airplane beacon was located at its summit, but only its foundation remains.

–threatened by quarrying, attention was called to its plight by Maxwell Anderson's 3-act play, "High Tor" (1936), which dramatized the area's natural beauty and history. After its owner, Elmer Van Orden, died in 1942, local groups and citizens rallied to the support of their renowned landmark. It was finally purchased for $12,000 through the fund-raising campaign of the New York-New Jersey Trail Conference, Rockland County Conservation Association, and Hudson River Conservation Society. High Tor was presented to the Interstate Park in 1943, the same

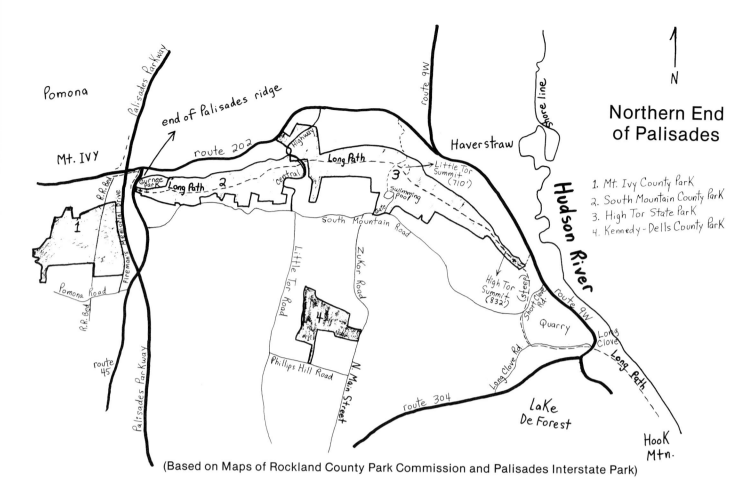

(Based on Maps of Rockland County Park Commission and Palisades Interstate Park)

year that 470 acres (Little Tor and much of the southern flank of South Mountain) were given to the Park by writer-philanthropist Archer Huntington. These gifts are all part of today's High Tor State Park.

Schedule—Park facilities open every day from mid-June to Labor Day (Long Path can be hiked all year); nominal parking fee and minimal fee for pool (open 10 A.M. to 6 P.M. weekdays, 9 to 7 weekends, holidays).

Facilities and Natural Highlights—picnic areas, refreshment stand, swimming pool, bathhouse.

–*highest peak of Palisades, with unparalleled views in 360-degree circle: Haverstraw and its 3-mile-wide Bay below; to east, Palisades ridge curving southeastward, and Hudson River and Westchester; to west, the end of Palisades (Mt. Ivy) and the Ramapo Mountains.

–top of High Tor is all bare rock, and exhibits large grooves and scratches ("striae") left by the last glacier; several large granite and

gneiss erratics were also dropped along ridge by glacier, and can be seen off Long Path (see page 11).

–the Long Path traverses the entire 4 miles across High Tor, Little Tor and to Central Highway where the Park ends and South Mountain County Park begins (Long Path continues through the latter also); side trails near Central Highway lead both down to the Park's facilities and up to the top of Little Tor.

–not far from swimming pool are two man-made impoundments with willows, cattails, aquatic vegetation, amphibians, kingfishers; also, a nice waterfall here cascades down from ridge top through talus ravine and into a valley of maples, hemlocks, sycamores near Park entrance road.

–most of forest along ridge including both Tors is young forest of mixed oak (red, white, black, and chestnut oaks), red maple, pignut hickory, with some black birch, white ash, flowering and gray dogwoods, witch hazel, shagbark and mockernut hick-

150

ories, maple-leaf viburnum, bush honey-suckle, and lots of mountain laurel and hemlock on the south flanks.

–more exposed summits and cliff edges have red cedar, choke and fire cherries, gray birch, aspen, chestnut oak, gooseberry, polypody fern, boulder lichens; west of Little Tor is a section of the Long Path which passes through a disturbed, "pioneer" forest with many of these same species plus lots of striped maple.

–in rockier areas, red elderberry, basswood, and bladdernut are common.

–swampy, flooded areas contain yellow birch, pussy willow, arrowwood, silky dogwood, skunk cabbage, and sphagnum moss.

–wildflowers include rue anenome, Dutchman's breeches, Solomon's seal, pussytoes, bush clover, lesser stitchwort, yellow false foxglove.

–High Tor and Little Tor are good vantage points to watch migrating hawks in autumn, and the young woods contain large numbers of migrating songbirds in spring and fall.

–bank swallows and pied-billed grebes (only the second regional nesting record) have nested in the former Haverstraw brickyard-claypit area below High Tor.

SOUTH MOUNTAIN COUNTY PARK

–273 acres, part of Rockland County (N.Y.) Park system.

Location –the northwestern end of the Palisades ridge, which is often called South Mountain in this region.

–at junctions of town of Clarkstown, Ramapo, and Haverstraw.

–eastern end is Central Highway (which is the western boundary of High Tor State Park); extends westward for 2 miles to the end of the Palisades ridge, where it dips beneath the ground in Mount Ivy, near the intersection of Routes 45 and 202; bordered on north by Route 202 and on south by South Mountain Road.

Directions –Route 202 (Exit 12 of Palisades Parkway) east from Mount Ivy to Central Highway, then south to parking area on east side of road just below the crest. Long Path enters east end of Park across the road.

–from Haverstraw and other points east, take 202 west to Central Highway.

–from south, Route 45 intersects South Mountain Road, which runs east to intersect Central Highway.

–also can be reached from its west end by parking at adjacent Gurnee Park (a former quarry, now a County Park) at Routes 202/45 intersection and then climbing into woods along Long Path.

Background –formerly private land, including the Gurnee Quarry at its west end, which was acquired by Rockland County by purchases and gifts in 1975–76.

Schedule –open for hiking all year, 8 A.M. to dark, no fee.

Facilities and Natural Highlights – 14-acre Gurnee Park and Amphitheater adjoins western end of Park, and this former quarry is planned to be developed by County into a site for outdoor theatrical and musical programs.

–*Long Path traverses entire Park, with views along the crest toward Haverstraw, Letchworth Village (a state institution),

Hudson River, and finally the end of the Palisades as the ridge descends beneath the ground in the Mahwah River valley in front of the Ramapo Mountains.

–most of the woods along this 2-mile section of the Palisades is a very young forest of oak, lots of cedar, some hickory, pitch pine, gooseberry (currant), with open grassy "balds."

–blueberry, raspberry, wild rose, columbine, smooth rock cress, small bittercress.

–uncommon falcate orange-tip butterflies visit the cresses in April to lay their eggs on the leaves.

–white-tailed deer, red fox, ruffed grouse, even an occasional porcupine.

MOUNT IVY COUNTY PARK

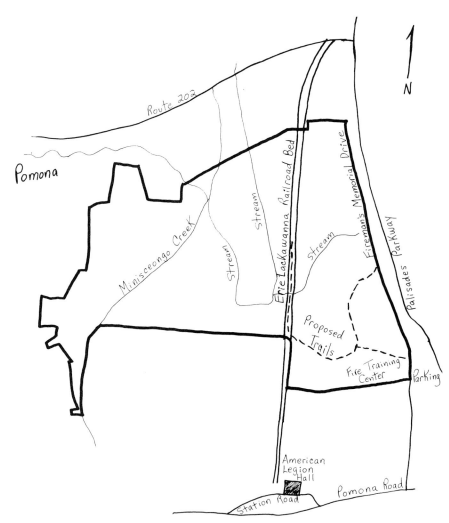

Mount Ivy County Park
(Based on Map prepared by Rockland County Planning Board for Rockland County Park Commission's 1985 Brochure

–255 acres in the Rockland County (N.Y.) Park System.

Location – Pomona, N.Y., in lowland just beyond where South Mountain sinks beneath the ground as the western end of the Palisades ridge – bordered on east by Palisades Interstate Parkway, west by Camp Hill Road, south by private school and Fire Training Center.

Directions – Palisades Interstate Parkway to exit 11, drive south to Pomona Road, turn right onto Fireman's Memorial Drive and continue past Fire Training Center and Animal Shelter to Park.

Background – a Quaker settlement (with Meeting House) in 18th century; acquired by County 1962–1963, with 43 acres of tax-delinquent land added in 1984.

Schedule – open every day, 8 A.M. to sunset; no fee.

Facilities and Natural Highlights – abandoned railroad bed (New York and New Jersey Railroad) cuts north-south swath through center of Park and provides access through swamp lowland; can be entered from parking area of American Legion Hall on Station Road (off Pomona Road).

–hiking trail also exists in southeastern portion, off Fireman's Drive extension.

–*composed mainly of swampy lowland forest and marshland, the headwaters of the Minesceonga River – named by DEC as a protected wetland area. At southern end of Park, the railroad bed is raised above a swampy floodplain forest, with lots of red maple and white ash, and some shagbark hickory, yellow birch, butternut, and beech near the streams. Farther north, away from the streams, it is boggier, with smaller trees growing from sedge tussocks and lots of shrubs like silky dogwood, honeysuckle, and meadowsweet.

–many nesting birds use the wetlands, including green-backed heron, wood duck, woodcock, eastern kingbird, red-bellied woodpecker, ruffed grouse, wood pewee, veery, yellow warbler, yellowthroat, etc.

–also, many amphibians and turtles.

KENNEDY-DELLS COUNTY PARK

–177 acres in the Rockland County (N.Y) Park system.

Location–in lowland below western slope of Palisades ridge, in New City, N.Y., off North Main Street.

Directions–from County Court House in New City, drive north on North Main Street for one mile to park entrance on left.

Background–once owned by famous movie producer Adolph Zukor; 80 acres purchased in 1969 by County, another 97 acres in 1975.

Schedule–open every day, 8 AM to sunset, no fee.

Facilities and Natural Highlights–large parking lot, parcourse fitness trail, bridle paths for horseback riding, horse corral, handicapped trail, soccer field, sledding, pavilion, field for radio-controlled model plane flying (by permit).

–*hiking trails in western portion along a stream valley through dense forests of hemlock, beech, sugar maple, mixed oak, white ash.

–deep sandstone ravine in northwest.

–lectures and guided tours (including farming demonstration at model farm) by park rangers available.

–most of tract is open, with 10 fields being farmed commercially for corn.

–wildlife includes white-tailed deer, red fox, woodcock, red-tailed hawk, woodchuck.

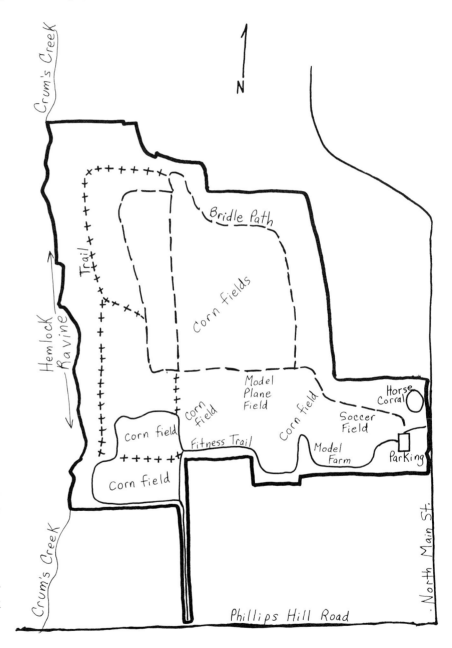

Kennedy-Dells County Park

(Based on Map prepared by Rockland County Planning Board for Rockland County Park Commission's 1985 Brochure)

153

BIBLIOGRAPHY AND FURTHER READING

A. General History of Palisades and Hudson Valley:

Abbott, A. 1914. (see Section E).

Adams, A. 1981. *The Hudson. A Guidebook to the River.* State Univ. of N.Y. Press, Albany.

Adams, A. 1983. *The Hudson River Through the Years.* Lind Publications, Westwood, N.J.

Bedell, C. 1968 (reprinted). *Now and Then and Long Ago in Rockland County.* Historical Society of Rockland County, New City, N.Y.

Boyle, R. 1979. (see Section F).

Carmer, C. 1968 (revised edition). *The Hudson.* Grosset and Dunlap, New York.

Cole, D. (ed.). 1884. *History of Rockland County.* J. B. Beers and Co., New York (reprinted 1969 by Rockland Co. Public Library Assoc., Nyack, N.Y.).

Collins, S. 1956. (see Section H).

Comstock, S. 1914. "Along the Palisades." *N.Y. Times,* Sunday, July 26, 1914.

Dickinson, R. 1921. (see Section E).

Greco, J. 1964. *The Story of Englewood Cliffs.* Tercentenery Committee, Englewood Cliffs, N.J.

Green, F. 1886. *The History of Rockland County.* A. S. Barnes and Co., New York. (reprinted 1969 by Rockland Co. Public Library Assoc., Nyack, N.Y.).

Lynch, D. 1977. *Rocklandia.* Morgan and Morgan, Inc., New York.

Mack, A. 1909. *The Palisades of the Hudson.* Palisades Press, Edgewater, N.J. (reprinted 1982 by Walking News, Inc., New York).

New Jersey History Committee. 1950. *Outline History of New Jersey.* Rutgers Univ. Press, New Brunswick, N.J.

New York-New Jersey Trail Conference. 1984. (see Section L).

O'Brien, R. 1981. *American Sublime.* Columbia Univ. Press, New York.

Palisades Interstate Park Commission. 1948. *A Story of History.* PIPC, Bear Mountain, N.Y.

Palisades Interstate Park Commission. 1960. (see Section E).

Sheridan, J. (ed.) 1962. *Beautiful Bergen.* (privately published). Englewood Public Library, N.J.

Sisson, E. 1939. *The Story of Tenafly.* Tenafly Trust Co., N.J.

Van Valen, J. 1900. *History of Bergen County.* Publishing and Engraving Co., New York.

Van Zandt, R. (ed.). 1971. *Chronicles of the Hudson: Three Centuries of Travellers' Accounts.* Rutgers Univ. Press, New Brunswick, N.J.

Westervelt, F. (ed.), 1923. *History of Bergen County, 1630-1923.* Lewis Historical Publishing Co., New York.

Wilstach, P. 1933. *Hudson River Landings.* Ira Friedman, Inc., Port Washington, N.Y.

B. Early History of Palisades (Indians, European Settlers):

Altshuler, J. 1969. *Dumont Heritage.* Borough of Dumont, N.J.

Bergen Council Boy Scouts of America. 1976. (see Section L).

Bergen County Historical Society. 1975. (see Section C).

Diamant, L. 1983. "First trip up the Hudson." *Columbia* (Columbia Univ., New York), 8(6): 22-23, 34-35.

Kraft, H. C. (ed.). 1974. *A Delaware Indian Symposium.* Anthropology Series # 4. Penn. Historical and Museum Commission, Harrisburgh, PA.

Leiby, A. 1964. *The Early Dutch and Swedish Settlers of New Jersey.* D. Van Nostrand Co., Inc., Princeton, N.J.

McCormick, R. 1964. *New Jersey from Colony to State 1609-1789.* D. Van Nostrand Co., Inc., Princeton, N.J.

Salomon, J. 1982. *Indians of the Lower Hudson Region. The Munsee.* Historical Society of Rockland Co., New City, N.Y.

C. The Palisades During the Revolutionary War:

Altshuler, J. 1969. (see section B).

Bergen Council Boy Scouts of America. 1976. (see Section L).

Bergen County Historical Society. 1977. *Position Paper on Location of Landing in New Jersey by the British Forces.* (unpublished). River Edge, N.J.

Bergen County Historical Society. 1975 (Annual).

Bergen County History. River Edge, N.J.

Bill, A. H. 1964. *New Jersey and the Revolutionary War.* D. Van Nostrand Co., Inc., Princeton, N.J.

Bradley, S. 1978. *Crossroads of History – The Story of Alpine, N.J.* Bicentennial Commission, Alpine, N.J.

Henderson, P. 1952. "Point O'Bluff overlooking the Hudson." *Press Journal* (Englewood, N.J.), Sept. 18, 1952.

Henderson, P. 1975. *Campaign of Chaos.* Archives, Ink, Ltd., Haworth, N.J.

Henderson, P. 1976. "A tale of two roads, or where did the boats land." *Sunday Bergen Record,* Sept. 26, 1976: D-3.

Leiby, A. 1980. *The Revolutionary War in the Hackensack Valley.* Rutgers Univ. Press, New Brunswick, N.J.

McCormick, R. 1964. (see Section B).

Mosley, V. 1977. *Fort Lee During the American Revolution, A Selected Bibliography* (unpublished). Tenafly, N.J.

Spring, J. 1982. "New trail at Huyler's Landing." *Trail Walker* (N.Y.-N.J. Trail Conference, N.Y.C.), April-May 1982:11.

D. The Palisades During the 19th Century:

Adams, A. 1984. "Annual ice harvest received a warm welcome." *Focs'le News* (Hudson River Maritime Center, Kingston, N.Y.), Winter 1984: 12–13.

Allison, J. 1937. "Vanished folk of the river." *Bergen Evening Record,* March 1, 2, and 3, 1937.

Geismar, J. 1982. *The Archaeology of Social Disintegration in Skunk Hollow.* Academic Press, Inc., New York.

Haring, J. 1924. *Floating Chips – Annals of Old and New Times.* Tenafly Public Library, N.J.

Humphrey, J. 1899. *Englewood, Its Annals and Reminiscences.* J. S. Oglivie Publ. Co., New York.

Lavigne, M. 1983. "The Hudson river." *Columbia* (Columbia Univ., New York), 8(6): 5–8.

Scott, J. 1976. "The slote, Piermont, and the Erie railroad." *South of the Mountain* (The Historical Society of Rockland County), 20(3): 5–21.

E. The Palisades Interstate Park – Its Creation, Development, and the Preservation of the Palisades:

Abbott, A. 1914. *The Greatest Park in the World, Palisades Interstate Park.* Historian Publishing Co., New York.

Clyne, P. 1985. "The Blauvelt rifle range – Camp Bluefields." *South of the Mountains* (The Historical Society of Rockland County), 29(4): 3–11.

Dickinson, R. 1921. *The Palisades Interstate Park.* American Geographical Society of N.Y., New York.

Grutzner, C. 1953. "Bird refuge on the Palisades." *N.Y. Times,* Aug. 23, 1953.

Mack, A. 1909. (see Section A).

New Jersey Association for Parks and Parkways. 1946. *Booklet* (opposing Palisades Parkway). Palisades Interstate Park Commission files, Alpine, N.J.

New Jersey Parks and Recreation Association. Jan. 1947. "The Palisades Interstate Parkway." *Your Parks,* 3(4).

O'Brien, R. 1981. (see Section A).

Oliver, E. 1964. *Background and History of the Palisades Nature Association.* P.N.A., Alpine, N.J.

O'Reilly, J. 1956. "Sanctuary for man." *Sports Illustrated,* July 30, 1956.

Palisades Interstate Park Commission. 1946. *References and Notes on Palisades Parkway.* Oct. 5, 1946. PIPC files, Alpine, N.J.

Palisades Interstate Park Commission. 1953. *Palisades Interstate Parkway.* (booklet for opening, Nov. 30, 1953). PIPC files, Alpine, N.J.

Palisades Interstate Park Commission. 1960. *Sixty Years of Cooperation.* Bear Mountain, N.Y.

Palisades Interstate Park Commission. *Annual Composite Reports, 1979–1984.* Bear Mountain, N.Y.

Perkins, G. 1945. *The Parkway Plan for the Preservation of the Top of the Palisades* (booklet). PIPC files, Alpine, N.J.

Rockefeller, L. 1957. *Palisades Interstate Park* (address to Garden Club of N.J.). PIPC files, Alpine, N.J.

F. The Hudson River – Its Biology, Natural History, Pollution:

Adams, A. 1981. (see Section A).

Boyle, R. 1979 (expanded edition). *The Hudson River.* W. W. Norton & Co., New York.

Hall, A. 1978. "The Hudson, that river's alive." *National Geographic.* 153(1): 62–89.

Lavigne, M. 1983. (see Section D).

U.S. Dept. of Commerce, N.Y. State Dept. of Environmental Conservation. 1982. *Draft Environmental Impact Statement – Hudson River Estuarine Sanctuary.* Office of Coastal Zone Management, Washington, D.C.

Vaux, M. 1983. "A strong brown god." *Columbia* (Columbia Univ., N.Y.), 8(6): 9–15, 40–41.

G. Geology of the Palisades:

Collins, S. 1956. (see Section H).

Harlow, G. 1984. "An introduction to the geology of the New York region." In *New York Walk*

Book. Anchor Press/Doubleday, Garden City, N.Y.

Horenstein, S. 1980. "Looking around Manhattan." *Seaport,* Spring 1980: 8–15.

Horenstein, S. 1982. "Father Knickerbocker the first." *Natural History,* 91(7): 74–75.

Isachsen, Y. 1980. *Continental Collisions and Ancient Volcanoes. The Geology of Southeastern New York.* Educational Leaflet 24. N.Y. State Geological Survey, Albany.

Leopold, E. 1982. "Palynology: the key to lost landscapes." *Nature Conservancy News,* 32(6): 22–23.

Lobeck, A. K. 1952. *Panoramic View of the New York Region as Seen from the Palisades.* Scenic Folder No. 1. Geographical Press, Columbia Univ., New York.

Lowe, K. 1959. "Structure of the Palisades intrusion at Haverstraw and West Nyack." *Annals of N.Y. Academy of Science,* 80: 1127–1139.

Olsen, P. 1980. "The latest Triassic and early Jurassic formations of the Newark basin." *The Bulletin* (N.J. Academy of Sciences), 25(2).

Schuberth, C. 1968. *The Geology of New York City and Environs.* The Natural History Press, Garden City, N.Y.

Sharp, H. 1962. "The geology of the Palisades." *New Jersey Nature News* (N.J. Audubon Society, Franklin Lakes, N.J.), 17(2): 50–54.

Subitsky, S. (ed.) 1969. *Geology of Selected Areas in New Jersey and Eastern Pennsylvania and Guide Book.* Rutgers Univ. Press, New Brunswick, N.J.

Thompson, H. D. 1959. "The Palisades ridge in Rockland County, N.Y." *Annals of N.Y. Academy of Science,* 80: 1106–1126.

Vaux, M. 1983. (see Section F).

Widmer, K. 1964. *The Geology and Geography of New Jersey.* D. Van Nostrand Co., Inc., Princeton, N.J.

Wolfe, P. 1977. *The Geology and Landscapes of New Jersey.* Crane, Russak, and Co., New York.

Wyckoff, J. 1971. *Rock Scenery of the Hudson Highlands and Palisades.* Adirondack Mountain Club, Glens Falls, N.Y.

H. Palisades Forests and Habitats:

Airola, T. and K. Buchholz. 1982. "Forest community relationships of the Greenbrook Sanctuary."*Bulletin of Torrey Botanical Club,* 109(2): 205–218.

Buell, M. et al. 1966. "The upland forest continuum in northern New Jersey." *Ecology,* 47(3): 416–432.

Charney, J. 1980. "Hemlock-hardwood community relationships in the highlands of southeastern New

York." *Bulletin of Torrey Botanical Club,* 107(2): 249–257.

Collins, S. 1956. *The Biotic Communities of Greenbrook Sanctuary.* Palisades Nature Association, Alpine, N.J.

Huth, P. and D. Smiley. 1985. "Flowering dogwood: decline in the Shawangunks." *Mohonk Preserve Research Report,* May 1985.

Lawrence, S. and B. Gross. 1984. (see Section L).

McDonough, W. and M. Buell. 1956. "The vegetation of Voorhees State Park, N.J.". *American Midland Naturalist,* 56(2): 473–490.

Moore, E. B. 1949. *Forestry Report of Greenbrook Sanctuary* (unpublished report). Palisades Nature Association files, Alpine, N.J.

Robichaud, B. and M. Buell. 1973. *Vegetation of New Jersey.* Rutgers Univ. Press, New Brunswick, N.J.

Serrao, J. 1981. "The magnificent Palisades forests." *American Forests,* 87(2): 30–34, 55–57.

Serrao, J. 1982 (a). (see Section I).

Serrao, J. 1983. *Palisades Forests–A Self-Guided Trail Booklet.* Palisades Nature Association, Alpine, N.J.

Serrao, J. 1985. "What's happening to our trees?" *N.Y. Times.* Sunday, Dec. 29, 1985: 18 (N.J. section).

Serrao, J. 1985. (see Section K-4).

Serrao, J. 1985 (b). (see Section L).

Stalter, R. and J. Serrao. 1983. "The impact of defoliation by gypsy moths on the oak forests of Greenbrook Sanctuary." *Bulletin of Torrey Botanical Club,* 110(4): 526–529.

Stimmel, J. 1979. "Elongate hemlock scale." *Regulatory Horticulture* (P.A. Dept. of Agriculture), 5(1): 13–14.

Talerico, R. et al. 1967. "Fiorinia externa, a scale insect of hemlock." *USDA Forest Pest Leaflet* 107.

I. Flora and Fauna of Palisades Region:

Arbib, R. et al. 1966. (see Section L).

Boyajian, N. 1966. "Warbler populations on the east slope of the Palisades, 1965". *Linnaean Newsletter,* 20(5).

Bull, J. 1964. *Birds of the New York Area.* Dover Publications, Inc., New York.

Bull, J. 1974. *Birds of New York State.* Doubleday, Garden City, N.Y.

Chrysler, M. and J. L. Edwards. 1947. *Ferns of New Jersey.* Rutgers Univ. Press, New Brunswick, N.J.

Dater, E. 1951. "First successful nesting of the cerulean warbler in New Jersey." *The Wilson Bulletin,* 63(2).

Deed, R. 1976. *Birds of Rockland County and Hudson Highlands, 1844–1976.* Nyack, N.Y.

Drennan, S. 1981. (see Section L).

Dunne, M. (ed.) 1982. "The woodrats are here." *Non-Game News* (N.J. Dept. Environmental Protection, Trenton). Fall 1982.

Heintzelman, D. 1975. *Autumn Hawk Flights.* Rutgers Univ. Press, New Brunswick, N.J.

Irvine, J. 1984. (see Section L).

Lawrence, S. and B. Gross. 1984. (see Section L).

Lehr, J. H. 1956. "Annotated preliminary catalogue of vascular flora of Rockland County." *Bulletin of Torrey Botanical Club,* 83: 435–438 (and 84(1–6) and 85(6)).

Lehr, J. H. 1967. "The marshes at Piermont, N.Y., a field report." *Sarracenia* (N.Y. Botanical Gardens), 11: 31–34.

Mueller, H. C. and D. D. Berger. 1961. "Weather and fall migration of hawks at Cedar Grove, Wisconsin." *The Wilson Bulletin,* 73: 171–192.

Palisades Nature Association. 1946–1983. *Breeding Bird Censuses at Greenbrook Sanctuary.* P.N.A. files, Alpine, N.J.

Pollock, E. 1980. "Birding the Piermont marsh and its environs." *The Observer,* (Rockland Audubon Society), May–June 1980.

Serrao, J. 1976–1979. "Autumn hawk migration counts in Greenbrook Sanctuary." Various *Members Bulletins.* Palisades Nature Association, Alpine, N.J.

Serrao, J. 1979. "Autumn hawk migration." *Biology Digest,* 6(1): 12–38.

Serrao, J. 1982 (a). *A Natural Resource Inventory of the Tenafly East Hill Natural Area.* Citizens for Green Acres, Tenafly, N.J.

Serrao, J. 1982 (b). "Palisades woodrats." *Members Bulletin* (Palisades Nature Association), Autumn, 1982.

Serrao, J. 1982 (c). "Woodrats trapped." *Members Bulletin* (Palisades Nature Association), Winter 1982–1983.

Serrao, J. 1984 (a). *The Birds of Greenbrook Sanctuary.* Palisades Nature Association, Alpine, N.J.

Serrao, J. 1984 (b). *The Butterflies of Greenbrook Sanctuary.* Palisades Nature Association, Alpine, N.J.

Serrao, J. 1984 (c). *The Mammals, Reptiles and Amphibians of Greenbrook Sanctuary.* Palisades Nature Association, Alpine, N.J.

Serrao, J. 1984 (d). *The Trees and Shrubs of Greenbrook Sanctuary.* Palisades Nature Association, Alpine, N.J.

Serrao, J. 1984 (e). *The Wildflowers of Greenbrook Sanctuary.* Palisades Nature Association, Alpine, N.J.

Serrao, J 1985. "Two rare plants on the Palisades of New Jersey." *Bartonia,* 51: 112.

Shapiro, A. 1974. "Butterflies and skippers of New York State." *Search* (Cornell Univ., Ithaca, N.Y.), 4(3).

Single, E. et al. (eds.) (various years). *The Newsletter of the Hawk Migration Association of North America.* Route 4, Salem, Virginia.

Snyder, D. and V. E. Vivian. 1981. *Rare and Endangered Vascular Plant Species of New Jersey.* Conservation and Environmental Studies Center, Browns Mills, N.J.

Thomas, S. et al. (ed.) (various years). *Annual Reports.* Society for the Preservation of Birds of Prey, Box 891, Pacific Palisades, CA.

U.S. Dept. Agriculture, Soil Conservation Service and N.J. Dept. Environmental Protection. 1980. *Endangered and Threatened Species of New Jersey.* N.J.D.E.P., Trenton.

U.S. Dept. Commerce and N.Y. Dept. Environmental Conservation. 1982. (see Section F).

Van Gelder, R. 1984. *The Mammals of the State of New Jersey.* N.J. Audubon Society Occasional Paper 143. Bernardsville, N.J.

J. General Field Guides for Identification:

The Audubon Society Field Guides (various titles). Alfred Knopf, N.Y.

The Golden Press Field Guides (various titles). Golden Press, N.Y.

The Pictured-Key "How to Know" Nature Guides (various titles). Wm. C. Brown Co., Dubuque, Iowa.

The Peterson Field Guides (various titles). Houghton Mifflin, Boston.

K. Modern Problems and Solutions:

1. Habitat Restoration:

Serrao, J. 1984. "Vernal ponds restored, amphibians introduced." *Restoration and Management Notes* (Univ. of Wisconsin, Madison), 2(2): 78–79.

Serrao, J. 1985 (a). "Meadow clearing created to increase wildlife diversity." *Restoration and Management Notes,* 3(1): 44.

Serrao, J. 1985 (b). "Reptile habitat created at Greenbrook Sanctuary." *Restoration and Management Notes,* 3(1): 44

2. Pesticides and Raptors:

Ford, G. 1983. "Rare falcons nest on Verrazano bridge." *Staten Island Advance,* Monday, May 9, 1983: A-1, 7.

Harper, T. 1981. "Peregrine's progress." *Defenders,* 56(4): 7–11.

Harwood, M. 1982. "Peregrine redux." *Audubon,* 84(5): 8–11

Hickey, J. 1969. *Peregrine Falcon Populations: Their Biology and Decline.* Univ. Wisconsin Press, Madison.

Kaufmann, J. 1976. "Soaring free again." *National Wildlife,* 14(2): 4–11.

Kelsey, P. 1965. "The peregrine disappears." *Conservationist,* 20(1): 2–5.

Loucks, B. and K. Kogut. 1985. "The peregrine returns." *Conservationist,* 39(5): 12–17.

Nye, P. 1982. "Restoring the bald eagle in New York." *Conservationist,* 37(1): 9–13, 48.

Ott, G. 1970. "Is the bald eagle doomed?" *National Wildlife,* 8(3): 4–10.

Peakall, D. and W. Spofford, 1965. "Pesticides and wildlife." *Kingbird,* 15: 5–12.

Postupalsky, S. 1978. "The bald eagles return." *Natural History,* 87(5):62–63.

Serrao, J. 1976. "Feathering their nests in Eden." *Hudson Valley,* 5(3): 10–13.

Steinhart, P. 1982. "The bird behind the symbol." *National Wildlife,* 20(1): 24–32.

Webster, B. 1982. "The bald eagle: flight from extinction." *N.Y. Times,* Tues., June 8, 1982: C–1, 6.

Zimmerman, D. 1975 (a). "That the peregrine shall live." *Audubon,* 77(6): 39–49.

Zimmerman, D 1975 (b). *To Save a Bird in Peril.* Coward, McCann, and Geoghegan, Inc., New York.

3. Migrant Songbird Declines:

Ambuel, B. and S. Temple, 1982. "Songbird populations in southern Wisconsin forests, 1954 and 1979." *Journal of Field Ornithology,* 53: 149–158.

Briggs, S. and J. Criswell. 1979. "Gradual silencing of spring in Washington." *Atlantic Naturalist,* 32: 19–26.

Fitzpatrick, J. 1982. "Northern birds at home in the tropics." *Natural History,* 91(9): 40–46.

Howe, J. 1983. "The vanishing birds of Veracruz." *Defenders,* 58(6): 18–28.

Keast, A. and E. Morton (eds.). 1980. *Migrant Birds in the Neotropics.* Smithsonian Institute, Washington, D.C.

Leck, C. et al. 1981. "Changes in breeding bird populations at Hutcheson Memorial Forest since 1958." *Wm. Hutcheson Memorial Forest Bulletin,* 6(1): 8–15.

Pasquier, R. 1982. "Whose birds are they?" *Nature Conservancy News,* 32(4): 12–15.

Robbins, C. 1980. "Effects of forest fragmentation on breeding bird populations in the Piedmont of the mid-Atlantic region." *Atlantic Naturalist,* 33: 31–36.

Serrao, J. 1985 (a). "Decline of forest songbirds." *Records of New Jersey Birds* (N.J. Audubon Soc.). 11(1): 5–9.

Serrao, J. 1985 (b). "Our forest birds are disappearing." *American Forests,* 91(4): 40–41, 61–62.

Steinhart, P. 1984. "Trouble in the tropics." *National Wildlife,* 22(1): 16–20.

Wilcove, D. and R. Whitcomb. 1983. "Gone with the trees." *Natural History,* 92(9): 82–91.

Wilcove, D. 1985. "Where have all the songbirds gone?" *The Living Bird,* 4(2): 20–23.

4. Land Development on Palisades:

Akst, D. 1983. "Real profit v. preservation." *The Sunday Record,* May 22, 1983: A–41, 42.

Canger Engineering Associates. 1967. *Engineering Report and Feasibility Study of the Blankman Property in Tenafly, N.J.* Fair Lawn, N.J.

Doane, C. J. 1983 (a). "Report urges preserving North Bergen river tract." *The Dispatch,* Thurs., Feb. 24, 1983.

Doane, C. J. 1983 (b). "North Bergen can lease preserve." *The Dispatch,* July 2, 1983.

Flynn, E. 1985. "Plans for scout tract OK'd." *The Record,* Wed., Dec. 11, 1985: C–3.

Gaffney, D. 1982. "151 acre sanctuary in the midst of chaos." *Valley Star,* Thurs., Nov. 25, 1982: 1.

Hanley, R. 1984. "Clash over Palisades legacy." *N.Y. Times,* Sat., Jan. 14, 1984: 23–24.

Hartung, W. 1974. "The East Hill remains the outstanding issue in Tenafly." *Tenafly Newsletter,* Jan. 1974.

Kohn, K. 1985. "NEW suit denied by judge." *North Jersey Suburbanite,* Wed., March 6, 1985: 1, 23.

Kuhn, J. 1983. "Park agency sues for scout property." *The Record,* Wed., Dec. 28, 1983: C–3, 4.

O'Dea, C. 1984. "Wildlife's battle with wild life." *The Record,* Wed., Dec. 26, 1984: C–3, 5.

Regional Plan Association (New Jersey Committee). 1985. "River City." *Regional Plan News,* 122: 31 pages.

Serrao, J. 1982 (a). (see Section I).

Serrao, J. 1985. *The Norwood Easthill Tract.* Report written for Norwood Easthill Watch, N.J.

Shapiro, E. 1982. "Non-profit group may purchase East Hill." *North Jersey Suburbanite,* Wed. Aug. 25, 1982: 3, 36.

5. Miscellaneous Problems:

Brodo, I. 1971. "Lichens and air pollution." *Conservationist,* 26(1): 22–26.

Serrao, J. 1981. "The gypsy moth in Greenbrook Sanctuary." *Members Bulletin* (Palisades Nature Association, Alpine, N.J.), Spring, 1981.

Serrao, J. 1985. (see Section H).

U.S. Dept. Agriculture et al. 1980. (see Section I).

L. Recreational and Scenic Opportunities Along the Palisades:

Adams, A. 1981. (see Section A).

Arbib, R. et al. 1966. *Enjoying Birds Around New York City.* Houghton Mifflin Co., Boston.

159

Bergen Council Boy Scouts of America. 1976. *Palisades Historic Trails.* River Edge, N.J.

Brown, M. et al. 1949. *Trails and Pleasant Walks in Rockland County.* Rockland County Audubon Society, New City, N.Y.

Dann, K. 1982. *Twenty-five Walks in New Jersey.* Rutgers Univ. Press, New Brunswick, N.J.

Deed, R. 1981. "The Piermont pier and marsh." *The Observer* (Rockland County Audubon Soc., New City, N.Y.), 34(2): 1–2.

Drennan, S. 1981. *Where to Find Birds in New York State–The Top 500 Sites.* Syracuse Univ. Press, N.Y.

Goodman, S. 1985. "Tenafly refuge: a bucolic secret." *The Record,* Sunday, Feb. 10, 1985: A–55, 57.

Heintzelman, D. 1976. *A Guide to Eastern Hawk Watching.* Pennsylvania State Univ. Press, University Park.

Irvine, J. (ed.) 1984. *Hook Mountain Hawk Watch.* Bi-State Hawk Watch Coalition, Park Ridge, N.J.

Lawrence, S. and B. Gross. 1984. *The Audubon Society Field Guide to the Natural Places of the Mid-Atlantic States, Inland.* Hilltown Press, New York.

Natural Science for Youth Foundation. 1984. *Directory of Natural Science Centers.* NSYF, New Canaan, Ct.

New York-New Jersey Trail Conference. 1982. *Guide to the Long Path.* 232 Madison Ave., New York.

New York-New Jersey Trail Conference. 1984 (5th edition). *New York Walk Book.* Anchor Press/Doubleday, Garden City, N.Y.

Palisades Interstate Park Commission. 1985. *Brochure and Map of Park.* Alpine, N.J.

Palisades Interstate Park Commission. *Fort Lee Historic Park* (brochure). Alpine, N.J.

Palisades Interstate Park Commission. *Annual Composite Reports,* 1979–1984. Bear Mountain, N.Y.

Palisades Nature Association. 1984. *Greenbrook at a Glance.* Alpine, N.J.

Pollock, E. 1980. (see Section I).

Serrao, J. 1985. "Greenbrook sanctuary." *Bartonia,* 51: 108–109.

Serrao, J. 1985 b. "The Wild Palisades." *New Jersey Outdoors,* 12(5): 18–20.

Tanner, O. 1975. *Urban Wilds.* Time-Life Books, New York.

Time-Life Books (eds.). 1971. *Photographing Nature* (pages 70–76). Time-Life, New York.

Upper Nyack P.T.A. 1965. *A Guide Through Rockland County.* Upper Nyack, N.Y.

Sundberg, E. et al (eds.) 1985. *Rockland County Park System.* Rockland Co. Park Commission, New City, N.Y.

Walking News, Inc. *Hikers Region Maps 's 2 and 18, and 24.* Box 352, New York City, 10013.

ADDITIONAL SOURCES OF INFORMATION AND CENTERS

Bergen Community Museum, East Ridgewood and Fairview Avenues, Paramus, N.J. 07652

Bergen County Audubon Society, 167 8th Street, Hoboken, N.J. 07030

Bergen County Historical Society, P.O. Box 55, River Edge, N.J. 07661

Bergen County Wildlife Center, Crescent Avenue, Wyckoff, N.J. 07481

Bi-State Hawk Watch Coalition, 58 S. 4th St., Park Ridge, N.J. 07656

Closter Nature Center Assoc., Box 80, Closter, N.J. 07624

Demarest Nature Center Assoc., Box 41, Demarest, N.J. 07627

Endangered & Nongame Species Program, Division of Fish-Game & Wildlife, CN 400, Trenton, N.J. 08625

Ferry Sloop, Inc., P.O. Box 529, Yonkers, N.Y. 10702

Flat Rock Brook Center for Environmental Studies, 443 Van Nostrand Avenue, Englewood, N.J. 07631

Fyke Nature Association, 90 East Orchard St., Allendale, N.J. 07401

Hawk Migration Assoc. of North America, Route 4, Box 205, Salem, Virginia 24153

Highlands Audubon Society, P.O. Box 337, Oak Ridge, N.J. 07438

Historical Society of Rockland County, Zukor Rd., New City, N.Y. 10956

Hudson River Fisherman's Assoc., Box 312, Cold Spring, N.Y. 10516

Hudson River Maritime Center, Rondout Landing, Kingston, N.Y. 12401

Hudson River Sloop Clearwater, Inc., 112 Market St., Poughkeepsie, N.Y. 12601

Hudsonia Limited, Box 96, Bard College, Annandale, N.Y. 12504

Lamont Geological Observatory, Route 9W, Palisades, N.Y. 10964

Linnaean Society of N.Y., 15 West 77 St., New York, N.Y. 10024

Nature Conservancy, Lower Hudson Chapter, Chestnut Ridge Road, Mt. Kisco, N.Y. 10549

New Jersey Audubon Society, P.O. Box 125, 790 Ewing Avenue, Franklin Lakes, N.J. 07417

New Jersey Environmental Lobby, Box 605, Teaneck, N.J. 07666

N.J. State Federation of Women's Clubs, 55 Clifton Ave., New Brunswick, N.J. 08901

New York-New Jersey Trail Conference, 232 Madison Ave. Suite 908, New York, N.Y. 10016

Palisades Interstate Park Commission, N.J. Headquarters, Box 155, Alpine, N.J. 07620

Palisades Interstate Park Commission, N.Y. Headquarters, Bear Mountain State Park, Bear Mountain, N.Y. 10911

Palisades Nature Association (Greenbrook Sanctuary), Box 155, Alpine, N.J. 07620

Rockland Audubon Society, P.O. Box 404, New City, N.Y. 10956

Rockland County Park Commission, 11 New Hempstead Road, New City, N.Y. 10956

Ridgewood Audubon Society, P.O. Box 395, Ridgewood, N.J. 07451

Scenic Hudson, Inc., 9 Vassar St., Poughkeepsie, N.Y. 12601

Tenafly Nature Center, 313 Hudson Ave., Tenafly, N.J. 07670

Torrey Botanical Club, N.Y. Botanical Garden, Bronx Park, Bronx, N.Y. 10460

APPENDIX – A SPRING CALENDAR OF EVENTS FOR THE PALISADES

The following natural happenings and dates are the results of ten years of the author's records. The dates are the averages of the earliest dates each event occurred during the years 1976 to 1985 in the New Jersey sections of the Palisades. Dates for New York sections of the Palisades may be one or two days later since they are a little farther north. This calendar is meant to be a general guide to many of the natural events and when they may be expected to occur along the Palisades.

Species	Date of First Emergence, Arrival, Bloom, Appearance, Etc.
skunk cabbage flower	March 1
smooth alder flower	March 15
spotted salamanders breeding	March 15
garter snake emerging	March 15
mourning cloak butterfly	March 15
wood frogs breeding	March 16
spring peeper calling	March 19
wood duck arriving	March 21
phoebe returning	March 21
painted turtle emerging	March 22
eggs of spotted salamanders	March 22
red maple in bloom	March 24
pine warbler migrating	April 3
myrtle (yellow-rumped) warbler migrating	April 5
spicebush in bloom	April 6
ruby-crowned kinglet migrating	April 6
spring azure butterfly	April 7
spring beauty in bloom	April 8
trout lily in bloom	April 8
palm warbler migrating	April 10
Dutchman's breeches in bloom	April 11
blue-gray gnatcatcher migrating	April 12
osprey migrating	April 12
American toads breeding	April 15
rufous-sided towhee returning	April 17
brown thrasher returning	April 17
broad-winged hawk returning	April 18
jack-in-the-pulpit in bloom	April 20
black and white warbler returning	April 20
black birch in bloom	April 22
highbush blueberry in bloom	April 23
solitary vireo migrating	April 25
wild geranium in bloom	April 26
ovenbird returning	April 27
barn swallow returning	April 27
flowering dogwood in bloom	April 27
gray catbird returning	April 28
American painted lady butterfly	April 28

wild pinks in bloom	April 29
wood thrush returning	April 29
black-throated green warbler migrating	April 30
northern (Baltimore) oriole returning	April 30
rose-breasted grosbeak returning	May 2
spicebush swallowtail butterfly	May 3
pink azalea in bloom	May 3
great crested flycatcher returning	May 3
veery returning	May 3
scarlet tanager returning	May 3
eastern kingbird returning	May 3
American redstart migrating	May 6
Canada mayflower in bloom	May 6
red-eyed vireo returning	May 7
pink lady slipper in bloom	May 8
royal Paulownia (princess tree) in bloom	May 9
blackpoll warbler migrating	May 12
eastern wood pewee returning	May 13
ruby-throated hummingbird migrating	May 14
bullfrogs calling	May 18
tulip tree in flower	May 21
maple-leaf viburnum in bloom	May 23
copperhead snake	May 23
ruffed grouse with chicks	May 27
mountain laurel in bloom	May 30
snapping turtle laying eggs	June 3

INDEX

The index lists only those plant and animal species that are significantly mentioned or described in the text.

Pages *in italics* contain photos of the subject.